VERA AND THE AMBASSADOR

Escape and Return

VERA AND DONALD BLINKEN

Published by
State University of New York Press, Albany

For information, contact State University of New York Press, Albany, NY
www.sunypress.edu

Production, Laurie Searl
Marketing, Fran Keneston

Library of Congress Cataloging-in-Publication Data

Blinken, Vera and Blinken, Donald.
  Vera and the ambassador : escape and return / Vera Blinken and Donald Blinken.
    p. cm.
  Includes index.
  ISBN 978-1-4384-2663-1 (hardcover : alk. paper)
   1. Blinken, Vera. 2. Blinken, Donald. 3. Ambassador's spouses—United States—Biography.
4. Ambassadors—United States—Biography. 5. Ambassadors—Hungary—Biography. 6. United
States—Foreign relations—Hungary. 7. Hungary—Foreign relations—United States. 8. Hungarian
Americans—Biography. 9. Hungary—Biography. I. Blinken, Donald. II. Title.

E840.8.B58A3 2009
327.2092'2—dc22
[B]   2009002528

10 9 8 7 6 5 4 3 2 1

In memory of Lili

and Senator Daniel Patrick Moynihan.

They made this possible.

CONTENTS

PROLOGUE

During most of the twentieth century, Hungary, a nation of approximately ten million people, was in the eye of political, ethnic, and military storms. Hungarians have never fully recovered from the 1920 Treaty of Trianon at the end of World War I that caused Hungary to lose two-thirds of its territory and almost half of its population. Moreover, the country could not escape its geographic destiny, poised between the Russian Empire to the East, the Balkans to the South, and a relentless pressure from an aggressive Germany in the West. For most of the twentieth century, Hungary was constantly vulnerable to external forces.

During World War II, having been promised the return of its lost territories, Hungary sided with the Axis Powers, and its home-grown Arrow Cross Nazi Party was complicit in the extermination of 600,000 Hungarian Jews. Following the expulsion of the Germans by Allied Forces in 1945, Hungary fell under the iron grip of a Soviet-controlled Communist regime.

In 1956, the Hungarians regained a sense of their identity because, even though their attempt to break free of a repressive regime failed, the world took notice. In the decades that followed, some of the most talented Hungarians escaped to the West, among them a number of world-class scientists. Those who remained at home were often pragmatic, managing to retain some of their special characteristics. In what came to be known as "goulash communism," private incentives and artistic dissent began to pierce the communist gloom. In 1978, the United States returned the Crown of St. Stephen—the symbol of Magyar independence—not to the government, but to the people of Hungary. (At the request of Hungary at the end of World War II, the United States had safeguarded the crown at Fort Knox.) Its return gave a strong symbolic boost to U.S.-Hungarian relations, even as the Cold War continued.

A decade later, Hungary's dramatic opening of its border with Austria triggered the November 1989 fall of the Berlin Wall. This in turn led to the breakup of the Warsaw Pact and the Soviet Union and signified the end of the Cold War.

By the time we arrived to take up our post in April 1994, Hungary had held free elections, mended relations with Western nations, and watched the last occupying Soviet troops leave in 1991. Hungary's prospects, however, while optimistic, were not yet assured. Would Hungary embrace free markets or fall back into a command economy? Could Hungary make a 180-degree turn from the Warsaw Pact to a Western system of collective security such as the Partnership for Peace or even NATO? With the demise of Nicolae Ceausescu, the Romanian dictator, and the breakup of Czechoslovakia—home to more than two and one-half million Hungarians—how would Hungary manage the ethnic tensions that were beginning to reassert themselves? What would Hungary be prepared to do about restitution to its approximately 125,000 Jewish citizens, some 20,000 of whom were Holocaust survivors? Would the Hungarian people be able to shake off forty years of a communist mindset and a reflexive reliance upon government to make decisions for them? Yes, the red stars were removed from public buildings and bridges, as the Soviet Union collapsed, but how and when would the lasting impact of those red stars be erased?

We were prepared to grapple with these challenges on our arrival. Vera as a small child had escaped Hungary in 1950 and related instinctively to the Hungarian people, not to mention speaking their difficult language. In 1988, she had established a nutrition program and underwritten the first European Peace Corps Conference held in Budapest in October 1989. Beginning in 1987, Donald had accompanied Vera on numerous trips to Budapest and, as chairman of the board of trustees of the State University of New York (SUNY), established a business management program there in 1990.

We were both ready and eager to make a difference. In the following pages we relate our personal experiences leading up to and then serving in Hungary. We take the reader behind the scenes of the operations of the embassy and describe diplomacy in a post–Cold War country taking hesitant steps toward economic and political freedom. In addition, we examine how the Bosnian conflict thrust Hungary into a pivotal role on the European stage.

Hungary today is vastly different from the Hungary of the 1990s, to the benefit of its people, its neighbors, Europe, and the United States. Our role in helping Hungary turn from the turmoil of the twentieth century to the challenges of the twenty-first is the story we now tell.

PART I

VERA

ESCAPE

"The war will be over some day, and we have to make sure that when it is, this child will have good nails, good teeth, and good hair."

"Run, Vera, run! Run as fast as you can!" I was ten years old. On that moonless night, Mother and I had traveled on a train to a bleak station far from our Budapest home and were now running through thick, dark woods.

"Faster, Vera!" she kept urging. "Faster!"

I ran as fast as I could over barely visible roots and around shadowy tree trunks. For what reason, I had no idea.

Only later did Mother explain. Like so many Hungarians before us, we were trying to escape by running through the woods and jumping onto the train after it passed passport control, slowing down around a curve before continuing into Austria and freedom. But I could not run fast enough. We could not catch up to the train and were left behind; so we had to go back to Budapest. I knew it was all my fault.

Now, more than four decades later, it seemed like a dream as we stood alongside Secretary of State Warren Christopher on a cold, gray, cloudy December morning in 1994. I was back in Budapest, standing on the tarmac of Ferihegy Airport with my husband, Donald Blinken, the United States Ambassador to the Republic of Hungary. We were awaiting the arrival of President Bill Clinton aboard *Air Force One*. Just five years after the fall of the Berlin Wall, historic changes were sweeping across Hungary and other former communist countries in Eastern Europe.

Heavy cloud cover enveloped the airport. Soon, far in the distance, we heard the thunderous rumbling of a jet approaching and, a short time later, the loud squeal of airplane tires touching down. Even on the ground, visibility was poor and we couldn't quite make out the jumbo jet. A few moments later, a gleaming white airliner appeared out of the grayness and slowly taxied toward us. The large black letters on its side proclaimed: United States of America.

This stunning and dramatic vision made me feel like a character in a novel. Only this was real, as Donald kept reminding me, and welcoming President Clinton as his ambassadorial husband-and-wife team in Hungary was the culmination of our uncommon journey. How had that frightened little girl trying to escape Soviet-occupied Hungary come to find herself in such a place?

BUDAPEST

My return to Hungary took many turns, and begins with my mother, Lili. The youngest of three sisters, she was vivacious, outgoing, and lovable. She had blonde hair and the most beautiful bright blue eyes that sparkled whenever she laughed, which was often. She was thin and petite, 5-feet 4-inches in heels. Her first husband died in an automobile accident after one year of marriage; left with few resources, she supported herself by giving French lessons. Her charming personality soon caused two men to fall in love with her: Jozsef Ermer and Paul Flesch. Jozsef was a banker of medium height, with brown hair and blue eyes; his demeanor was formal and serious, hiding a keen sense of humor. Paul was the son of a rural veterinarian who yearned to be a doctor. He was unusually tall for a Hungarian, six feet, three inches, a gentle giant of a man. When laws were passed prohibiting Jews from attending medical school, Paul went to Austria, learned

German, completed medical school, and passed his qualifying exams. Upon returning to Hungary and passing the exams again, this time in Hungarian, he began an internship in pediatrics.

Lili chose to marry Jozsef and was determined to have a child. With war threatening to erupt in Europe, her cautious husband thought the times were too dangerous to bring a child into the world. Fortunately for me, Lili got her way. Her marriage to Jozsef and my birth, along with the passage of anti-Jewish laws and Germany's saber rattling, drove Paul to emigrate to America.

I was named Veronica but have always been called Vera because Mother thought it was a diminutive of Veronica. Actually, they are two entirely different names, and started my early duality. Mother loved me so much that she wanted to be everything to me. To prove how much she wanted me, she often recounted the exchange in which Father said this was not the time to bring another person into the world. I honestly believe she had no idea that she was inadvertently imparting the impression that Father *didn't* want me, as if she had selected me beforehand and he had rejected the choice.

We were a happy little family in Budapest, but on March 19, 1944, life changed irrevocably. An infection behind my ear, which today would be cured by an antibiotic, had required the removal of the mastoid bone. While recovering at home after the surgery, I began to bleed through the bandages, and Mother quickly set off with me to the hospital. Our progress was suddenly blocked by crowds of people, and we saw regiments of German soldiers and armored vehicles moving in formation down the wide boulevard. For a child, frightened by the bleeding and unable to get to the hospital, this threat was very personal. Hungary had become part of the Axis Powers after Germany promised to restore the two-thirds of Hungarian territory lost after the 1920 Treaty of Trianon. Now, the Germans were occupying Budapest because they had discovered the Hungarian government was secretly negotiating with the Allies to switch sides.

On Christmas Eve, 1944, nine months after we watched the German Army enter our city, awareness of the war became inescapable even to a child. Mother and I were dressing for a family dinner to be held at her sister's house in Buda, in the hilly, residential area across the Danube from our apartment in Pest. Father planned to meet us there. I had stubbornly insisted on wearing a favorite dress that was late coming back from a seamstress and, as a result, we were delayed leaving the apartment. Bypassing the heavily damaged Margit Bridge, closest to our home, we had almost reached the bridge to its north when planes suddenly attacked, killing everyone on it. We fled in terror. Mother's hair soon turned white, and she always believed this was caused by the shock of our close call.

Soon afterwards, German authorities commandeered our Hollan Street apartment building and turned it into a temporary hospital. Father had not been able to cross the Danube and we had no idea where he was, yet we had to leave our home. By now, Pest was overcrowded with people fleeing from the countryside, all desperate for shelter from the fighting and the frigid cold. Somehow, my resourceful mother found an apartment at 2 Becsi Street, overlooking Erzsebet Square.

Mitzi, my nanny, was with us because her husband was in the Army. In her wonderful Teutonic way, Mitzi kept me very busy. It was a harshly cold winter and we had no heat, but the layers of clothes I wore at all times were no obstacle to Mitzi, who was always washing some part of me with very cold water, and saying, "The war will be over some day, and we have to make sure that when it is, this child will have good nails, good teeth, and good hair." I bless her for that.

As the Germans retreated and the Allies advanced, the fighting reached Pest. Each block was fought for, each street became a battleground, and the fighting was house to house. There was looting, the stores were empty, and, like everyone else, we had no food left. As a last resort, Mother would run the few blocks from Becsi Street to the hotels along the Danube where food was sometimes still available. It was a very dangerous run, but she always took me with her. "If we are going to die," she would say, "we are going to die together." We lived with constant fear and hunger.

Later, deep into the siege, to keep us from starving, Mother began to interpret for the Germans in exchange for food. While interpreting, she would always ask, "Where are you coming from?" They replied with the name of one or another section or street in the city. In mid-January, a wounded German soldier said he had just come from the front.

"How far away is the front?" Mother asked.

"Erzsebet Square," the soldier replied, and pointed to the street. The fighting was literally in front of our house.

Budapest was pounded by bombs almost daily and each time the sirens sounded, we had to rush to the basement, which had been turned into an air-raid shelter. We often had to spend long hours in those tight, dark quarters. A dim candle or two substituted for the electrical power that was an early casualty of the siege. Mother, Mitzi, and I had been assigned seats on benches along a wall; other occupants filled benches in the middle of the room. A typical little girl, I tired of sitting in the same place every day; so, on one occasion, a very nice older gentleman and two other kind people sitting next to him on a bench in the middle of the room offered to change places with us. Suddenly, a bomb struck the apartment house next door, setting it on fire and causing a wall in our building to collapse. Everybody sitting along that wall, where we had been sitting just moments earlier, died instantly.

We threw ourselves to the floor with our arms covering our heads as the rubble fell on us. Through a gaping hole in the wall and ceiling we could see the fire raging in the adjacent building. All the adults knew that the Germans were using the building behind ours as an ammunition depot. If the fire reached it, the whole block would blow up. We were desperate to find a way out, but mounds of debris blocked us, and we thought we would soon die. Miraculously, a heavy snow began to fall, putting out the fire. The snowstorm and a child's whim had saved our lives, but three people had died for doing something nice for a little girl.

On January 16, 1945, Soviet soldiers entered our air raid shelter. They had come to liberate us, and one of the soldiers came over to shake my hand. Even stranger than his desire to shake the hand of a little girl were the wristwatches he wore all the way up his arm. Most of the Soviet advance soldiers were from rural areas, had never seen wristwatches before, and didn't know that they had to be wound. Whenever a watch stopped, they threw it away and grabbed some more. Meanwhile, the Germans had retreated over the remaining bridges into Buda and then blown them up. The battle would continue on the Buda side for another month, until the Soviets finally overran the last Germans, who were holding out in the royal castle on the hill above the city.

What the Soviets would do afterward to Hungary and the other countries of the region was tragic, but in those first days we were grateful to them for reaching us before we died. Unaware of what the future held, at that moment we truly felt liberated. After our liberation from the Germans, Mother's first thought was to search for Father. She assumed that he had been caught on the Buda side on Christmas Eve. Thinking his brother might know where he was, Mother dressed us both in all the clothes we had to protect us from the terrible cold, and we ventured outside to find my uncle.

We found the city in ruins. Many buildings were only heaps of brick, stone, and plaster, and every window was shattered. In front of one building rows of dead bodies were piled up. The building had been a holding center for Jews awaiting deportation. Before retreating, with no time to ship them to concentration camps, the Germans shot their captives and stacked the corpses outside. As Mother and I walked on, I bumped into someone I thought was sprawled in the street. He failed to respond when I excused myself.

"He is not very polite," I told Mother. "He didn't say anything."

"He can't," Mother replied. "He is dead."

We walked on and saw people crowded around a dead horse. They were carving it up for food.

To our great joy and relief, we found Father at my uncle's apartment. He had indeed been caught on the Buda side, but later walked across the frozen Danube to look for us at home. Nobody knew where we had gone, so he went to his brother's apartment. Only six blocks away from us during the siege, he might have been in a different country until the Soviets fought their way from his street to ours. He and my uncle had somehow acquired a single, extraordinary food supply: a very large sack filled with chunks of white sugar. This was the first nourishment Mother and I had eaten in several days. Not very good for the teeth, but we were overjoyed to have it. That sack of sugar would sustain us for quite some time, and to this day, I always have at least ten pounds of sugar at home—just in case.

My parents and I started back toward our old apartment in a heavy snowstorm. Beside me on a child's sled were our few possessions. Father pulled the sled along Szent Istvan Avenue, a once-grand boulevard now dark and heavily damaged. Not a single vehicle was on it, just people like us walking or pulling children and belongings on sleds. Mother had been deprived of cigarettes during the war, but had now located a few and wanted to stop for a smoke. Father put the rope down and courteously went over to light her cigarette. At that instant, a stray bullet whistled down through the space where my father's head had been a few seconds before. An act of providence had spared him. I still have that bullet.

Our apartment was miraculously undamaged, and its contents were mostly intact. We pushed most of the furniture back into place and tried to resume our lives. For the first night in weeks, although hungry, I went to sleep in my own bed in my corner room on the top floor of the six-story apartment building. A few hours later, the German bombers sounded overhead and then explosions rocked the city. One bomb struck the roof of our building, slicing off a corner of my ceiling. The bomb landed alongside the building without exploding. Heavy rain poured through the gaping hole in my bedroom, but I was alive. Earlier, my childish whims had kept us off a doomed bridge and away from a deadly wall collapse. Now, for the third time, I had been miraculously saved. Years would pass before I would begin to wonder why.

Whispers among survivors said the Soviets were savages, raping and murdering wherever they went. It was to our horror, therefore, that the next night several Soviet soldiers looking for a place to sleep chose our apartment. My mother's perfume bottles had somehow survived the war. Perfume was another item most Russian soldiers had never seen before, and thinking it was a kind of whiskey, they drank it down. Of course, the perfume burned their throats terribly and they became enraged. Their anger threatened to turn violent, but they left us alone. Late that night, I peered through a keyhole into our living room, where the soldiers were sleeping on the floor with their guns beside them. It was a frightening sight.

The soldiers soon left our apartment in the morning and we were safe, but we were also very hungry. We had nothing to eat, and the only available food was in the countryside. Father feared being rounded up by the soldiers and sent to a Russian labor camp if he went outside, so Mother made her way to the country by train. Often the trains were so overcrowded that she was forced to cling to the roof of a rail car. As always, Mother showed remarkable ingenuity and courage.

The Hungarian Communists who had fled to Moscow after their failed coup at the end of World War I now came back to Budapest and took control of the government. Foreseeing that the end of the war would be followed by Soviet domination and repression, Mother urged Father to arrange our family's emigration, which would have been possible just after the war. Not given to rash action, Father told her he thought the harsh times were only temporary. If things got really bad, with the help of his good friends and banking connections in Great Britain, we could escape to London. Soon, however, the government began to nationalize companies and financial institutions, among them father's bank. He returned to join his brother at his family's export-import company, where, on a cold winter day in 1947, Mother was visiting him when government officials entered.

"We will have your keys," they said to Father.

Everyone knew what that meant. The company was being nationalized. Mother had already stopped wearing red nail polish, having been warned that the "bourgeois" color would bring undue attention. Now, when she went to put on her fur coat, an official said, "No, that stays, too." Mother walked out into the freezing cold, knowing that her coat would end up on the shoulders of the man's wife or girlfriend.

In 1948, the Communist Party openly took control of the government. All land was collectivized, industry was nationalized, and a "planned economy" was imposed.

In the spring of that same year, Father became ill although Mother and I were not told how serious his illness was. By summer, Father was hospitalized, Mother was spending all her time with him, and I was sent to a friend's country house at Lake Balaton. In August, though, I was told that Father was getting better and that he and Mother were coming to visit.

The night before their planned arrival I had a very strange experience. My friend Marika and I were sleeping in separate beds in a corner of the room with a wall behind her bed and a wall to the side of mine. A tremendous banging in that side wall woke me up in the middle of the night. Frightened, I woke Marika and asked her what was happening, what was causing the noise. Marika heard nothing. "You're imagining things," she said. "Come on, we'll change beds." We changed beds, and Marika went back to sleep. I soon heard the noise again, this time coming from behind the bed to which I had switched. After awhile it stopped, but it took a long time for me to get to sleep because I was so excited about seeing my parents after such a long separation.

The next morning, we all went to the train station to meet my parents. Instead, my mother's eldest sister, Aunt Erzsike, stepped off the train. She always had played a motherly role in the family, and now she took me for a long walk. She told me my father's condition had suddenly worsened, and he had died the night before. I am convinced that he came to me during the night to say goodbye.

Hoping to shield me from the loss, Mother kept me away from the funeral, which was held before I returned to Budapest. Because I had never seen Father looking ill and was never taken to his grave, I never completely accepted his death; something felt uncertain, unfinished. In my young mind, I imagined Mother's phrase "He left us" to mean that he had left because he didn't want to have me in the first place and perhaps now he didn't like me. When I told her this later in life, Mother was devastated, realizing that she had innocently used an unfortunate phrase to add to my sense of unresolved emotions and loss.

Thirty-four years later, in February 1982, Mother was in the hospital dying. She was in a coma, and the doctors said she would never open her eyes or speak again. I would not leave her side and was sitting by her bed looking at her and crying when her eyelids suddenly fluttered open. She stared at me with those clear blue eyes, looked around the room, and asked, "Am I still here?" Speaking in Hungarian, she then looked at me lovingly and said, "Don't cry. It's all right. There will be more of us there to look after you." She closed her eyes and never spoke again. I am convinced that, just like my Father in 1948, Mother came back from another place to say goodbye.

Mother saw Father's death at forty-four as a sign that she had been right about wanting to leave Hungary. Why else, she asked, would God have taken such a fine man so young? By the summer of 1948, however, the Communist government had sealed the borders, condemning its citizens to life imprisonment. That was when Mother began seeking a way to escape, testing possible means, like our futile run to catch the train before it crossed into Austria.

Mother had always spoken openly to me, but now she began to keep things to herself. If I had known her objective was escaping from Hungary, I would certainly have approved. Even though I liked school, it felt oppressive: All education had been recast in accordance with communist ideology and Soviet needs, communication had been cut off with countries on the other side of the Iron Curtain, and Russian became the only foreign language taught in the schools. Even as a child, I disliked the authoritarian orders and the many restrictions placed on what we could do. I disliked the drabness of the Little Pioneers' tan uniform and red scarf. I also resented being responsible for the grades of our building concierge's lazy daughter. Communism, we were told, meant share and share alike, and supposedly we all were born with equal capabilities.

Mother assumed that the appropriation of both my father's businesses meant we were on the government's watch list. Thousands of citizens considered untrustworthy were on the list by then. The secret police couldn't send everyone to Siberia. Instead, people who got caught trying to escape were forced to report on others; you became a *besugo* or "whisperer," in other words, an informer. The secret police, however, wouldn't believe you if you accused strangers. One had to denounce people one knew, friends and neighbors, which created an atmosphere of tension and betrayal.

After nearly two years of failing to find a slit in the Iron Curtain for our escape, Mother was losing hope. Unexpectedly, the government provided a way to slip through when it passed a law in 1949 ordering all foreign citizens to leave the country. Giorgio Benzoni, the Italian ambassador, a friend of my parents, came to Mother in early 1950 with an escape plan: He would arrange for her to marry an Italian widower whom the law was expelling from Hungary. She and I would leave with her "husband." Because the marriage was being undertaken for humanitarian reasons, the Vatican would annul it once we were all safely out of Hungary.

I first learned of the plan the afternoon my mother came home with an Italian widower named Leo Comis. A good-looking, dark-skinned man with gray hair, he spoke Hungarian with a heavy Italian accent and owned a pastry shop in Budapest, where he had lived a long time. He and his son were now returning home to Piave di Cadore, a small town north of Venice. Mother introduced him to me as her new husband and my new father. Angry and appalled, I broke into tears. At first, I refused to speak to her, and then I wanted to know how she could betray my father's memory by getting married so soon after his death, and to a man who didn't even speak proper Hungarian.

Fearing that keeping the truth from me might destroy our relationship, Mother explained that Leo was helping us to leave Hungary, so we could go to America. The marriage wasn't a real one and would last only a short while. Wanting my friends to understand that my mother wasn't being unfaithful to my father's memory, I informed them the next day that she was getting married as a ploy for us to escape to America. Then I proudly reported to Mother that I had upheld her honor. My poor mother must have been horrified. With everyone in Hungary being forced to inform on everyone else as the price for their own freedom, she immediately diagnosed a terrible virus that required my staying home—and having no contact with my friends because I was extremely contagious. At the same time, concerned that our neighbors would begin to grow suspicious about why Mr. and Mrs. Comis were not living together, Leo and his son moved in with us, which added to my emotional turmoil at the prospect of leaving home forever for a destination that was only a name to me.

These events took place during a dreadful time in Hungary. As in China's Cultural Revolution, which sent city inhabitants to farms in the countryside, Hungary undertook a mass relocation scheme to switch the "disloyal" and "rebellious" city bourgeoisie with presumably more loyal country peasants. We knew several families who were given just two hours to pack up whatever they could and move out of their houses to distant farms. The government then divided their houses into tiny apartments and moved in several country families who shared the kitchen, Soviet style. Mother thought there was an imminent possibility that we, too, might be forcibly relocated to live on what we forever afterward referred to as the "chicken farm."

Although Mother's marriage was for humanitarian reasons, there was a financial side to it as well. We were very fortunate. Mother's sister Manci and her Greek ship-owner husband, Dimitri, who lived in New York, made it financially possible for us to leave Hungary by transferring funds into Leo's Swiss bank account. Letters full of hidden meanings shuttled to and from New York regarding our escape plan. "The package will be arriving shortly at the snowy country" meant Leo's payment had been wired to his Swiss bank account. Much of the communication went through my grandmother in Budapest. She was a great letter writer and, to her credit, kept her three daughters closely connected during the many years of separation.

In April, the newly-formed Comis family finally went to the Western railroad station for our trip to "our new home in Italy." My grandmother, Aunt Erzsike, and her family came to see us off. No one knew if we would see each other ever again. At the last moment, I heard Mother whisper to her sister something I was too young to decipher: "Take good care of her if they send her back." Only many years later did I find out its meaning. Mother did not allow Leo to adopt me because the Catholic Church would annul a marriage but not an adoption. She was adamant that my father did not die at the young age of forty-four for his child to be somebody else's daughter for the rest of her life. So, I remained Hungarian and, being under age, was included on my mother's new Italian passport, but only as "Daughter—minor." The risk was that if the border guards requested my papers and learned that my last name was not Comis, they might force my now-Italian Mother across the border into Austria, but send me, her Hungarian daughter, back to Budapest.

Those expelled by the Communist regime were not allowed to take out of the country any valuables, including jewelry, but Mother was not leaving without the treasured ring Father had given her at my birth: a wide gold band with the initial *L* for Lili in pavé diamonds. Once aboard the train in our sleeping compartment, she hung it on a necklace around my neck and slipped it inside my pajama top. Then she gave me a sleeping pill. If I were asleep, I could not be questioned. I awoke as the train was pulling into Vienna and heard that we had successfully passed through the Hungarian border checkpoint; we were out of Soviet-occupied Hungary, and we were free. On the station platform, Mother purchased oranges and bananas. Never before had I tasted—or even seen—an orange or a banana. They were heavenly.

Our euphoria was short-lived. As the train was traveling through the Austrian countryside, it suddenly stopped. Through the window Mother and I could see Soviet soldiers marching toward us. Both of us were sure the Hungarian authorities had learned of our escape and sent word to take us off the train. Mother knew that they could force her to continue onward and send me back to Hungary. Our hearts were racing, but we tried to appear calm as the soldiers moved through the train toward the "Comis family." A Russian soldier took Mother's Italian passport and began to study our photographs. The soldier looked sharply at us for what seemed like forever. Then he snapped the passport shut and gave it back to Mother. The soldiers moved on, and the train soon started moving again.

A little farther on, the train suddenly stopped again in the middle of a field. This time, British soldiers came aboard and wanted to see our passports. Mother asked one who spoke German what was going on. He explained that we had left the Soviet zone and were entering the British zone. We had been so isolated in Hungary that we were unaware that Austria had been divided after the war into four zones controlled by separate allied forces: the British, the Americans, the French and the Soviets. Our train had simply gone through routine passport controls. We were safe and we were free. We later learned from Aunt Erzsike that shortly after we left Hungary, the authorities seized our apartment with orders to relocate us to the countryside. We had escaped with little time to spare.

ZURICH

When the train reached Zurich, Mother and I said goodbye to Leo, whose obligation had ended after we crossed the border from Hungary. He and his son continued on, home to Italy. We took a taxi to the only hotel in Zurich that Mother knew: the elegant and stately Baur au Lac, where she had stayed with Father in happier times. The sensation of riding freely through a bustling, colorful city after gray and gloomy Budapest seemed surreal to us.

Anxiety soon returned. Mother immediately phoned her sister Manci in New York, who had been expecting the call for days and was overjoyed to hear that her little sister's escape was successful. The two had been unable to speak with each other since the outbreak of the war because in Hungary phone calls abroad were problematic. They could be made only at the post office, and were reported to the Ministry of the Interior, who undoubtedly listened in on them. We had expected Manci to fly to Europe on the very next plane, as she had assured Mother, in code of course, that she would take care of everything from then on. On the phone, however, Manci said, "I'll get there as soon as possible, but you and Vera are going to be expensive for me, so I'm going to travel on one of Dimitri's freighters. I don't know how long that will take. It may be a month or so."

Mother was devastated, but could not say so. She was embarrassed to tell Manci that we had no money because we had only been allowed to take out of Hungary the equivalent of a hundred dollars. What to do? To conserve cash, we had all our meals at the hotel and charged them to our room, stalling for time. A chance encounter at our hotel briefly lifted Mother's spirits. She was happy to meet an old friend from Budapest, the pianist George Feyer. George left Hungary right after the war and made his way to New York, where he gained renown performing at the famous Café Carlyle in Manhattan. Mother told him how despondent she had become at our seemingly hopeless situation in Zurich, and of my homesickness for Budapest. "You should bend down and kiss the ground you are walking on because you are free," he said, his voice rising with emotion. He was so right.

In desperation, Mother telephoned Leo in Italy to ask if he would send us some money, which she would pay back when Manci arrived. Like the Italian ambassador, people always wanted to help Mother. The charm that radiated from her once again stood us in good stead. Instead of sending money, good, kind Leo came to Zurich himself, paid our hotel bill, and took us to Venice, even stopping off in Milan to take the homesick child sightseeing. Remarkably, Leo was being family to us.

VENICE

In Venice, Leo gave us some money and found us a room at the Wildner, a small, reasonably priced hotel near St. Mark's Square, with a view of the Grand Canal. Venice thrilled me; the world was much larger and more beautiful than I could have ever imagined in war-torn Hungary.

Mother tried to be frugal. Seeing a café that announced a low price for *café con panna*, she ordered it for us. Knowing French, but not Italian, she assumed that with our coffee we would get bread (*pain* in French). What the waiter brought out was coffee with whipped cream. Bread, it turned out, was *pane*. One inexpensive way we occupied our time was by teaching each other English from a book. Among the few phrases we learned were "I don't speak English" and "Please speak slowly."

Less than a week after we arrived, Manci phoned to say she was flying to Milan and would be arriving in Venice by train in two days. Mother had told me many stories about my glamorous aunt, including that we had an identical birthmark on the side of our legs. My first sight of this vision stepping down from the train, however, far surpassed anything that a shy little girl from postwar Hungary could have imagined. She was the most glamorous, most elegant, most striking being I had ever seen! Aunt Manci had auburn hair, a stunning smile, and a dramatic presence. I was transfixed by her big, full skirt, which was the style that year, the shimmering blouse with long puffy sleeves, and her chunky gold bracelets. Just for traveling! That this divine goddess and I could share a birthmark felt overwhelming.

Sweeping into our Venice hotel like Auntie Mame, Aunt Manci instantly and permanently changed the lives of her two penniless relatives as if she had waved a magic wand. She paid all our bills and soon moved us to the elegant Grand Hotel des Bains on the Lido, the resort island between Venice and the sea. With the summer season approaching, Manci was sure that awaiting Mother's annulment from the Vatican would be far more enjoyable by the sea. Eventually, Manci admitted the real reason for her delay in leaving New York: clothes. Knowing the hardships Mother had endured in Hungary and the risks she had taken to escape, Manci was embarrassed to reveal that she had delayed her trip because her summer wardrobe was not ready. As soon as it was delivered, she was on the next plane to Europe and us. Clothes and her appearance were very important to Aunt Manci.

The Korean War broke out on my birthday, June 27, 1950. Many Americans in Europe immediately headed home. Sure that another world war was about to start, Manci's husband Dimitri kept phoning and sending telegrams, imploring her to come home. "Absolutely not," she told him. "After what my sister has been through, I'm not leaving her and her child behind." In August, the Vatican granted Mother the annulment of her marriage to Leo Comis. The United States had set quotas for the number of persons from each country allowed to emigrate there. The quota for Italians was quickly filled and there was a long waiting list. Because so few people were able to escape Hungary, the Hungarian quota was empty. Now that both Mother and I were Hungarian again, America would accept us. Our problem, however, was getting there. The Korean War had put a strain on flights and shipping, so Aunt Manci decided we should go to Paris, Her husband had an office there, and they would help us obtain transportation to America.

PARIS

The Champs Elysees with all its lights was the most dazzling sight Mother had seen since before the war, and certainly the most dazzling that I had ever seen. It took us a long time to summon the courage to cross that wide, busy boulevard. Aunt Manci had installed us all at the luxurious Georges V Hotel and bought us new wardrobes for our new lives in America.

One afternoon Mother and Aunt Manci were having drinks at the hotel with me tagging along when Jolie Gabor entered. She and her beautiful daughters, Zsa Zsa, Eva, and Magda, had left Hungary before the war. My mother knew her from Hungary, and Aunt Manci from New York, where Jolie had a jewelry store that had become very successful selling replicas of famous designers' jewelry. I still remember how impressed I was when a telephone was brought to our table. Zsa Zsa was calling from Hollywood to ask her mother what she should wear to a dinner party that evening and which dinner partner she should concentrate on.

NEW YORK

In August 1950, Mother, Aunt Manci, and I finally sailed for New York on the *S.S. America*. Even the ship's name proclaimed not only my destination but my destiny. An early-season hurricane made the trip difficult but could not diminish my excitement or my apprehension. Except for Niagara Falls, I knew nothing about America, and Mother knew little more. Frightening to contemplate as I stepped off the ship and onto a New York City pier was that I was a stranger here, without roots and without a home. I was a homesick little girl, but I knew that Communist Hungary was not the home I wanted.

Uncle Dimitri had not seen Mother or me since I was born. Naturally, Mother was very concerned about how he would receive us, for my coming into his life would be a shock because he and Aunt Manci had no children. Dimitri turned out to be the kindest man, immediately welcoming and loving, and he jokingly told me that he would have to get to know me because the last time he saw me I was just a "little piece of red meat." Aunt Manci did some quick research on private schools, and the Lenox School for Girls accepted me, even though the school year was starting in a few short weeks. School was difficult at first. A child doesn't want to be different and fitting in was difficult for a little girl who spoke no English, wore an immense wristwatch to which she was unreasonably attached, and had long pigtails with bows that were fashionable only among the Little Pioneers in Hungary. These were superficialities to be sure, but they provoked teasing from my classmates that needed no translation and caused me a great deal of anguish. One girl assigned to shepherd me around took malicious pleasure in leaving me in the wrong classroom, and if you weren't in the right place on time, you got a demerit. I didn't know what a demerit was, but she made sure I got a lot of them. I occasionally see her at large social events, and the pain I felt at the undeserved demerits and the mocking laughter still resonates.

On several occasions the math teacher asked if anyone knew the answer to the problem she had just written on the blackboard. I did, but dared not raise my hand because I could not have said it in correct English. Another time, at a poetry reading contest, I pronounced the word *desert* as *dessert*, eliciting laughter from my fellow contestants. Wanting so badly to be understood and accepted, I became determined to be 200 percent American and forget everything Hungarian. Hungary was in the past. America was my future. Conversations with my mother became bilingual: I spoke to her in English, and although she learned to speak English very well, she spoke to me in Hungarian, so as not to impart her accent to me.

Six months after entering the Lenox School, I won the American history prize and was awarded a book, Ralph Waldo Emerson's *Self-Reliance*, which I still treasure. My rapid mastery of the English language was not only a necessity but also a source of great pride and has persuaded me that, however respectful bilingual education may be toward a child's cultural heritage and first language, it is a huge mistake. If the Lennox School had been able to educate me in Hungarian, I would never have learned to speak English well enough to further my education and get ahead in life. By hearing my native language at home, as immigrant children do, I retained that as well.

After my father died and knowing that my mother wanted to leave Hungary, Aunt Manci had telephoned my mother's former suitor, Paul, who had left Hungary with a broken heart after my mother married my father. Paul was now a struggling doctor in New York. Manci asked him to return to Hungary, marry my mother in order to bring us out, and then get a divorce if they wished. If he would, Manci offered to set him up in an office anywhere he wanted, which must have been tempting for him. Yet, too hurt by Mother's earlier rejection, Paul refused, saying, "I never want to see that woman again and especially not her child." I was, of course, living proof that she had chosen the other man.

Soon after we arrived in New York, Mother phoned Paul, saying, "Here we are, Paul. No thanks to you, but here we are."

"Welcome to America," he said. "I'm married."

"That's wonderful. Good for you."

"But I'm separated." I went along on their first date.

It took some time for Paul's divorce to come through, but two years later Mother and he were married, and they lived happily ever after. Paul was a good man with a deep love for America. Even before becoming a citizen, he had enlisted in the U.S. Army and served in Europe throughout World War II under General Eisenhower, whose photo he carried in his wallet for the rest of his life. When the war ended, Paul went back to Hungary to locate his family and discovered that all of them—his mother, father and brother—had perished in a mass grave the Nazis had forced them to dig. Ironically, Mother's decision to marry my father drove Paul, heartsick, from Hungary, and thus saved his life.

Because Paul loved my mother—and she loved him—he accepted me in the bargain. Sadly, Paul, who was so fond of children that he had become a pediatrician, did not have any children of his own. Paul's life had been marked by hardships that he overcame with fortitude, and he was afraid that I would be spoiled by Aunt Manci's luxurious lifestyle. What kept me from becoming spoiled was a desire to live up to my mother's high expectations of me. She had risked so much to bring me to America that I believed I owed her my best efforts at whatever I did.

I arrived at Vassar College six short years after leaving Communist Hungary. I did not own the de rigueur Bermuda shorts or button-down shirts that everyone else was wearing, although I had several exquisite Pierre Cardin suits Aunt Manci had bought me in Paris. My European upbringing had not prepared me to live with girls who had attended prep schools and knew each other from country clubs; who carried themselves with an insider's confidence I couldn't begin to emulate. Once again, I felt totally out of place. My unhappiness and the resulting sleepless nights made me a prime target for that freshman bane, mononucleosis. By mid-October, I was back home, confined to bed and on my way to gaining twenty pounds.

On October 23, 1956, my bedside radio brought the electrifying news that university students in Budapest were demonstrating for greater political freedom and the withdrawal of Soviet troops stationed on Hungarian soil. The uprising quickly spread to other regions and other segments of the population. Demands were made to liberalize all aspects of the oppressive political and economic systems. When the government's security forces proved incapable of quelling the unrest, the

Hungarian Army was called in, but the soldiers joined the revolt and distributed weapons to the insurgents. At the cost of many lives, Soviet troops were forced to withdraw beyond the country's borders.

Freedom fighters took control of radio stations to keep the population informed and rally others to their cause. American-sponsored Radio Free Europe not only beamed information into the country but also, many would later contend, assurances that U.S. troops would come to the freedom fighters' aid. Instead of sending in troops, the United States turned the matter over to the United Nations, and nothing was done.

On November 4, 1956, Soviet forces rolled back into Hungary to suppress the uprising. Behind the radio reporters' voices I could hear the sounds of the uprising: guns firing, tanks rolling, and even Hungarian voices crying out, "They're coming! They're coming! This is our last broadcast."

In the six years since leaving Hungary, as I was building a new life, I had not thought much about my childhood years. Now, I felt guilty. While I was safe in New York, young people my age—teenagers, college students, perhaps even former classmates—were engaged in gun battles and were throwing homemade Molotov cocktails at advancing Soviet tanks. Each day the uprising continued, my guilt increased: for not being there with my contemporaries, for having survived the war when thousands didn't, for having escaped when millions couldn't, and even for being alive when so many were now dying for their beliefs. I think it was at that point that the idea began to grow within me that there had to be a reason I had been saved when others perished, and perhaps even a reason for my being in America.

Twenty-seven hundred insurgents were killed in the fighting, and nineteen thousand were injured. Thousands of Hungarians were imprisoned, executed, or deported to Soviet labor camps, and during the ten days the borders were open, two hundred thousand Hungarians fled the country. Thanks to my indomitable Aunt Manci, our family was among them. Manci could treat a broken fingernail as a tragedy of vast proportions, but when serious action was called for, she rose

to the occasion and acted gallantly. At the first report that the border
was open, she rushed to Vienna and arranged to have someone drive a
truck into Hungary and bring out the rest of our family still trapped
in Budapest: my grandmother; Aunt Erzsike and her husband, Lajos;
their architect son, Peter; Peter's pregnant wife, Susan; and their young
daughter, Ann. All but grandmother, who lived with us for the few
remaining years of her life, emigrated to Canada.

After my graduation from Vassar College in June with a bachelor's
degree in art history, I did what was expected of me: I got married
in July. Because my parents did not approve of a young woman living alone in New York, my only other choice would have been to
go home to live with them and so I went through with a wedding
I had already sensed might be a mistake. After a difficult few years,
I obtained a divorce. By then I had earned a graduate degree from
the New York School of Interior Design and was working as an assistant to a very traditional decorator doing what I called "Upper Park
Avenue chintz," not my favorite look. But my salary allowed me to
embark on the lively, single life that finally helped me grow up and
become independent.

However hard we try to direct our lives, I believe that fate plays
an important role as well. At a cocktail party, an architect approached
me because he liked the way I tied my scarf around the handle of my
Hermes Kelly bag. He was the head of the Interiors Department at
the renowned architectural firm of Edward Durell Stone. He offered
me a job and I accepted on the spot.

At the Stone office, I worked on several interesting projects,
such as the interior designs of the General Motors building in New
York and the Kennedy Center in Washington. Client meetings with
Mr. Stone could be embarrassing because he never called me by my
name. He did not remember the names of blondes; his affinity was
for brunettes. At meetings he would say, "Blondie, what's the color

scheme for this?" or "What are the fabrics for that, Blondie?" He could not get away with that today.

The firm did not decorate private residences, but when an important Stone client requested this, I was assigned to do the interiors. So it followed that in 1967, when a friend of mine moved to Greenwich, Connecticut, her house became the first project of Vera Evans Interiors.

With my business going well in the early 1970s, and my private life busy, if not happy, I began to feel a growing need to pay back the debt I owed God or fate for my good fortune. I was already doing interesting and useful volunteer work on the boards of arts organizations, but that was fun, not repayment. After doing some research, I found an organization to whose mission I related: The International Rescue Committee, which helped resettle refugees who had fled totalitarian regimes. If I hadn't had an Aunt Manci, I might have been among them. The IRC was founded in 1933 at the suggestion of Albert Einstein to assist intellectuals fleeing Nazi Germany. Its founders hoped that after World War II ended, the IRC could be disbanded because the world would no longer have refugees. However, after the 1956 uprising opened Communist Hungary's borders long enough for thousands of Hungarians to escape, it became sadly obvious that refugees would be fleeing totalitarianism for many decades to come. The IRC's mission was still relevant. I informed the IRC that I would do anything to help—stuff envelopes or whatever was needed. In 1978 I was asked to join the board of directors, and the IRC has been an important part of my life ever since.

Despite my earlier resolve to become 200 percent American, I carry my past within me like every other refugee. This refugee mentality resurfaced during the 1962 Cuban Missile Crisis. When war between the United States and the Soviet Union appeared imminent, Mother worriedly phoned and told me to go right out and stock up on sugar, and of course I immediately did. From our wartime experience, we knew that sugar would save us from starvation.

Mother often lamented my unmarried state, but I was in no hurry to wed and possibly make another mistake. My interior design business was going well and one day I phoned Mother to tell her that I had bought myself a mink coat. "Aren't you proud of me, that I could do it on my own?" I asked.

Mother broke into tears. "No, no, no, a husband should buy you a fur coat."

So, just to please Mother, on May 11, 1971, I went out on a blind date. It was with Donald Blinken. We had a very pleasant dinner at a neighborhood French restaurant, and the following morning I phoned two close friends and said, "I just met the man with whom I would like to spend the rest of my life. But it will take some time."

Donald and I were married on October 15, 1975. I received a wedding band inscribed "D.B. to V.E. with all my love." This simple gold band and my American passport are my two most treasured possessions. Donald's son, Antony, who had been nine years old when we first met and was then thirteen, gave me the best possible wedding present when he told me how grateful he was to me for making his father so happy. And I am thankful for the close and loving relationship that Antony and I have continued.

Marriage to Donald provided me with emotional security for the first time in my life. I felt that our marriage was meant to be. My sense of security grew out of Donald's genuine sincerity and his absolute reliability. "He's like the Rock of Gibraltar," I explained to my mother. Donald has a brilliant, complex mind, but he is admirably simple in this way: When he says something, he means it. When he says he will do something, he does it. That kind of reliability is very important to me, probably because of the uncertainty and turbulence of my childhood. In addition to our shared interests, we bring out the best in each other. We complement and support each other without competing.

Looking back, I can see that both of us came into our own and our horizons expanded after we married. I don't think it was accidental that good and interesting things outside business began happening for Donald when I entered his life. His modesty causes him to downplay his accomplishments, but I have taken it upon myself to remind him how he shines at whatever he does. I hope that it was in part my unwavering belief in him and my encouragement that has provided Donald with a serenity that allowed him to take on new and exciting challenges.

Vera with her mother in Budapest

Vera with her father

Vera with Mitzi in Budapest

Vera with Lili and Leo Comis, Venice, 1950

Vera with Aunt Manci, New York, 1950

Lili, age 9

Lili and Paul

Uncle Dimitri

Donald as urban cowboy

Donald reading the Sunday funnies

Donald with parents Ethel and Maurice, Nye Bevan, Jennie Lee, and Israel
Sieff, outside London, 1950

Donald in his Army Air Corps uniform

RETURN

"What am I doing taking myself back to this dangerous place? What if they know Mother and I left illegally and won't let me out?"

In 1986, Donald and I were invited to a farewell party for our friends Ronald Lauder and his wife, Jo Carole, who were leaving for Vienna, where Ronald would be taking up his duties as ambassador to Austria. Ronald had always been interested in Central Europe, Viennese culture, and his Hungarian heritage through his mother, Estee, who was born in New York to Hungarian parents.

Ronald invited his friends to visit him and Jo Carole in Vienna, and, to me, he added, "There will be a price to pay. You have to promise me that when you come to visit us in Vienna, you're going to go back to Budapest."

By that time, I was getting interested in exploring my roots. So, I replied, "Ronald, it's a deal."

Hungary was still a communist country and a satellite of the Soviet Union, but outsiders had long been permitted to visit. Twice in the 1960s I obtained an entry visa, but both times got cold feet and found excuses to cancel the trip.

BUDAPEST, 1987

On June 11, 1987, at the conclusion of a delightful stay with the Lauders in Vienna, Donald and I left by car for Hungary. Ronald insisted that it was important to drive and not to fly as I had planned because I must be aware of actually crossing the border. He was very prescient because that was exactly what I was trying to avoid.

We drove up to the same checkpoint at Hegyeshalom that Mother and I had tried to bypass in our run through the woods on that dark night in 1949. Now, it looked like a toll booth on a bridge. The moment I had dreaded turned out to be anticlimactic. The guard looked at our American passports, glanced at us, lifted the pole, and said, "Okay." Not even "German" or "Hungarian." Just, "Okay."

As we drove on and entered Hungary, I burst into uncontrollable tears. *What was I doing taking myself back to this dangerous place? What if they know Mother and I left illegally and won't let me out?* Overcome with fear and thoughts of my mother's sacrifice, I cried all the way to Budapest, and Donald tried in vain to comfort me.

We checked into the Forum Hotel, which was built on the site of the bombed-out Ritz, the hotel my mother and I had run to for food during the siege. As we were unpacking, I noticed that there was only one tiny soap in the bathroom, so in Hungarian I asked the maid for more soap. "New," she replied, "or will a used one do?" It broke my heart. Her reply illuminated the chasm between my life in the free world and those trapped behind the Iron Curtain, and I was reminded of why I had not returned earlier, the guilt of the survivor having just surfaced.

Donald and I went out to find the place where I had lived. All the street names had been changed under Communism. My street, Hollan, was now Furst Sandor. "I think we're getting close," I said, as I got a whiff of freshly baked bread and suddenly remembered that a bakery had been on the corner. We got out of the car and walked the rest of the way. I remembered every store we passed. Around the corner from the bakery had been a movie theater, and it was still there. When we reached my former apartment house, the umbrella shop still occupied the corner, with the same sign still there. The toy store that had been across the street, however, was gone. The space had been converted into ground-level apartments.

The fear of being overpowered by my emotions prevented me from entering my old apartment building, but a family friend had asked me to take a look at the building where she had lived. The concierge at our hotel had either not recognized the old street name, as he claimed, or pretended not to know, so as not to be considered subversive by remembering it. He advised me to ask someone over the age of forty when I was in the neighborhood. So, I stopped a woman who looked to be about the right age and asked if she knew what the old street name had been changed to.

Indeed she did. Before I could thank her, she asked her own question. "How is it that a foreigner, I assume an American, is in this neighborhood and speaks Hungarian?" I told her that I was born in Budapest and had lived in the neighborhood, pointing back to my building. Without missing a beat, she said, "Oh, then you must remember the toy store."

I stood there dumbfounded. Here was somebody I had never seen before who shared the same distant memories. But I had escaped, and she had not. The feeling I had had all my life was now piercingly poignant: How lucky I was to live in freedom, to have such a full life, to be able to travel all over the world, to see and experience so much that to this woman were just dreams, perhaps not even dreams.

I guess my thoughts showed on my face because she said, "Don't look so sad. It's better than it used to be." She insisted on buying us ice cream and we exchanged addresses, but I knew she would not want to write or want to receive mail from the United States. That would still be too dangerous. My heart filled with sadness.

After the encounter at Hollan Street, I decided to seek out a place that I feared and confront it. Donald and I walked to Erszebet Square, then along its periphery until I came upon the familiar building at 2 Becsi Street. More than forty years earlier it had contained the basement air-raid shelter to which Mother, Mitzi, and I had been assigned. With my heart pounding, my mind raced back to those distant times. Once again, I saw the faces of German and Russian soldiers, I remembered streets Mother and I had raced along in search of food, and later, streets littered with frozen bodies. I thought about the bullet that didn't kill Father because Mother wanted a cigarette. I recalled the bridge that exploded in front of Mother and me, and I remembered the people who were buried beneath the falling wall of this building those many years ago. And I remembered—no, I felt—the frightened little girl who survived.

Because the door to 2 Becsi Street was locked, I turned away and crossed the street to Erszebet Square. It had been a battlefield. War had raged here and now it was a peaceful park and playground. Sitting down on a bench, I looked around and saw children younger than I had been then, laughing and calling out at the imaginary danger as their swings arced up and down. Happily, they were so safe, and so was I.

Yet, I could not control a recurring nightmare in the twilight zone before waking: a small girl alone in Budapest, usually cold and hungry, without a place to live, always without a home.

I had spoken very little Hungarian since arriving in New York as a little girl, but heard it spoken at home by my mother and stepfather Paul. Now, as I began to speak my mother tongue again, my emotions surged. I felt disoriented: in place and out of place, on intimate terms with strangers. Memories I had repressed for thirty-seven years flowed back, and so did the guilt and fear, now mixed with enormous sadness. Tears erupted as each new sight exposed another hardship imposed by an oppressive regime. We had a letter of introduction to the American ambassador, Mark Palmer, from our friend John Whitehead, who was then deputy secretary of state. Upon arriving in Budapest, we learned that the ambassador was out of the country. It was just as well, since under the circumstances I was not fit company.

It matched my mood that Budapest looked so sad and grey. The government had done little maintenance and only necessary repairs since taking power and nationalizing private property after the war. Walking back to the hotel after dinner one evening, we saw Soviet military vehicles, windows darkened and military insignias removed, ferrying troops around the country in secret convoys.

As a child, I had never been allowed to visit my father's grave. Before leaving Budapest Donald and I went to the cemetery where he is buried. My memory of my father had faded over the years, in part because my mother had not spoken of him in an attempt to protect me from the loss. The sight of his gravestone brought back how much he and I had loved each other and confirmed my belief that on the night he died he came to me to say goodbye. Along with his name and the dates of his birth and death, my mother had a single word carved on the tombstone. I recognized a child's handwriting as my own. The word was *Apukam.* "My Daddy.

From the cemetery, Istvan, our driver, drove us to the airport. We met Istvan when we requested at the hotel a driver who spoke English and was clever enough to help us locate a grave from forty years ago. Istvan fit the bill. He personifies the irrepressible Hungarian spirit. Before he dropped us off at the airport, he told us to call the hotel if we needed him again because he didn't have a telephone. A hotel employee was his neighbor and would relay our message.

The next time Istvan drove us, on a later visit to Budapest, he informed us that he had had a phone installed at his home after a ten-year wait under the previous regime, but it had not yet been connected. Then, he asked us to pay him in U.S. dollars. Because he couldn't be seen accepting foreign currency in public, we stopped on the side of the road before we reached the airport and gave him dollars.

On our next trip, Istvan's telephone was connected and he said he could accept U.S. cash openly because he had a legitimate foreign currency occupation. On the next visit, he asked if I wanted a receipt because he knew I had a foundation for which it might be a tax-deductible expense. Today, he operates a fleet of cars and has e-mail and a Web site. Our experience with Istvan was emblematic of how quickly Hungarians can adapt to capitalism, given the opportunity.

SOUTHAMPTON, 1988

In the summer of 1988, George Soros invited us to a lunch in South-ampton that he was giving for Hungary's Prime Minister, Karoly Grosz. George, a Hungarian-born American financier, established a foundation in Hungary in 1984 to promote a more open society. The foundation's first activity was to distribute free photocopiers to dissidents to help them publicize their views. Accompanying the prime minister on his trip to meet with American officials was the American ambassador to Hungary, Mark Palmer, who had not been in Hungary when Donald and I made our first visit to Budapest in the summer of 1987. A charismatic career diplomat, Ambassador Palmer urged me to return to Hungary for another visit, promising, "Next time I'll make sure that I'm there."

"That's very kind of you, Ambassador," I replied, "but I really doubt that I will be returning in the near future."

Donald had satisfied his curiosity about the place where I was born, and I had no reason to go back to a place that made me feel so sad and guilty, a place I did not think I could do anything to effect positive change.

BUDAPEST, 1988

Only six months later, however, in December 1988, fate took me back to Budapest. Donald was chairman of the board of trustees of the State University of New York and, together with the new SUNY chancellor, Bruce Johnstone, and his wife, Gail, we went to Moscow to renew a student exchange program with Moscow State University. We had planned to visit Warsaw, where SUNY has programs, but no seats were available on any flights, so the Johnstones asked us to show them Budapest. At the airport, I saw how much luggage the four of us had and looked for two taxis. But a taxi driver made a counter offer: If he could fit all four of us and all our suitcases into his small car, would we pay him double the fare? He did and we did. Welcome to "goulash communism."

Ambassador Palmer set up meetings for Donald and Bruce with Hungarian educators. Because "goulash communism" had brought a degree of free enterprise to Hungary, Donald and Bruce came to the conclusion that what the country needed most was a basic business management school that would teach essentials about balance sheets, cash flow, and business organization. SUNY committed to developing a business program, along with supporting educational materials, and I was happy that Donald had established a connection to Hungary.

That December, all Budapest was gray, gray, gray! Walking down Vaci Street, the major shopping street, we saw few street lights and only limited lighting inside the stores. Tiny squares of glass were set into the shop windows, all you were allowed of a peek into the shop's interior. The shelves were mostly bare and the goods unappealing. The staff would get their weekly salaries even if nothing was sold, as would the factory workers, who had presumably achieved their production quotas. The hard-currency stores, which could earn foreign exchange for the struggling Hungarian economy, were better supplied but off-limits to locals, who were not allowed to have the foreign currency necessary to shop there. When we went out shopping on a Saturday afternoon, so the Johnstones could buy souvenirs, we were disappointed to find out that all the stores were closed until Monday morning. It was a command rather than market economy, and not at all customer friendly.

Ambassador Palmer invited the Johnstones and us to dinner at the residence and asked me, "Vera, why don't you buy an apartment in Budapest and get involved here?"

I replied, "No, Ambassador Palmer, I will not. The Communists took everything away from my family. I don't want to own anything here that can be taken away from me again, and I don't know how I could get involved, or with what."

Knowing that I was a member of the Board of Directors of the International Rescue Committee, Mark Palmer invited me the next evening to accompany him to a church, where he would be welcoming ethnic Hungarians who had fled across the border from Romania, where they faced persecution because of their background. Several Romanians recounted harrowing stories of their escapes and told of how children and parents were often separated when parents pushed their children under the barbed wire to freedom before they themselves were seized by Romanian border guards.

Back in the ambassador's car, the only American Cadillac in Communist Hungary, driving through dark and gloomy Budapest, with the American flag flying from the fender, tears were running down my cheeks when Mark asked, "Now will you get involved?"

"Yes, yes," I sobbed.

My expertise, however, was in the arts, which I felt was not an urgent need in Hungary at that time. So what could I do? I told Mark how dismayed Donald and I were that nearly every dish we encountered was cooked with lard and swimming in cream. "I wish I could do something about that, but I don't know anything about nutrition," I said.

Mark smiled and took out his card. On the back he wrote his wife's name, Sushma Palmer, and her phone number in Washington. Sushma was a nutritionist, and he told me to phone her. With all of Hungary's problems, I had the good luck to identify a need in which the wife of the ambassador was an expert.

Sushma and I established a program to educate Hungarians about the dangers of their diet, which was killing more men under forty with heart attacks than in any other country in Europe. To fund it, I set up the American-Hungarian Friendship Forum. I now had a reason to return to Hungary on a regular basis.

In June 1989, the first President Bush visited Budapest and announced that the Peace Corps would be coming to Hungary to teach English, the international language of business and technology. It was to be the organization's first entry into a developed country. In New York, I was glued to the television set as Peter Jennings reported on the President's visit from the roof of the Forum Hotel, a view that was familiar to me from our recent trip.

A few weeks later, I received a phone call from the Peace Corps asking if the American-Hungarian Friendship Forum would underwrite a symposium the Peace Corps was planning to hold in Hungary that fall. Because this was to be the Peace Corps' first program in a developed country, the organizers wanted to be careful about consulting with Hungarian educators on the parameters of the proposed English language curriculum. However, the Peace Corps was authorized to fund only programs, not conferences.

Before deciding, I went down to Washington to meet Paul Coverdell, who had headed Bush's election campaign in the South and was now director of the Peace Corps. I asked why the Peace Corps had approached me and not George Soros. Paul admitted George had turned the Peace Corps down because he was already sponsoring English-language programs in Hungary. Mark Palmer, a tireless cheerleader for improving Hungarian-American relations, had suggested they try me next.

I was delighted with Paul. He had the zeal of a missionary, which was contagious. I found very appealing his hope that an English-teaching program in Hungary might start to redress in a small way America's failure to come to the aid of the freedom fighters in 1956. I said I would think about the matter for a few days and get back to him.

A day or so later, as I walked into the International Rescue Committee's offices for a meeting, the chairman, Leo Cherne, said, "I need to talk to you, confidentially." We stepped to one side, and he whispered, "Do it!"

"Do what, Leo?"

"You know what I'm talking about. Do it. We'll talk after the meeting."

Pure cloak and dagger! All during the meeting, I was thinking, *Leo is on the President's Intelligence Committee, so he was probably told to convince me to provide the funds for the conference. The Peace Corps Program must be a cover for some secret operation they don't want traced back to the CIA. George Soros is a lot smarter than I am, and he's turned it down. I am definitely not going to do it either!*

After the meeting, I warily asked Leo, "How do you know about it? You're on the Intelligence Committee, right?"

"Yes, I am," he said.

"I'm not doing it."

Leo burst out laughing, then said, "My niece works for the Peace Corps and typed the official letter to you. She knew you were on the IRC board, so she asked me to 'please encourage Mrs. Blinken to do it.' "

The story sounded bizarre enough to be true, and I believed it. Our longtime friend, Senator Daniel Patrick Moynihan, for whom I worked as Special Assistant for the Arts and Cultural Affairs in the late 1980s, also encouraged me to fund the conference. I phoned Paul Coverdell and told him, "Yes, I will do it."

BUDAPEST, 1989

The Peace Corps symposium took place October 15–17, 1989 in a beautifully restored castle just outside Budapest. We flew to Hungary for the conference with Paul Coverdell, and Donald also became involved, locating SUNY English-studies faculty interested in providing input on programs and texts for teaching English. The Peace Corps proposed a five-year plan for the program, but Hungarians objected, not to the length but because of the bad connotations of five-year plans in Soviet-bloc countries. The program was lengthened to six years.

Ambassador Mark Palmer gave a dinner at the embassy residence in honor of the Peace Corps, Paul Coverdell, and the Blinkens. After we climbed the stairs, nearly hitting our heads on low-hanging light fixtures, we entered the public rooms and saw the neglected condition of the furnishings under overly bright lights. My first reaction was, *"Can this be how the United States wants to present itself to the people of Hungary?"* My interior designer's mind began considering the changes I would make, never dreaming that I would actually get the chance to do so.

The first person I saw upon entering the reception hall was Estee Lauder and her son, Ronald. Ronald had been responsible for my first visit back to Hungary, more than two years earlier. Estee and Ronald, no longer ambassador to Austria, were there to open the Estee Lauder boutique on Vaci Street. Estee invited us to the ribbon-cutting ceremony the following day.

The next morning, Donald and I walked over to Vaci Street and saw a large crowd of government officials, reporters, TV crews, and people gathered to watch Estee cut the ribbon. Hungarian women have always been interested in fashion and cosmetics, and were known for taking good care of themselves even during the dark period of Communism. So having glamorous Estee Lauder in Budapest and bringing her world-renowned products to Hungary was a major event.

One reporter asked Estee to demonstrate something for the cameras and seeing my familiar face in the front row, she called out, "Vera, come here." So, with TV news cameras rolling and photographers from the various newspapers clicking away, Estee touched up my makeup. That evening, a photo of Estee applying my lipstick appeared on the front page of Hungary's best-selling newspaper, *Nepszabadsag,* which was still called the "Socialist Daily." Donald teased us about the two good Socialists: Estee Lauder and Vera Blinken. For a while, the company used the video of Estee applying my makeup in its international advertising. My fifteen minutes of fame.

Because of my support of the symposium, Paul Coverdell recommended that I be among the first recipients of the Peace Corps' Partners for Peace award, which was presented on June 15, 1990 in the Rose Garden at the White House by President Bush. It was a very moving experience for this naturalized American citizen.

WHITE HOUSE DINNER, 1990

I was invited to my first White House state dinner by Paul Coverdell, director of the Peace Corps, after Donald and I returned from the 1989 Peace Corps symposium in Budapest that I had helped organize and fund. Paul's wife was unable to accompany him to a White House dinner hosted by President George Bush in honor of the Prime Minister of Poland, Tadeusz Mazowiecki, on March 21, 1990. Paul invited me to go in her place because he thought I would enjoy it. I replied that I couldn't go without Donald, but Paul explained he could bring only one guest. Donald, who had previously accompanied me to the White House for a concert by the dissident Russian pianist Vladimir Feltsman, encouraged me to go, adding, "Go because we will probably not see a Democratic president in our lifetime." He said this just after the first Gulf War when George H. W. Bush's approval ratings were off the charts.

So I went, joining Paul and the 130 other guests who filled the White House State Dining Room. President Bush recalled his visit to Poland the previous summer, spoke of the rebirth of the Solidarity movement, and praised the election of its leader, Lech Walesa, as president of Poland in 1989. President Bush also used the dinner to honor famous Polish-Americans in attendance, including former U.S. National Security Advisor Zbigniew Brzezinski and best-selling author James Michener. Paul was right. It was a magical evening and I truly enjoyed it. As for Donald's prediction, events would prove otherwise.

Almost immediately after opening the border to the West in May 1989, Hungarian government officials began revoking the repressive laws that had imprisoned their country as much as the barbed wire around it. There was a new freedom to speak openly, and it brought heady elation to a population gagged for decades.

This change in the atmosphere became apparent to me when I was sitting in a hotel lobby and was startled by the sound of a small group of Hungarians breaking into laughter. In former times, one never heard people laughing. Laughter aroused suspicion. Hearing it, one might think: *What does he possess that makes him happy that I don't?* Hungarians have always understood that the first rule of survival in an occupied country is to keep one's head down and not to make waves.

SISTER CITY PROGRAM

Already involved with the nutrition program, my foundation, The American-Hungarian Friendship Forum, considered other projects, as a new Hungary emerged. Usually they were art exhibits or educational projects for a Hungary eager to see and learn new things. In a different vein, in 1990 I received a request from Nadine Hack, president of the Sister City Program for the City of New York, a program that promotes economic and cultural relationships between New York and its sister cities. Nadine said they were looking for a sister city in Central Europe and were thinking of Prague. She wanted to know if I was interested in helping with the project.

"Not if it's Prague," I told her. "But I would if the city is Budapest."

She said if I could show them why the choice should be Budapest, they would consider it.

Knowing how valuable this recognition would be for Budapest so early in its emergence from Communist rule, I flew to Budapest and met with its mayor, Gabor Demszki, who enthusiastically supported the idea. His staff and I wrote a strong proposal and, on March 16, 1992, a year after the process commenced, simultaneous press conferences in the two cities announced their new sister-city relationship. I was appointed chairman of the New York–Budapest Sister City Committee. What most impressed the New York selection committee was the key role Budapest played in bringing about the end of the Cold

War. Democracy had been reborn in Eastern Europe when Hungary opened its borders with Austria in the spring of 1989, causing the dominoes to fall. Six months later, that process culminated in the fall of the Berlin Wall on November 9, 1989.

When the Senate approved Donald's nomination as Ambassador to Hungary in February 1994, according to the regulations of the State Department, I resigned from the boards I was serving on and suspended the activities of the American-Hungarian Friendship Forum. A new stage of my public service was about to begin.

PART II

DONALD

GETTING THERE

*"I told one and all that we were the right people for Hungary.
I was not interested in simply being an ambassador. Our
country had important work to do in Hungary."*

In the summer of 1988, Vera and I were hosting a small dinner party for friends at our Easthampton home. One of the guests was our friend Liz Robbins, a very successful lobbyist in New York and Washington. A few days earlier we had attended a birthday party for the governor of Arkansas at her home. Liz asked if she could bring along her house guest who was staying with her. Of course her guest was welcome. She was an old friend, Liz said, Hillary Rodham Clinton, wife of Bill Clinton, the governor of Arkansas.

Vera worried that Hillary might feel uncomfortable at our table of eight, all old friends, so she seated Mrs. Clinton next to me. Hillary and I had a pleasant conversation about a mutual interest, higher education. I was chairman of the board of trustees of the State University of New York at the time, and she was deeply involved in issues involving colleges and universities in Arkansas as the state's first lady. I remember that she was bright, articulate, and knowledgeable about current issues in higher education. I corresponded with Hillary and wrote to Bill Clinton congratulating him on his leadership in the Democratic Party. I had been supporting Democratic presidential candidates for decades.

Bill Clinton phoned me in September 1991. He said he was thinking of running for president and asked if I'd support him. I wasn't at all optimistic about a Democrat winning—President Bush was still basking in the reflected glory of the quick victory in the Persian Gulf War. My feeling, though, was that Clinton was impressive and had the sort of personal appeal it would take to make an impact on the electorate. From my conversation with Hillary, I had some idea of where he stood on domestic matters, but I wanted to gain some sense of how he would react if American interests were threatened abroad.

I asked, "If you'd been in the Senate last year, how would you have voted on the Persian Gulf Resolution?"

There was a pause as he decided how best to respond. Then he said, "I would have voted for it."

"In that case, Governor," I said, "I'll support you for President."

I raised considerable funds for the Clinton election campaign, was one of the four co-chairs at a record-setting dinner at New York's Hilton Hotel that raised close to five million dollars, and of course I contributed personally. I believe however that a nonmonetary contribution that I made was at least as important.

With little evidence to support his claim, President Bush had been seeking to convince the electorate that he was the "Education President." I organized the Academics for Clinton program, which was helpful in refuting that. Our full-page ad in the October 1992 issue of the *Chronicle of Higher Education* bore endorsements of the Clinton/Gore ticket by several hundred university and college scholars, professors, chancellors, presidents, trustees, and academics, the first time this had been done. This helped him too, I believe, in winning the November general election.

Election night in 1992, the entire world seemed to be gathered in the Arkansas capital and the crowds around the statehouse were claustrophobic. Being in Little Rock was thrilling for all of us who had been working for so many years to put a Democrat back in the White House. I also had a personal reason to welcome the victory; I realized that in a Clinton Administration, I might have an opportunity for a new public service role. My work at the state level had immersed me in a wide range of political, economic, and cultural issues. Now I had to decide what sort of federal role to seek. I concluded that my experience in business, cultural matters, and public policy could be best put to use as an ambassador, representing our nation's affairs in a foreign country.

More specifically, however, why and how did I seek the ambassadorship to Hungary? Upon returning from a visit to Hungary in November 1989, I wrote a memo to my Warburg Pincus partners outlining possible business opportunities in that country, and I had a long talk with Lionel Pincus about leaving the firm. I had been in investment banking for exactly thirty years since Eric Warburg first hired me. By the late 1980s, the profession had become very transactional and impersonal, a hard-nosed, numbers-crunching game. That didn't appeal much to me, and I had been spending more time on SUNY; public service had become increasingly fulfilling for me.

The late Angier Biddle Duke, a former United States Ambassador to four countries, told me: "An ambassador is responsible for all Americans working or visiting his host country, whether they are civilian or military. He or she speaks for the United States, tries to explain the United States to the host country, and, in turn, explains the host country back to Washington." About one-third of our country's ambassadors have traditionally been political appointees, rather than career Foreign Service officers. Clinton's election campaign had focused on strengthening America's economy and on increasing trade with other countries (hence its slogan: "It's the economy, stupid."). I thought my business experience as a partner and cofounder of a successful venture capital firm made me ideally suited to do that. Moreover, in business and as chairman of SUNY's board of trustees, I was used to working closely with others in a large organization, yet I was also used to taking responsibility for decisions.

Hungary seemed the obvious post for Vera and me. We already knew the country and its people and were familiar with its problems. She spoke the language and had made important contributions to initiating Peace Corps activities there and to remedying the country's nutritional shortcomings. For my part, I had introduced SUNY, which had founded a full-time business education center in Budapest. All in all, it seemed to me that Vera and I had jointly established our credentials and could make a compelling case for the ambassadorship in Hungary.

One obstacle had to be overcome: Hungary had traditionally been served by a career Foreign Service officer. With that country no longer under Soviet subjugation, however, I thought I could make a convincing argument for an ambassador from the private sector. My broad knowledge of economics, politics, and culture could promote American business interests, strengthen Hungary's fragile democratic institutions, and guide the transition from a failed Communist command economy to a vigorous capitalistic market economy that welcomed increased investment, trade, and, above all, openness.

Senator Daniel Patrick Moynihan was truly the Renaissance man of American politics. He would have been my first choice for the person I would most like to have spent time with on a desert island—my wife Vera, of course, excepted. Through Vera's work for Senator Moynihan, I, too, had become good friends with him and his remarkable wife, Liz. Because of our endeavors in Hungary, we had also gotten to know Hungarian-born Congressman Tom Lantos and his wife, Annette. Tom

Lantos was an extraordinary individual: he later became a great friend and invaluable resource. Right after the election, I discussed my aspirations with these two strong and influential legislators, and they agreed to support my candidacy for the ambassadorship with the Clinton transition team that was filling slots in the new administration.

I also found we had an unexpected ally. Dr. Clifton R. Wharton, former SUNY Chancellor and currently CEO of TIAA-CREF, the teachers' insurance and investment company, had participated in Clinton's economic summit in Little Rock after the election. Cliff is very personable, attractive, and smart. He obviously made a strong impression because Clinton immediately appointed him deputy secretary of state, the second in command at the State Department, who is also customarily in charge of personnel. No one knew my abilities better than Cliff; we had worked closely for many years and had kept in touch after he left SUNY. We received additional strong support from Roy Furman, who had served as National Finance Chairman during the 1992 presidential election.

Nearly all the noncareer ambassadors I have met whom President Clinton appointed were highly capable and conscientious. Yet the suspicion somehow prevails that posts go to the highest bidder. I know of one very competent political appointee who, soon after taking up his duties at his host country, was rudely asked at a dinner party, "Mr. Ambassador, how much did you pay for this post?"

Rightly insulted, he replied, "To have gotten such a small country, obviously not enough."

My actual campaign to be named by the president—and it requires a campaign—began with my letter to Pat Moynihan a couple of days after the election. "My background in both venture capital and public service, combined with Vera's significant contributions to a struggling Hungary, present a very strong case for our representing the United States in Budapest during this time of change," I wrote. The letter set out Vera's and my qualifications and our reasons for believing that we would make an excellent team for the Administration to send to Hungary. Pat then used that information in his approach to the White House, which we felt would expedite the process. I congratulated the President-elect on his victory and said "that it would be a great privilege for me to serve in the Clinton Administration." A congratulatory letter went to Vice President–elect Al Gore.

During the months that followed, I was asked to attend a number of meetings and conferences with members of the executive branch, which I believed were a prelude to my nomination. Pat's office kept assuring me that I had nothing to worry about because the White House was on board. So I never anticipated the problems that were beginning to obstruct my nomination.

Although I thought the transition team was clear about the details of my very early and active support for Bill Clinton, I later learned that their records were not accurately compiled. An additional source of confusion was what became known as "the two brothers issue."

My brother, Alan, was a longtime Al Gore supporter. He had been Gore's New York finance chairman in 1988 and his active supporter during the 1992 primaries. Unlike Clinton, Gore had many fewer obligations, and he was also more meticulous about his relationships with supporters and more scrupulous about rewarding the people who had helped him. Alan had indicated that he wished to be considered for an ambassadorship, and Gore endorsed his request. Thus, there were two Blinkens up for ambassadorial posts, and the White House wasn't clear on which of us was which.

Weeks and months went by with no definitive word from anyone in the administration about my candidacy. By March 1993, four months after Clinton's election, I was expecting a phone call, and I finally did find a message on my answering machine with a call-back number at the State Department. I was elated.

When I dialed the number, however, I realized State wasn't look-ing for me, but for my son, Antony. Antony had graduated *magna cum laude* from Harvard, received a law degree from Columbia Law School, worked for a top New York law firm, and published a book on foreign affairs, *Ally Versus Ally: America, Europe, and the Siberian Pipeline Crisis.* A mutual friend had suggested him for a position with Steve Oxman, the Assistant Secretary of State for Europe, and the caller had been seeking Antony in order to set up an interview. So, "my" first call from Washington and the State Department was for my son.

Vera and I went abroad in early 1993, accompanying the New York Philharmonic on a Central European tour. Kurt Masur, the music director, took the orchestra to his old home base of Leipzig, Warsaw, and Budapest. Because the orchestra was American, Charles Thomas, Mark Palmer's successor as American ambassador in Budapest, arranged a reception on April 1 for some of the orchestra members and the board. At one point during the reception, he pulled Vera and me aside and said, "I hear you're going to be succeeding me. Would you like to see the upstairs, the family quarters?"

Vera had seen the family quarters, located on the third or top floor, but I never had, and I was grateful to him for his kind gesture. Clearly he had been informed that I was the leading candidate; this seemed to confirm everything we had been hearing about my immi-nent nomination.

"Has the White House called yet?" It was April 28 and we were at a National Gallery dinner with Cliff Wharton, and while the answer was no, I took his expectation as another favorable sign.

In mid-May, I met with Mark Gearan, the president's deputy chief of staff, and his special assistant, Mark Middleton, who assured me that although the White House had just nominated my brother Alan to be ambassador to Belgium, no "two brothers issue" existed.

Gearan said he regretted that Hungary had not come up at the first round of decision-making and added that he hoped to visit us in Budapest before long.

Ten days later, on May 24, Congressman Tom Lantos called Vera to say that he had received a phone call from the highest authority to discuss my candidacy and was confident that it would soon happen. Although the phone call had doubtless been confidential, we were sure that "the highest authority" could only have been the president himself. Later that week, John Whitehead, the former deputy secretary of state, told me that the career foreign-service officer who had been interested in Hungary had informed him that the post was slotted for someone who was not with the State Department, someone on the White House list.

On June 9, everything fell apart. We read in the *New York Times* that Melvyn Levitsky, director of the State Department's antinarcotic program, was nominated Ambassador to Hungary.

Vera and I were devastated. What had gone wrong? Despite all the assurances about the lack of conflict between Alan's and my candidacy, it seems that in the White House's collective mind, the belief may have taken root that one member of the Blinken family getting an ambassadorship was enough. Also, in the wake of the Lani Guinier debacle, which left the administration embarrassed in its failed campaign to name her Assistant Attorney General for Civil Rights, President Clinton did not want to stand up for another political appointee.

Someone out of work and needing to feed a family would rightly have little sympathy for Vera and my dismay at being passed over for a job we did not need for economic survival. Nevertheless, attaining a position where we could make a difference for our country and for the people of Hungary was a matter of great consequence for us. For that to happen we needed Clinton's attention.

I spoke to Cliff Wharton and I phoned Pat Moynihan. The White House owed Pat a great deal. As chairman of the Senate Finance Committee, he had been doing a lot of heavy lifting for the Clinton administration, most significantly by gaining Senate approval of their first budget. He had heard nothing about this new development and was outraged. I was later told that he went "ballistic" in his angry phone call to the White House, castigating them for what he took to be the personal insult of their rejecting his recommendation of an excellent candidate.

Despite Pat Moynihan's efforts, nearly every knowledgeable person I spoke to told me that I no longer had a chance for the Hungary appointment, that once the White House and State had made a choice public, changing their minds was virtually impossible. People counseled that I should indicate my willingness to seek a different post in another country. Continuing to insist on Hungary, already promised to Melvyn Levitsky, might eliminate me from consideration for some other job. As one friend put it, "You're not leaving any options open. If you don't get Hungary, that's it; you've had it."

"It's either Hungary or nothing," I told one and all. Vera and I were right for Hungary, and that was where we should be sent. I refused to encourage anybody to think about any other place. I wasn't interested in simply being an ambassador. Our country had important work to do in Hungary, and I believed that, with Vera, I was the right person for them to send there to do it.

Tom Lantos was among the few who disagreed with the pessimists. He felt the ambassadorship was not a done deal until the president signed the nomination paper, and that was a long way off because the background check every candidate had to go through was not a quick process.

In a June 21 fax, I recounted to Pat Moynihan the names of those in the Clinton administration who in recent months had indicated that my candidacy was on track. I also stated my belief that State had slipped in their own candidate at the last minute, using the "two brothers issue" as a ploy to find another career slot for one of their own. I continued that I have always based my candidacy not on how much money I raised, but, more importantly, on how early I committed myself to President Clinton and on what Vera and I could bring to the Budapest post. We offered an extra dimension that could not be matched by any Foreign Service officer. Pat used the information in my memo to re-emphasize to the White House that someone had intervened at the last moment to derail an outstanding candidacy.

Two days later, John Emerson, deputy director of personnel at the White House, called. "Don," he explained, "Eastern Europe is being restudied." It was a face-saving way to say that the White House was prepared to switch from a career Foreign Service candidate to a political appointee. He told me that he knew I was highly qualified for Hungary and would not present a confirmation problem. To minimize negative comments, however, my nomination would have to wait; the White House did not wish to run my nomination and my brother's Senate confirmation too close together—another face-saving statement.

In mid-July, John Emerson called to confirm the president's intentions, but again mentioned the need for time to separate my nomination from Alan's. At that point Vera and I finally felt I was going to get the nomination. Now it was just a question of timing and the White House doing the paperwork. We could only wait.

In August, the president went off to vacation on Martha's Vineyard without having signed my nomination papers. In early September, we were invited to a White House dinner, but Vera was reluctant to attend, declaring, "If this invitation is simply a consolation prize, I don't want to be there." I persuaded her to go, but by the time we checked into the Madison Hotel, Vera was so upset that she went for a walk.

At 4 P.M., I could take the uncertainty no longer and decided to phone the White House. I was able to reach John Emerson and told him of our concern of being put in an uncomfortable position at the dinner if the president had decided not to sign my appointment as ambassador. Emerson sounded surprised. "You mean nobody called you? The president signed the nomination paper yesterday."

The White House dinner turned out to be a genial evening, with approximately seventy-five guests from business, government, and the arts. Hillary Clinton seemed to know about the appointment because she congratulated Vera as we walked along the receiving lines. Vera and I felt at ease for the first time in a very long while.

We then went from one kind of limbo to another as I began the process of filling out innumerable forms in anticipation of Senate confirmation hearings, preparing for questions the senators on the Foreign Relations Committee might ask me. The State Department cautions nominees to keep a low profile during this period and to refrain from any activity that might prejudice the senators against a nomination. For example, you shouldn't accept dinners in your honor—they might be considered attempts to win your favor. You can consult experts on your assigned country *within* the State Department, but not *outside* it. Until confirmed by the Senate, a nominee cannot act as if he or she were the ambassador in waiting.

I had no concerns that the FBI's background investigation would turn up damaging information about Vera or me, but it did require filling out voluminous paperwork, a long process for people outside the system who have never before gathered all that information. Like a complex income tax return, it's too complicated to prepare without professional help. I had to engage an accountant and a Washington law firm to prepare the three sets of required papers, each fifteen to twenty pages long: one for the White House, one for the State Department, and one for the Senate. They cover exactly the same material, but the forms are different, so the paperwork has to be separately completed three times. For years, people have been trying to induce the three institutions to agree on a single form, but due to pride of ownership, they won't.

The Iron Curtain had come down several years before, but the Cold War mentality still pervaded the questionnaire. Vera and I like to travel, and we travel a lot. Now, we had to document exactly where we had traveled during the past fifteen years. Fortunately, Vera is very organized and had all her appointment books going back twenty-five or thirty years; she was able to reconstruct exactly where we had been every day for the past fifteen years.

Among the information one submits are the names of twelve to twenty-four people you know well for the FBI to interview. They will invariably be friends who will say nice things about you. Most of these background checks are done by retired FBI agents. Several weeks after I submitted our papers, one of the agents arrived at my office. He said, "I wish I had as many good friends as you do. They all speak so highly of you. Is there anything I should know?"

"No," I replied.

He said, "Thank you very much. Goodbye."

I appeared to have passed my background check and now the president could formally announce my nomination, subject to Senate confirmation.

More advice then issued from the State Department: Continue to keep a low profile; don't go near the host country's embassy; continue to avoid parties in your honor, but it's now appropriate to say that it would be an honor to accept the post if confirmed by the Senate. The ambassadorial nominee is also expected to make calls on Congress, various agencies, and perhaps cabinet members, and to attend all the appropriate briefings. It's also useful to speak to former ambassadors, which I did, sometimes accompanied by Vera. I consulted with Phil Kaiser, who had been ambassador to Hungary in the 1970's, and with Mark Palmer. I had lunch with Angier Duke, who had been ambassador to Spain, San Salvador, Denmark, and Morocco, and called on former Federal Reserve Chairman Paul Volker to elicit ideas on fiscal and monetary matters. I spoke to professors in the so-called "Hungarian Experts Community" and applied myself to a reading list. These activities kept me busy while I awaited my hearing with the Senate Foreign Relations Committee.

By November, the process was far enough along for Vera and me to attend the State Department's ambassadorial seminar for candidates and spouses that is familiarly known as "charm school." The course is intended to teach newly appointed envoys how to be effective emissaries of the United States. Vera and I went down to Washington and checked into the Watergate Hotel for two weeks of total education about our new life. We were new to this profession and had a lot to learn.

On Monday, November 29, 1993, the weather was beautiful, so we strolled the short distance from the Watergate to the State Department, where we were given State Department IDs, and photos were taken for our diplomatic passports. As Jeff Levine, the desk officer for Hungary, walked us through the process, I'm sure Vera felt the same sense of unreality about what was happening that I did.

Our first session started promptly at 8:30 A.M. Because more than a year had passed since President Clinton's election, we were one of only five couples. The small class size was an advantage because more information could be imparted and we could get to know our classmates well.

Coincidentally, Mel Levitsky and his wife, Joan, were in the group. When I received at my office the list of who would be attending with us, I called Vera at home and said, "You won't believe who's in our class, both ambassadors to Hungary!" In fact, Levitsky was en route to Brazil as ambassador designate.

We were lectured on a variety of topics, including the extent of an ambassador's authority, which office at State should be approached with which request, what is required of an ambassador and what is optional, and how to divide one's time among department heads. The others in the class, career Foreign Service personnel, already knew just about everything we were being taught, but much of the information that would be useful for a political appointee like me was too detailed either to convey or to master in so short a time. A good example of that were the classifications of the written communications between diplomatic posts. (They are still called "cables," although they are now faxes or e-mail and are sent at least as often by satellite as by a cable laid under the Atlantic.) These communications are stamped with one of a sliding scale of designations, such as *secret* or *top secret*. In actual practice, however, the deputy chief of mission, a career foreign service officer, designates the cables when they go out. If a cable were truly highest security, top-most secret, or whatever, there would be no question about what to stamp on it.

One briefing concerned the functioning of each country's contingent of the United States Information Agency, the USIA, which deals with the local press and is an important force for shaping our country's image in the host country. Another briefing on "consular affairs" reviewed that a consul reports to the ambassador at every embassy and deals with visas and passports. We were warned that people who know the ambassadorial couple will frequently plead for special favors in obtaining a visa. Under no circumstances, the briefing warned, were we to get involved. Were we to do so, we would have been personally responsible for those travelers once they were in the United States.

We also learned two new words: "clientitis" and "ambassadoritis." Clientitis is the disease of those so enthralled by a host country that they promote its interests, rather than their own country's. Ambassadoritis is mistaking the influence and respect one receives for being the United States' representative for what one has earned as an individual. Ambassadors and their spouses lead privileged lives, often in beautiful places, are looked after and up to by staff who cater to them in all possible ways and appear to be admired for their wit and brilliance. Upon return to private life, a chronic disease like ambassadoritis can inflict feelings of depression and impotence. Vera and I were determined to keep in mind that this would be a special period in our lives with a beginning and an end.

Of course, a good ambassador strives to earn the respect of the host country, but that takes awhile. I always kept in mind the saying, "It's not the applause when you arrive that counts; it's the judgment when you leave."

After four days, we ambassador designates were separated from our spouses. While they would be learning how to budget their time, we were flown to Fort Bragg, North Carolina, to be exposed to the

skills of our Special Forces, who are headquartered there, and the uses
to which those skills could be put if our embassy or residence were
to come under attack. Fort Bragg is an enormous base, the size of
a small state, with every conceivable facility for training in military
and security tactics.

Later, we were taken to the CIA's headquarters in Langley, Virginia. Most of the training there focused on protecting against illicit
eavesdropping and mail intercepts. We were shown hidden microphones and a variety of other devices that the Soviet Union had
used to spy on us. It was fun and interesting, but I'm sure none of
it was a complete revelation to any of us, who were well aware that
our phone lines might be tapped and microphones hidden in our
embassies or residences.

The last three days of the seminar were devoted to a media
workshop, only one day of which included our wives. Under the
tutelage of the former musical comedy star and now highly regarded
speaking coach Dorothy Sarnoff, we practiced giving speeches and TV
interviews. Our wives watched and served as interrogators. At the end
Dorothy praised my performance but told me to bring a lot of glue
to Hungary—"to glue your hands together."

The final approval for a presidential nomination comes from the
Senate, and the schedule for when that determination will be made
is also the Senate's. One can only await the call from the Senate
Foreign Relations Committee and continue to prepare for its hearing, which is a precondition for submitting one's name for a vote
by the entire Senate.

The Hungarian press by now had become aware of my nomination as the next U.S. ambassador. On February 23, 1994, the *Magyar
Nemzet* wrote: "Donald Blinken will be U.S. Ambassador . . . Blinken
is not a career diplomat but a businessman close to the Democrats.
His nomination suggests that since the 1989 changes Budapest has

become politically important, but it needs an ambassador with economic expertise as well as the necessary contacts." The phrase "the 1989 changes" was polite shorthand for Hungary's shift from communism to democracy. In articles like this, one could sense an unspoken concern that although I knew the financial world, I was a political novice.

The Foreign Relations Committee's hearing took place on March 2. Pat Moynihan was so confident that my appearance would go smoothly that he stayed only long enough to introduce me to the committee and then left to take care of other business. His wife, Liz, however, remained and held Vera's hand throughout the hearing.

The principal questioning came from Senator Joseph Biden of Delaware, who brought up a sensitive foreign-policy issue that had recently arisen: Hungary had permitted the United States, which was acting for NATO and the United Nations, to use its AWACS (Airborne Warning and Control System) radar planes in Hungarian air space to monitor the U.N.–mandated no-fly zone to the south in Bosnia. The goal of the AWACS flights was to keep Serbia's fighter jets from aiding ethnic Serb militias, who had initiated a murderous war in Bosnia. One AWACS plane, after spotting four Serbian fighter planes entering that zone, had taken offensive action by guiding our fighter jets in shooting them down when they failed to leave after repeated warnings. Expressing concern that a combative Serbia might retaliate militarily against Hungary or against the 400,000 ethnic Hungarians living in northern Serbia, the Hungarian government had retracted its permission for the AWACS to use Hungarian air space. Senator Biden asked whether that might mean Hungary was not prepared to be the firm ally we thought we could count on, perhaps to the point that it might not be as ready to join NATO as we had all hoped.

A seasoned career Foreign Service officer probably would have given an equivocal answer to Senator Biden's provocative question, concluding with a promise that once on the job as ambassador in Budapest, he or she would attempt to persuade the Hungarians to withdraw their objections. While I tried to phrase my response to Senator Biden diplomatically, I frankly asserted my belief that the Hungarian government's ban of AWACS planes was an attempt to allay the fears of voters before the nation's upcoming election and would be rescinded shortly afterward.

In the back of my mind, my nagging concern was that if my take on the issue was wrong, a Hungary we expected to rely on us as a military partner in uncertain times might back off when some more threatening incident tested its loyalty to America and the West. Such a scenario could undermine everything we were hoping to accomplish. Alas, my reply brought a sharp rebuke from the Hungarian government. A Budapest newspaper disputed my opinion, editorializing that any change in Hungarian policy was unlikely. "Most major parties have endorsed this policy as a good way of avoiding military retaliation from Serbia," the newspaper editorial began. "Hopefully, the new ambassador will have a better understanding of Hungary's concerns in this area after he spends some time in Budapest." Another Hungarian paper wrote that it was refreshing to be getting an ambassador who speaks his mind, although it made no effort to support my opinion.

The complicated response to my brief, extemporaneous remarks was a harbinger of the highly charged, complex web of holdover disputes, historic bad blood between neighboring countries, simmering ethnic disputes, and other political issues I would later encounter as ambassador. Adding to the pressure and high stakes was the looming date of May 8, 1994, when elections for positions to the National Assembly, the first since the end of the Communist era, would be held. There was a lot at stake, and I found myself at the center of delicate diplomatic behind-the-scenes work at a time when Hungary watched warily as the brutal Bosnian War raged in its backyard.

Regardless of how it troubled Senator Biden and other U.S. leaders, the Hungarian officials' election campaign maneuvering and public relations ploy were a shrewd move. Polls at the time revealed that only a small majority of Hungarians actually favored joining

NATO. Many feared that siding with NATO might trigger a reprisal from bellicose Serbia and, more worrisome, from Russia, which had pulled its troops out of Hungary only three years before and might decide to march them right back in.

As matters turned out, the ban on AWACS vanished once the major elections were over. The issue was never raised again, confirming my rather undiplomatic but accurate prediction.

The Senate Foreign Relations Committee forwarded my nomination without reservation and sent it to the full Senate for confirmation. The State Department recommended that we begin to pack our belongings for shipment to Budapest because the sea shipment to Rotterdam would take up to six weeks. We should take our essential clothing with us in suitcases.

A few days after the hearing, Vera received a note from Paul Coverdell, the former Peace Corps Director, who was now a senator from Georgia and on the Foreign Relations Committee. He wrote:

> *Dear Vera,*
>
> *Today, I voted for Don to be Ambassador to Hungary. He will be a good one. I feel that we are sending two ambassadors, as I know what a good job you will do. This has certainly been a long process. I do wish you both the very best.*
> *Your friend,*
> *Paul*

Our relationship with Paul had come full circle.

On the day on which the Senate's vote was expected, we sat by the phone and waited for word on my confirmation, but that body had a very full agenda. The phone finally rang at one in the morning.

Liz Moynihan was excitedly calling to tell us that the full Senate had just voted to approve my appointment.

Once the Senate sends notice of its approval to the president, the State Department dispatches a document called an *agrement* to the host country, a request for the appointee to be accepted as the next ambassador. At that point, the host country can voice an objection and indicate that it will deny entrance to the nominee. In practice that rarely happens, but it was one more formality to fulfill.

In the meantime, I had to sever all my business, charitable, and cultural board ties. The requirement that I resign my affiliations with charitable and cultural organizations, such as the New York Philharmonic, was puzzling to me. The ethics officer explained State's concern that an ambassador's name on an organization's fundraising letterhead might be construed as an endorsement by the United States or an invitation for others to curry favor with the ambassador by making a contribution. So, I resigned from the Philharmonic board and others on which I served, including the New York Public Library and the National Gallery Trustees Council. Vera also resigned from several boards and suspended the activities of the American-Hungarian Friendship Forum.

Nearly three weeks into March, my desk officer at the State Department finally worked out with the vice president's assistant a date for our swearing-in that was convenient to him. Vice President Gore would swear me in at the end of the month in the Indian Treaty Room of the Executive Office Building. If we wished family and friends to attend, we would have to get out the invitations immediately. "Not to worry," we were told. "There's a stationery store named Copenhaver that's been specializing in just that sort of thing for a hundred years and knows exactly what the cards should look like and can make them quickly. Everybody in Washington goes there."

On March 29, 1994, Vera and I arrived at the Executive Office Building where the swearing-in was scheduled to take place. For a few minutes it looked like I wouldn't make it to the event because my name had been omitted from the list of invitees, and the officer manning the security desk in the lobby refused to allow me in. Fortunately, Assistant Secretary of State Pat Kennedy was able to persuade the security officer to let me through.

Finally, in the presence of Vera and Antony, who was now working for Assistant Secretary of State for Europe Steve Oxman, and many of our family and friends, Vice President Gore swore me in as United States Ambassador to Hungary. Antony delivered moving remarks that added pride in my son to all the other emotions I was feeling.

At that time no American airline flew directly to Hungary, so the next evening, a year and a half after Bill Clinton had been elected president and I first indicated my interest in becoming our nation's ambassador to Hungary, Vera and I stepped onto an airplane headed for Frankfurt, Germany—as far as an American carrier could take us—where we would change planes for Budapest.

EARLY DAYS

"It is not the applause when you arrive that counts, it is the judgment when you leave."

Vera and I arrived in Budapest on March 31, 1994. We were tired after an overnight flight, but we felt invigorated nonetheless. This was an exhilarating, yet uncertain, time in Hungary. The Clinton Administration was hoping to show the world that the political and economic freedoms that characterize the American way of life would generate prosperity in this former Iron Curtain country and make it a reliable commercial and military partner to the United States. We would strive to revive a once enterprising national spirit that had produced towering figures in science and the arts, but which had been crushed into timidity and conformity by nearly one-half century of totalitarian rule. Unfortunately, the freely-elected Hungarian government's failure to improve the standard of living for Hungarians was providing pessimists with ample evidence for their prediction that Hungary would soon collapse back into iron-handed, one-party rule and a command economy. The Clinton Administration considered the situation precarious and the stakes high.

We were greeted at the airport by senior staff members of the embassy, who led us into a press conference for TV and newspapers reporters. I immediately began hearing Dorothy Sarnoff's authoritative, distinctive voice from seminar sessions echoing in my jet-lagged mind. Luckily, the reporters seemed more interested in hearing a few words from Vera, whom they knew was born in Hungary and spoke their language. We both felt equally comfortable for Vera to speak directly and openly in order to begin the process of gaining the Hungarian people's confidence in us as America's representatives.

After the press conference, we were driven in a motorcade to the U.S. embassy, which sits in the heart of Pest, the administrative and commercial western side of the city. Buda is situated on the other side of the Danube River, the eastern portion of the capital, and is the seat of an ancient royal castle and other historic landmarks, as well as a residential district. This striking contrast between the two halves of the Hungarian capital often takes first-time visitors by surprise.

When our motorcade reached the embassy, my first task was to sign the book that officially put me in charge. Although I would not be considered duly accredited until my credentials were presented to an appropriate Hungarian official, this signing of a ceremonial book allowed me to assume charge of the embassy for administrative purposes.

I had been forewarned that career diplomats were apprehensive about the motives and skills of political appointees, whom they feared might be at best ignorant, at worst arrogant, and, in the end, only in it for the prestige. My immediate predecessors in Budapest were skilled, professional diplomats. Richard Baltimore, the embassy's Deputy Chief of Mission, or DCM, my second-in-command, had been in charge since Ambassador Charles Thomas departed at the end of 1993.

I did not want to appear overzealous, and my remarks to the staff lasted only a few minutes. With Vera at my side, I tried to convey a tone of firm leadership and a broad outline for my goals as ambassador. I spoke of placing a priority on teamwork. I said that I had no intention of making my tenure a one-man show; we were all in this together and the entire embassy would share credit for our success. I concluded by saying that Vera and I were both looking forward enormously to working with all of them. After shaking a lot of hands and trying hard to remember names, we left for the residence.

Back in the car, alone in the back seat, Vera and I wondered aloud what impression we had made. Vera was, as usual, supportive and encouraging. This was one of those days we would never forget, marking the start of a life-transforming experience. The driver brought us to the ambassador's residence, which is located across the Danube River from the embassy, in the residential Buda hills to the east. The residence is a three-story brick building constructed on a sharply inclined, fenced-in property at the base of a small mountain. The small household staff was waiting for us. As they showed us around, and we saw how rundown this relic of the Cold War had become, I sympathized with what Vera was facing in renovating and upgrading the residence.

Entertaining occupies a large part of an ambassador's schedule, and the bulk of it takes place in the ambassador's residence, which is as much a catering establishment as a dwelling. Vera, an interior designer by profession, had agreed to undertake the task of transforming the residence into a warmer, more inviting environment that would convey the American spirit of openness. She also would work to improve the building's ability to handle a demanding schedule of receptions, luncheons, and dinners that Hungary's new prominence now demanded. Vera would oversee our entertaining, a role to which her warm and engaging personality was well suited. We hoped that together, over time, we would chip away at the Hungarian apprehension that America was but another mammoth, faceless bureaucracy like the former Soviet Union. Instead, we intended to build trust in America and its foreign-policy aims, as well as in the two of us as its representatives.

We realized that Hungarians had good reason to be suspicious of America. The United States had opposed them in both world wars.

More recently, America had been allied with West Germany during the Cold War, when Hungary was a captive ally of the Soviet Union. More significant, perhaps, was America's failure to come to the aid of Hungarians in their uprising of 1956 against the government of their Communist occupiers and the Soviet Army. Many Hungarians believed that Radio Free Europe, the American government's broadcast service set up to counter propaganda behind the Iron Curtain, had provoked and then misled the insurgents in 1956 by promising American military backing that never came. Now, both our countries had an opportunity to forge a fresh, new beginning.

Vera and I spent the rest of our first day in the third-floor living quarters of the ambassador's residence. We unpacked suitcases we had brought on the plane and boxes we had shipped ahead of our arrival. "How do you think it went this morning at the embassy?" Vera asked.

"I particularly liked that people stood whenever I entered a room," I quipped. "I'd appreciate your doing it, too." She allowed that she now understood why we were warned in the seminar about "ambassadoritis."

As we reflected on the series of coincidences and fortunate circumstances that had led us both to this moment, we discussed our goals. Mine was pragmatic—to help guide Hungary from its Communist shackles to a free-market economy integrated into Western Europe. While my objective came from the head, Vera's intentions came from the heart. She talked about trying to comprehend why she had miraculously escaped death on several occasions during World War II and was spared along with her mother, when so many others had been killed during the fighting. Vera attributed her good fortune to fate. She wouldn't give up the thought that her survival was part of some larger purpose she was meant to accomplish. "If there *was* any kind of purpose, it was probably to get you here to help Hungary's transition," Vera said.

After a much-needed night of sleep, Vera and I set off early the next morning for the office of Hungary's president in the Parliament building. I still needed to present my credential to the Hungarian government. Political power in Hungary is centered in the National Assembly, which elects the prime minister by a majority vote of its legislators, who are known as deputies. Every five years, members of the National Assembly also elect a president, a largely ceremonial post. The Hungarian president during our time in Budapest was Arpád Göncz, whose warmth, strong record of supporting humanitarian initiatives, and expertise in political statesmanship had managed to make the position quite influential. President Göncz, who had a small mustache and graying hair, exuded a fatherly sensitivity. Prior to entering politics, he was an accomplished poet and playwright. He survived lengthy periods of imprisonment by both the Nazis and the Communists, while maintaining his sharp mind and open heart. During his years in prison, Göncz taught himself English and translated Faulkner, Hemingway, and the work of other American writers into Hungarian. We had met him during a previous visit to Budapest and liked him from the start.

On this ceremonial first morning of my ambassadorship, Vera and I entered President Göncz's dark-paneled office in the Parliament building. None of us could have predicted the important and historic events that lay ahead. The relatively small size of Hungary belied the key role the country would soon be asked to play by the President of the United States in collaboration with some of the free world's most powerful countries.

As a mark of respect for the position that the United States occupies on the world stage, Göncz had volunteered for the ceremonial task of credentialing me on my first morning in Budapest. By contrast, an ambassador arriving for a new posting in Washington, D.C., can wait several weeks until someone in authority makes the time necessary to accept formally his or her credentials. I wasn't required to wear a tuxedo or tails and a top hat as I would have been in many Western European capitals (typically wherever a royal court exists). Still, my official title and my duty to deliver a formal opening statement were drawn from a century-old diplomatic ritual. My full title was: *Ambassador Extraordinary and Plenipotentiary of the United States of America to the Republic of Hungary.*

According to custom, I made a brief statement in the Parliament building at the formal credentialing ceremony. "Mr. President, it is with deep personal satisfaction and great anticipation that I present to you my letter of credence as ambassador of the United States of America and the letter of recall of my predecessor," I said. A relic of an era when news of an appointment would travel no faster than a messenger could carry it on horseback, the letter of credence was the "credential" that proved I truly had been sent by my government to become Hungary's ambassador. The letter of my predecessor's recall was a technical detail, making it clear that I was the only American ambassador on the scene, even though everyone knew that the previous ambassador, Charles Thomas, had left months earlier.

President Göncz and I exchanged short remarks praising each other's countries and the relationship between them. My statement appeared on the front pages of Hungarian newspapers across the country the next day, along with an interview I had given to a Budapest daily at my swearing-in ceremony four days earlier in Washington. The flood of attention I was receiving was a surprise introduction to the spotlight. Vera and I quickly realized that the American ambassador would always be under the glare of publicity in Hungary, which underscored the sound advice about how to handle media affairs we had received at our orientation.

President Göncz and I were scheduled to meet in a private, one-on-one session, but he graciously took Vera's hand and insisted that she join us in his private chambers, a kind and considerate gesture that was also a preview of how Vera's appealing personality would win people over in her native country as we moved forward. Afterward, President Göncz and I traveled in a limousine as part of an official motorcade, while Vera followed in a separate car as we drove to Heroes Square, the revered public and historic heart of the city. Our visit was accompanied by somber music performed by a military band as I was invited to lay a wreath at the tomb of Hungary's unknown soldier.

Our first morning was an exciting beginning for two people who wanted so much to serve the United States and to make a difference in people's lives after wondering for long, strained months if we would ever get that chance. Now, we had an opportunity to accomplish more than we ever imagined, and as the newly credentialed *Ambassador Extraordinary and Plenipotentiary of the United States of America to the Republic of Hungary,* I was happy to get started on the work at hand.

The first thing I discovered on my first day as the fully credentialed U.S. ambassador to Hungary was a long line of Hungarians snaking around the outside of our embassy building. This was a troubling sight. It suggested poor customer service and did nothing to improve our country's public image in Hungary. There was no emergency or crisis that caused the long queue of people. It was the routine situation faced by Hungarians applying for a visa to visit America. (The United States requires visitors from a foreign country to obtain a visa if ten percent or more of that country's visitors do not return home, a calculation known as the "refusal rate.")

The U.S. Consulate in Budapest is the unit of the embassy with which most people in Hungary come into contact with U.S. officials because the consulate processes visa applications, replaces lost and stolen American passports, and generally looks after the welfare of Americans who are in the country. At this time, the consulate, which was housed in the embassy building, was already experiencing a large number of visa applications. More and more Hungarians in the post-Communist era wanted to travel to the United States. For the first time, many Hungarians finally had the opportunity and the means to do so. The consulate's staff could not process visa applications fast enough, causing the long line to grow longer. I made a mental note to address the problem. Given the large size and bureaucracy of the embassy, which included a staff of four hundred spread across several sections and various agencies, it would take a sustained effort and some re-organization. Still, I vowed to cut down the excessive waiting time in line.

My first broad goal was to survey the diplomatic landscape, to get a good read on the embassy's staff, to assess its strengths and weaknesses, and then to prioritize a plan of action. The ambassador's "Country Team" is made up of a dozen heads of departments that include political, military, commercial, economic, security, and intelligence sections. I set up a new schedule that called for three Country Team meetings each week. My DCM and I met with the Country Team at nine o'clock sharp on Monday, Wednesday, and Friday mornings. My first innovation was having a map of Hungary permanently on the wall; up to then, no one had thought to produce a map of the country we were serving in.

The highly sensitive Country Team meetings took place in the embassy's fourth-floor conference room, known as "The Bubble," a space that was tightly secured and frequently swept for electronic devices. To an outsider, this may seem like cloak-and-dagger, but in any U.S. embassy in a foreign country—particularly a former Communist country just a few short years after the fall of the Berlin Wall—making a space secure from electronic eavesdropping was not a sign of paranoia, but a very practical and necessary consideration.

Security as a whole was taken very seriously. The embassy itself was guarded by a team of eleven U.S. Marines, four of whom were on duty at all times. Their official assignment was not to protect the embassy personnel but rather the building and its contents, as a matter of national security. This realization put matters into perspective.

The Bubble was not the only space in the embassy where security was essential. Two kinds of cables arrived on my desk each morning, this being the era before e-mails had become the standard of communication. One folder assembled for me contained cables from the State Department or other embassies conveying information, news, updates on programs, and requests for various items. I learned to read those quickly. Many of these cables weren't particularly relevant to Hungary, but they added to my perspective of what was happening worldwide.

A second folder was personally handed to me by a security adviser. It was the "red book," containing classified cables and other confidential information. The intelligence briefings I received from the embassy's security team were still very Russian-focused, tinged with a Cold War perspective. A heavy emphasis was placed on what our former adversaries were doing. If those who sent the cables also felt that outlaw nations with a presence in Budapest, such as Iran or North Korea, were acting counter to U.S. interests, they would inform me.

I was never sure how many CIA personnel were attached to the embassy in Budapest. The overt agents were known to me, of course, since they were intelligence officers who established relations with their host-country counterparts. While I may have suspected that certain other people working there were covert CIA agents embedded in other embassy jobs, I chose not to pry. Within two days of my arrival, however, I called the principal CIA personnel into The Bubble and laid out the way I intended to handle things. "Here are the ground rules," I said. "I'm a staunch supporter of the Agency and its work. But I don't ever want to be embarrassed. If anything ever goes on or is planned that you feel could potentially embarrass me or, more importantly, the United States government, ask my approval in advance—*before* you do it." They listened attentively. No further discussion was necessary. They understood my guidelines and since I articulated them early and clearly, I never had a problem with CIA matters.

During the meetings inside The Bubble, my style with my team was one of collaboration. I went around the conference table and asked each section head what was going on in his or her area and what the issues and concerns were. I considered myself fortunate to have taken over the ambassador's position at a time when an outstanding group of State Department, military, and intelligence specialists were already in place.

It was immediately evident to me that the political adviser, William Siefkin, and economic adviser, Chuck English, were first-rate Foreign Service officers. So were the two Volkers: Kurt, deputy to the political and military section, and his wife, Karen, an important player on the economic side. All the department heads kept me well informed, while providing their colleagues with a sense of the larger organization in which they were operating. It may have seemed like a subtle change, but I felt that I was bringing a new approach to running a large embassy that strengthened a sense of teamwork and accountability while I made sure everyone was on the same page.

On the other two mornings each week, Tuesdays and Thursdays, my nine o'clock meetings were held with the capable Donna Culpepper, who headed the United States Information Service. USIS is the former press relations and information service that is now part of each U.S. embassy. The other principals at these meetings included Thomas Cornell and his successor, Patricia Lerner, the heads of the United States Agency for International Development. USAID administers assistance programs to the host country and in the early 1990s often partnered with the Peace Corps. Because USAID was involved in so many programs to assist Hungarian institutions and operations in the country's new democratic, entrepreneurial environment, I decided it was important to set up a separate meeting with that agency each Friday. USAID's operations in Hungary were far-ranging at the time; they enlisted employees from the U.S. Treasury Department, as well as volunteers from U.S. companies, to carry out their myriad programs across Hungary. When I arrived, their wide-ranging efforts included developing new banking regulations, building modern water systems, and aiding new business enterprises.

There was no operator's manual for how to run an embassy. The styles were as varied as the ambassadors holding the posts. At least my new schedule of brief, daily morning meetings provided a framework and structure for an ambassador's long and often exhausting schedule. Most of my staff members were much younger than I was; nevertheless, as a "morning person," I started the day early and set a brisk pace.

A challenging internal situation I faced at the outset was working with my Deputy Chief of Mission, whom the State Department would be rotating to a new posting within a few months. The DCM is the embassy's second in command and acts for the ambassador when the ambassador is out of the country. Handling most day-to-day administrative and personnel matters, the DCM is a key figure and the ambassador's go-to person. He had served as acting ambassador for Hungary after Charles Thomas departed, and my arrival placed him in the difficult position of dropping back to the number two slot. Smart and active, he ably carried out whatever was asked of him, but it was human nature for him to be less than enthusiastic at my arrival. Who would expect him to start new initiatives when he would soon end his tour of duty in Budapest? That made it particularly difficult for me to raise a certain sensitive issue.

I had inherited a very irksome secretary. For example, when I asked her to make a reservation for Vera and me at a London hotel, she coldly responded that the ambassador's personal arrangements were not within the official scope of her duties. Such resistance came frequently and usually in a tone that sounded like a rebuke for even asking. It was a less-than-comfortable situation. I was made to feel that I was committing transgressions against State Department regulations and perhaps even her civil rights by calling on her to do simple tasks that related to our official duties. Concerned about starting my tenure entangled in a sticky personnel controversy, I kept the matter of her irritating behavior to myself, except for privately venting to Vera.

Some weeks later, on a summer holiday trip to Rome, Vera and I spent an evening with the U.S. ambassador to Italy, Reginald Bartholomew. Reggie was a seasoned veteran of the U.S. diplomatic corps and he had served in a number of key positions, including Spain and Lebanon. It was helpful for me to tap Reggie's expertise, and I sought his advice on what to do with my obstinate secretary.

"Fire her," Reggie said.

"Can I do that?" I asked. "I have the feeling she might raise problems regarding State Department personnel guidelines and that she might make a fuss about how I had infringed on her rights."

"Nonsense," Reggie reiterated. "Fire her."

I soon had a new secretary, the very able and helpful Terry Tedford. Immediately, my work environment improved immeasurably.

United States Army Colonel Arpad Szurgyi, a native of Hungary, headed the embassy's staff of high-ranking and capable military aides, including three who spoke Hungarian. Their primary role was to work with the Hungarians under the Partnership for Peace initiative. That program, begun by President Clinton, was a unique military collaboration between existing NATO members and aspiring NATO candidates who had formerly been on the other side of the Iron Curtain—starting with Hungary, Poland and the Czech Republic.

Some cynical pundits considered the Partnership for Peace program a meaningless diplomatic bone thrown to former Communist satellite countries. The reality, however, was that NATO countries realized the newcomers were totally unprepared to join a sophisticated military alliance that had evolved over forty years. For starters, the archaic Soviet system was top-heavy with generals who made all the decisions and did not delegate responsibility to the lower levels of the military, which was where the best and quickest decisions would have to be made when the bullets started flying. I worked closely with the U.S. military attachés in upgrading Hungary's military hardware and methods, and in shifting the Hungarian military mentality from the old Soviet ways to progressive Western thinking, democratization, and civilian control. Hungary needed an armed force that would serve the country, not threaten it.

Before my first meeting with Prime Minister-elect Horn, I had attempted to put Hungary's situation into a meaningful perspective. I did not want to see a repetition of what I had observed in the summer of 1946, a year after World War II ended. It had left a strong and lasting impression. I was a student at Harvard at the time and a staff member of the *Crimson*. I'd won the opportunity to report from Great Britain on the state of the economic recoveries of England and France. The *Crimson* assignment dovetailed nicely with my academic work as an economics major. I traveled to England at the invitation of Simon Marks and Israel Sieff. They were partners in the British department store chain Marks & Spencer and friends of my father, who served as their U.S. atttorney. The three men had been close ever since they invited my father to look after their company's U.S. interests during World War II. They also shared a keen interest in Zionist affairs, and each played a significant role in the founding of the State of Israel.

I arrived in London two years after D-Day. Large parts of the city still lay in rubble from sustained heavy bombing. Instead of trying to rebuild cities devastated by the war, the socialist Labour government was intent on earning hard currency to repay the nation's war debts by selling Britain's industrial output, including construction materials, in overseas markets and by heavily taxing luxuries to reduce demand at home. British officials reinforced the policy by imposing price controls and strictly rationing meat, sugar, and other staples, forcing everyone to sacrifice.

Crossing the channel to France, I came upon a very different landscape. By swiftly capitulating to the German invaders, France had suffered little physical damage. The French economy was already up and running on most cylinders, and the presumably individualistic, self-centered French were back doing their thing the French way by making the black market king. Money under the table could buy just about any item you wanted. I also foresaw the high psychic price the French would pay for choosing that route. I incorporated my first-hand observations of the postwar economies of England and France in a series of three articles for the Harvard *Crimson*. Moreover, my senior thesis at Harvard, which was published as a book, *Wool Tariffs and American Policy*, enabled me to graduate *magna cum laude* with a degree in economics. My book received a good review in England in the Manchester *Guardian*, and after graduation, I returned to London and worked for Marks & Spencer.

Those early international experiences helped in unforeseen ways during my posting as U.S. ambassador to Hungary. The most important preparation, however, was my career as an investment banker. My father introduced me to Eric Warburg, who had started up a small investment firm on Wall Street after his escape from Nazi Germany, where his family's 150-year-old M. M. Warburg Bank was a legendary institution. My earliest assignment was to join Eric Warburg in Hamburg, Germany, where he was engaged in regaining legal title to the family bank from the "trustworthy" Christian employee to whom it had been transferred for safekeeping before the war. My year in Germany afforded me a good look at an old-fashioned form of merchant banking (letters of credit, financing imports and exports, advising long-term customers) and at how another freed-up national economy was roaring back from total destruction. I then spent the summer of 1960 at a groundbreaking London investment bank started by Eric's cousin, Sigmund Warburg, which was like trading in a Model T for a Ferrari.

By the time I began to advise Gyula Horn, Hungary's new Socialist leader, I had studied economics in academia, examined socialism and capitalism in action, observed firsthand how nations build thriving economies—or fail at it—and spent three decades engineering complex financial transactions on Wall Street. Furthermore, my decade as chairman of SUNY provided me with ample public policy experience. By contrast, Horn had spent a lifetime committed to the Communist economic system, where profit was irrelevant. Central planners ordered each factory to meet a specific quota of production. Whether the goods they turned out were good, bad, or indifferent, or whether anybody would want to buy them in a free market didn't matter, only that the quota had been met.

Gyula Horn was poised to become Hungary's next prime minister. He was a tough-minded, highly intelligent politician with a dour demeanor who had been a prominent official during Hungary's Communist regime. Told to be wary about Horn's intentions, I attempted to understand my interlocutor by taking a deeper look at his background. This revealed a man far more complex than a one-dimensional, hardline ideologue. On one hand, he had been a member of the Communist militia that helped suppress the 1956 uprising. On the other hand, as the new foreign minister in 1989, he had authorized the opening of the Hungarian-Austrian border to permit a large number of waiting East Germans, who had been allowed unrestricted travel to Hungary, to cross into the West. This wide-open escape route made the Berlin Wall irrelevant and hastened its fall six months later. (As a token of appreciation, Germany sent the government of Hungary a piece of the graffiti-scrawled Berlin Wall, which is displayed in a Budapest park.)

Here was my challenge: negotiate with a skilled politician who had helped maintain Soviet control over his country but later personally pulled the plug on the Soviet empire. Rash assumptions about how he might act in any given situation would be ill-advised. My greatest concern, however, wasn't Horn's political leanings, but the dire state of Hungary's economy. I was convinced that unless the incoming government took drastic action and made fundamental reforms that would shift the economy onto a more prudent track, Hungary could well plunge over a financial cliff.

I sat down with Horn in mid-April, accompanied by my DCM and political section head, and laid out the facts as I saw them. Hungary was burdened by high unemployment, an outmoded industrial sector, declining economic growth, and excessive indebtedness. In addition, years of rigid state control had produced an unfortunate passivity in average Hungarians. Unable to make decisions and act on their own, they still looked to the central government to solve all their problems. This subservient attitude would doom a private business and, on a larger scale, the nation's efforts to become competitive in world markets. Adding to the bleak checklist I itemized for Horn was a lack of management training and marketplace tools. Another major problem was that the nation's industrial and office equipment was badly outmoded.

Horn's instinct, I knew, would be to keep workers employed by continuing to subsidize the many outdated, noncompetitive businesses owned by the government and to spend heavily on generous social programs. In fact, his Socialist party was leading in the polls in the run-up to the national election by promising to do just that. Their economic policies, which I had seen fail so miserably in Great Britain, would inevitably deepen the budget and trade deficits, elevate the crisis, and hasten an economic collapse. I expressed empathy for the workers who might lose their jobs, but I knew Hungary's salvation lay in selling or closing down its antiquated government-owned companies, cutting back severely on government spending, and attracting direct foreign investment and management. Only a solid, invigorated, competitive industrial and service economy would provide Hungarians with sustainable jobs and income and produce much-needed tax revenue increases for the government.

In short, I was prescribing for Horn and his country short-term pain in exchange for long-term gain. To help make my point, I mentioned Margaret Thatcher's book describing the drastic measures she had taken to awaken Britain's slumbering economy and restore initiative, including shutting down inefficient factories and closing nonproductive facilities such as coal mines. Had he considered taking such bold steps in Hungary, I asked. "Hungary isn't Britain," Horn replied.

I held my tongue but wanted to say he was right. The situation in Hungary was far worse than it had been in Britain when Thatcher took over. I left the meeting not knowing if I had gotten through to a man whose thinking was antithetical to mine or if he regarded my unvarnished assessment as the predictable bias of a capitalist banker.

I would have been in a better position had I arrived in Hungary with the new government in place, but I had to play the hand I was dealt. Elections were scheduled for April and May. I scheduled a dizzying series of meetings with incumbent government ministers although they would all shortly be voted out of office and replaced by Horn and his crew. I listened dutifully to these lame-duck officials, getting to know their issues and discussing mutual concerns. I understood that ignoring these officials on their way out would be shortsighted because I might need to enlist their support one day if they returned to office.

At the same time, my schedule was jammed with the time-consuming custom of making introductory "courtesy calls" on all the other ambassadors in Hungary, even though the United States really did business with only about twenty of them. Avoiding those introductory sessions would have been taken as a snub and an insult to their countries. As a result, my calendar was overloaded with a second series of meetings.

An ambassador's first courtesy call is traditionally made to the dean of the diplomatic corps, the longest-serving envoy in the capital. In Budapest it was the Papal Nuncio. Visits to each of the other ambassadors from NATO countries would follow, regardless of the fact that we had been meeting monthly anyway as a group at the British embassy. In a stroke of luck, the ambassadors of Norway and Portugal were leaving, and Iceland and Luxembourg didn't have offices in Budapest, so my list of courtesy calls was reduced to eleven.

The chairmanship of the NATO country meetings rotated, and all but one of the sessions was conducted in English. The dissenting tongue belonged to the French ambassador. Although he spoke fluent English, when it was his turn to chair our group, he insisted on speaking French and had an interpreter on hand to translate our English into French. (It spoke volumes about the French.) On the other hand, the ambassadors who met every few months to discuss Hungary's relations with Asian nations, including myself, held all of our meetings in English. It was the one language all the ambassadors spoke.

I likened my schedule to a relay race, rushing from one embassy to the next, as I added an additional twenty non-NATO ambassadors to my growing list of courtesy calls. Meetings conducted through interpreters were particularly taxing. I soon learned that while interpreters allowed me the luxury of extra time to think about the answer to a question, proper diplomatic manners required that I not look at the interpreter. Instead, I should direct my eyes at the foreign-language speaker, as if the translation was coming to me through ear phones. It was an awkward skill to acquire. Although this round of meetings was tiring and many were of marginal value, some helped to broaden my understanding of the situation in Hungary. Meeting these emissaries at future diplomatic functions would prove useful to me.

As I made the rounds of courtesy calls and continued to hold meetings with my team, I soon realized that our offices were too spread out. The size of the embassy had grown substantially since regime change in Hungary in 1990. As a result, the embassy's new departments and sections were housed all over both Buda and Pest, on both sides of the Danube, some as far as a thirty-minute drive away from the chancellery. The much-expanded commercial section, for example, was under the auspices of the U.S. Department of Commerce across the city, even though the section and its director, the very capable John Fogarasi, an American who spoke fluent Hungarian, needed to be in constant contact with me. USAID, USIS, the agricultural assistance unit, and the medical unit were also located great distances from the embassy.

I grew frustrated by how distant the various offices were from the embassy itself, which made attending meetings difficult and time-consuming. Quick meetings to discuss issues that had suddenly arisen were totally out of the question. Moreover, we lacked the high-tech telecommunication infrastructure that would have allowed us to meet through teleconferences or by other electronic means.

One example involved our 8:40 A.M. press briefings. I set them up to learn what the Hungarian newspapers were saying each day, as a way of keeping on top of what was happening and public senti- ment. Susan Elbow, a delightful and skilled woman, gave the brief- ings. Susan, who learned Hungarian, arrived very early each morning at the USIS's offices along with Edit Kovacs, a Hungarian woman in the press section. The morning's papers had been delivered, and they began clipping news articles, including human-interest stories Susan thought I should read. She then took the clippings and traveled half an hour or more, depending on traffic, to arrive at my office in time for the briefing. Afterwards, she traveled back to her office. So each workday, the embassy was needlessly losing an hour of her valuable services because of the commute time. Multiply that one example many times and the scope of the inefficiencies are obvious.

I didn't need a Harvard degree in economics to realize that this shuttling back and forth was a drain on resources, morale, and productivity. Bringing the far-flung offices closer, both geographically and operationally, was a priority. Three years earlier, the embassy had purchased a large parcel of land just two blocks from the embassy. Architect Robert Stern had designed a large multistory building to house our commercial, cultural, educational, and other units. By 1994, however, Congress had placed severe budget restrictions on the State Department, preventing construction of our much-needed building after it was already on the drawing board. The embassy sold the property to a Korean bank. I wasn't ready to give up, and directed our commercial and general services teams to continue scouting for an appropriate site to centralize the embassy's offices.

I didn't need to convince the General Services Office, or G.S.O., of the need for consolidation. It rented space in three locations, each twenty to thirty minutes away from the embassy, to garage all the embassy's trucks, vans, and cars, as well as to store extra furniture, equipment, and supplies. It was a logistical nightmare. By chance, just a few days after I arrived, the G.S.O. was presented with an opportunity to lease property just fifteen minutes from the embassy that had ample garage, warehouse, office and parking space. The G.S.O. could merge its three sites into a single location, with the added advantages of close access to a railroad facility and a perimeter security fence topped by barbed wire. It was an ideal location. A decision had to be made quickly, however, or the landlord would find a different tenant.

No approval to sign the lease was required from the State Department. A career ambassador, careful to go through all the channels, might have held off and sought higher approval so as not to risk being second-guessed later on, possibly slowing his or her climb up State's career ladder. (The opportunity was dropped in my lap and required an immediate decision.) Now the landlord was insisting on a prompt answer. For a noncareer ambassador, such as me, running an embassy is a temporary assignment, part of a long professional life. I had no intention of making a career out of foreign service, and neither did my fellow ambassadorial appointees in the Clinton administration. I was impressed by the high level of conscientiousness, achievement, and enterprise among the political appointees. Their knowledge gained in the professional world was not bound by the sometimes narrow customs and regulations of the State Department, whose members are often risk-averse and prone to bureaucratic infighting. On the whole, the appointees I encountered were more willing to do what they believed was right, to speak their minds about policies with which they disagreed, and to recommend innovative ideas.

At my confirmation hearing, Senator Hank Brown had encouraged me to "be aggressive at acquiring the properties we need to properly house your staff there and properly dispose of the responsibilities you will have." Observing that prices were lower at that time than they likely would be in a few years, he added: "I hope you urge the State Department to get off the dime and make sure that the appropriate facilities will be provided."

Senator Brown needn't have underscored the point because he was preaching to the converted. Quick thinking and decisive action are necessary traits in investment banking. Those are qualities I admire in our best military officers, and they are ones I felt confident I brought to Hungary. After taking a day or two to examine the particulars, I gave G.S.O. the go-ahead to lease the property for their support operations. The facility improved efficiency enormously and saved us a considerable amount a year in rent.

That point was underscored again for me early in my ambassadorship when I had the opportunity to resolve an impasse that was adversely affecting numerous American businesses in Hungary. The embassy's commercial section alerted me that perishable food items and other products trucked to and from adjacent countries, particularly Romania and Bosnia—Hungary had uneasy relations with both countries—were being held up at the borders sometimes for hours due to inadequate customs facilities. The food was spoiling at the inspection gates. Bill Siefkin and Chuck English suggested we consider taking a proactive position in getting the Hungarians to enlarge their border crossing infrastructure.

I decided to drive to a border crossing to the south to see for myself what was happening. Despite the vast increase in commercial and other traffic since the end of the Communist era, there was only a single inspection gate for vehicles seeking to enter Hungary. Lines of trucks stretched for miles. There was plenty of property for additional gates, and I saw no reason why the Hungarian government couldn't expand its border crossing checkpoint without a loss in security.

We arranged a meeting with the outgoing foreign minister, Geza Jeszenski, to explain the problem. We described how long lines of vehicles at the border crossing were hurting Hungary's businesses, undermining its Partnership for Peace initiatives, and upsetting neighboring countries. We had to make him understand that for businesses, time means money. The fact that I had made a previous courtesy call on Jeszenski helped, and I was able to level with him. "These are no longer Communist times," I told him. "You've got to make it easier for trade to move."

We spread out maps on a table in his office and pointed out where border bottlenecks were causing problems. I'm no expert on border crossings, but we had people who were, and they produced a schedule of what could be achieved. Jeszenski agreed with us and ordered the expansion of border crossings. I offered to find some U.S. grant money to help pay for it.

As soon as the new border crossing gates were in place, the process for inspecting vehicles speeded up. The lines decreased, attracting more foreign trade. Our practical, decisive, businesslike approach had proved effective.

Other decisions my predecessors had left for me to make concerned improvements in the embassy and its physical work conditions. I wasn't afraid to tackle such challenges head-on instead of passing them on to my eventual successor. The U.S. embassy building in Budapest was distinguished-looking on the exterior, but its interior was cut up into a warren of small rooms with antiquated electrical and substandard communications technology. Built as a bank in 1903 and converted to other uses several times, it was acquired by U.S. authorities prior to

World War II because of its central location in downtown Budapest, near the Parliament and Central Bank. It is also across Szabadsag Square from the Hungarian national television building, formerly the stock exchange. The oppressive heat that blanketed Budapest in the summer of 1994 demonstrated how poorly equipped the embassy was. The only rooms with air-conditioning were the ambassador's and DCM's offices, located across a hall from each other. The stifling temperatures forced the rest of the staff to leave at 1 P.M. to escape the oppressive conditions. I later found out that the embassy had air conditioners but not enough for every office; so they were kept in storage in State Department bureaucratic fashion with the G.S.O. refusing to parcel them out.

"This won't do!" I told the G.S.O. section head. "Please get those air conditioners in here, and we'll buy more for everyone else." I immediately authorized the purchase of portable air conditioners for the rest of the embassy, which should have been done years earlier. That simple, obvious move, I later learned, won me a lot of gratitude.

While visiting other American embassies across Europe, I observed displays of photographs and plaques describing the tenures of prior ambassadors. In Budapest, however, no such display existed, as if the contributions of past ambassadors had been forgotten. I ordered a large marble plaque engraved with the names of my predecessors and had it hung in a prominent location in the embassy's new entrance. I also had photo portraits of past ambassadors placed chronologically in the main corridor outside our offices. These reminders of the embassy's history helped to enhance a sense of continuity and pride in our mission.

Eventually, I helped draw up plans for a full-scale renovation of the embassy, which was long overdue; a full decade after my arrival, construction finally began.

Just a few weeks into my posting, came a summons to all of the U.S. ambassadors to European countries to attend a mid-April conference on

European policy in Brussels. Some of the speakers looked interesting, but I could have put those three days to much better use in Budapest, where a heavy workload and bureaucratic demands called for attention. What made the conference enjoyable was that Vera and I stayed with my brother, Alan, and his wife, Melinda, in Brussels. Alan was the U.S. ambassador to Belgium. That made us the first brothers who had ever simultaneously served as American ambassadors. While our dual appointments were historic, we tended to downplay the fact.

Being in the economic epicenter of Brussels stirred many memories. In 1966, I convinced my partners at E. M. Warburg, a small investment firm, to merge with my friend Lionel Pincus and his firm. In a few years, our merged company, Warburg Pincus, was at the leading edge of a new method for investing in private deals. By raising a pool of investment capital first, instead of seeking to raise funds for each separate transaction, Warburg Pincus helped create the modern venture capital business and would become one of the leaders in that field throughout the world.

At the same time, I was deeply involved in a family-controlled public company, the MITE Corporation. My brother, Robert, did a fine job managing MITE, which we sold successfully in 1985. It was a comfort for my father to know that the company which he had a major role in creating provided his three sons with an additional measure of financial security. When my father died two years later, it was an immense loss in my life.

Back in Budapest, I had changes to make at the office and Vera at the residence. Change can be hard for anyone, but the emotions were compounded for those who had grown accustomed to decades of Communist inertia.

One big change involved transportation. The driver assigned to me was an elderly gentleman named Istvan Bihari, who had driven

American ambassadors in Hungary for several decades. He took his job, its responsibilities, and the attendant formalities quite seriously. Before our arrival, the ambassador's aging black Cadillac limousine was replaced with a new white Ford Crown Victoria. When I found out that the color of the car assigned to me seemed better suited to Florida, I requested that it be painted black—the appropriate color for an official car. Washington agreed, and the newly painted Ford was ready on our arrival.

The car's diplomatic license plate, however, remained distinctive with the very conspicuous 01 designation. At that time of transition, free of Soviet control, the American ambassador was considered first in diplomatic importance in the country and, after the Hungarian prime minister and president, probably the most influential individual in the entire country. In addition, flags flew from the car's front fenders.

During our first hours in Budapest, Vera got into the car's rear right-hand seat and I into the left-hand seat beside her—thereby committing a diplomatic gaffe. Istvan would never have presumed to correct the ambassador directly, but afterward, he explained to Vera privately, speaking in hushed Hungarian, that protocol dictated that the ambassador always sits on the *right* side of the car because the ambassador's flag is attached to the *right* fender—opposite the American flag on the left fender.

A few days later, when we encountered heavy traffic in Budapest, Istvan demonstrated undesirable behavior. Apparently, under Communism, VIPs had been accustomed to have other cars get out of the way for them. In this instance, Istvan did a quick maneuver around the traffic jam by driving down the center lane trolley tracks. He switched on a blue flashing light and spoke into a loudspeaker. A shocked look appeared on Vera's face as she translated Istvan's commands. "He's telling all the other drivers that if they know what's good for them, they'd better get out of our way," Vera told me.

Without discussion, I decided on the spot to call an end to this public relations disaster. Except on a few special occasions, I told Istvan, there would be no more flags flown on the fenders, and there would be no more blue flashing lights or loudspeaker threats. He seemed to understand although he looked crestfallen.

Truth be told, I am not a patient man and wasting time in transit has long been one of my pet peeves. Throughout our stay in Hungary, I never failed to be frustrated by the hour or more spent each day commuting between the embassy and the ambassador's residence. Consequently, I'm only slightly embarrassed to admit that I quietly endorsed Istvan's shortcuts along the trolley tracks from time to time if he could make the maneuver safely without the blue flashing lights or the loudspeaker. It was a small hypocrisy, perhaps, but easier to bear than the expectation of inching along in traffic and possibly arriving late for important diplomatic meetings.

PART III

VERA

BEING THERE

"This house is the United States of America. When visitors come here, it is often their one and only opportunity to see America. So, we must always be hospitable and gracious."

On April 2, 1994, upon waking on our first morning at the residence of the American Ambassador in Budapest, I opened the bedroom shutters and was surprised to see, right outside our third-floor window, the American flag billowing in the wind. I was deeply moved, and filled with gratitude. I remembered the little girl unable to catch up with the train to freedom on that dark night in the woods 46 years ago. From somewhere deep inside me I could still hear my mother's voice saying, "Run, Vera, Run."

CATS!

Our first day at the embassy residence almost turned out to be my last. When I walked Donald to the car as he prepared to begin his official duties as Ambassador, I saw a pack of mangy, wild cats in our driveway. I ran back to the house and burst into tears. I have been terrified by any sort of cat for as long as I can remember, and over the years, it has become a phobia.

I was so upset! After all we had gone through to get here, the place was crawling with cats. I did not know what to do, but I was certain that I could not stay in the residence. I waited for Donald to reach the embassy and then called him, sobbing. "I'm moving to a hotel. I'll come back to entertain when I have to be here, but I'm not going to live here with all these cats. I can't!"

He tried to calm me down and promised that he would take care of the cat problem when he returned home, but I was not easily reassured. I imagined a scenario in which the wild cats could slither into the residence through an open door or even a ground-floor window.

When he came home that evening, Donald tried to confront my fears with logic and reasoning. "The cats must be coming here to be fed," he said. "We need to find out who is feeding them." Donald first questioned our chef, Tomas, who said he hadn't been feeding the cats. He then turned his gaze to the restaurant next to the ambassador's residence. It drew a steady crowd of locals and tourists because it was located near the entrance to a cable car that carried sightseers to the top of a mountain. Donald invited the restaurant manager to the residence to discuss the cat problem. Meanwhile, I barricaded myself behind locked doors and closed windows.

It was the manager's first time inside the embassy, and Donald immediately put him at ease by showing him around. He admitted that his staff had been feeding the cats and promised the practice would stop. He left on cordial terms, and I decided to give it some time.

Donald wanted to make absolutely certain that the cats would no longer torment me. So, in addition to the agreement with the restaurant manager, we asked Tomas, who owned a large dog named Danny, to bring his dog to work. (Dogs dislike cats about as much as I do.) Tomas was happy to oblige, and Danny's automatic response whenever he spotted a cat was a high-speed chase.

The morning Tomas started bringing Danny to work, I looked out the bedroom window, scanned the driveway and grounds, and discovered a most pleasant sight: no cats anywhere. I smiled as I opened the windows to let in some fresh air, breathing deeply and feeling finally at ease.

HOUSE AND HOME

With the cat problem solved, I was now ready to undertake the daunting task of bringing the residence out from behind the Iron Curtain. I would transform this neglected property below the State Department's radar, ushering it out of a Cold War mode and into a new era of elegance and comfort. I wanted to create a welcoming atmosphere for our visitors and to present to the host country our best "face" as Americans. In other words, I set out to make the residence user-friendly.

The villa had a rich history that dated to 1941 when businessman Jeno Hubay III completed construction of a new, red-brick summer residence on ten acres of sharply sloping land in the Zugligeti section of Buda. The area was countryside then, away from the city's bustle, and the air was clean. It is part of greater Budapest today, but many people prefer to live there because the air quality is better than in other parts of the city. Very little refurbishing had been carried out since the United States bought the property in 1948. I had visited it several times in recent years and was always surprised by its neglected condition. Now, I had a chance to make it attractive, welcoming, and efficient for entertaining, as well as a comfortable home to live in. After nearly fifty years behind the Iron Curtain, the place needed extensive restoration. If I had not been a professional interior designer, I suspect the embassy would have had to hire one. Some essential construction began before our arrival, including electrical work, the installation of air-conditioning units, and the repainting that was standard practice for incoming ambassadors.

Over the years there had accumulated various styles of furniture in the house, so I grouped compatible pieces together: French-style pieces went into the living room, the imitation English furniture went upstairs to our bedroom, and I asked the General Services Office—the embassy's maintenance department—to take the excess pieces to the warehouse. A truck was dispatched and the unwanted furniture vanished. A few days later, however, a General Services officer phoned back to say, "Sorry, Mrs. Blinken, we have to return all the furniture because once something is in the ambassador's residence, it has to stay there." The furniture went up to the attic, and I had my first lesson in bureaucracy.

One of the most dramatic and easiest changes to make at the residence was the lighting. In Hungary, lighting was traditionally provided by only one source, a chandelier. The entrance hall contained a lovely big brass chandelier and sconces, but their illumination was bright enough for night tennis. To control the light levels there and throughout the public areas, I had the switches changed to dimmers. A previous ambassador had purchased several beautiful Herend vases and had them made into lamps. Because lamps were not used in Hungary, shades were not available, so I bought some in New York and carried them back with me on the plane to Budapest. I also had Levelor blinds installed to protect the artwork from sunlight.

The residence's bathrooms, installed in the early 1950s, had a communist prison look. There was a drain in the middle of my bathroom floor for the overflow water from the bathtub! After my first bath, I never used it again, and showered in Donald's stall shower. I substituted more flattering incandescent bulbs for the harsh fluorescent lighting, added new chrome plumbing fixtures in place of the brown plastic ones, and provided such basic but previously missing items as wastebaskets, soap dishes, cups, towel racks, hooks, and shower curtains, all brought from the United States. These small, inexpensive changes made a big difference. A few years after we left, the State Department finally renovated all the bathrooms and the kitchen.

After decades of scarcity under Communism, most consumer goods were unavailable in Hungary, so while in New York I purchased fabric to reupholster the furniture in the public areas and yellow moiré fabric for curtains. I designed floor-to-ceiling closets for the guest suite and had folding luggage stands made by a local carpenter from a photo. As a final touch, I provided a folder for overnight guests that explained what an appropriate tip would be for staff tending to their needs, how to use the telephone system to call the United States, and other practical matters. Such amenities were standard in other residences, but as I kept reminding myself, Hungary had been behind the Iron Curtain for nearly half a century.

The centerpiece of the residence is a beautiful Bosendorfer piano that once belonged to Jeno Hubay, a famous violinist and the uncle of the residence's first owner. The American government bought the piano along with the house and signed an agreement prohibiting that national treasure from ever leaving Hungary. I gave it a place of honor in the living room where its beautiful sound was often enjoyed by our guests at musical events we held. The world-renowned pianist Murray Perahia played on it, for example, when we had the pleasure of hosting him and his wife, Ninette.

Donald and I enjoyed selecting art for the residence. Artwork is important both as décor and to get conversations started, often serving to break the ice. Ambassador designates can request curators at the State Department's Art-in-Embassies program to gather a collection to install in their residence for the duration of their stay. The State Department insures, ships, and often sends a registrar to help hang the art. Because of our relationships in the art world, Donald and I enjoyed choosing the art ourselves. Most of the works we selected could have been there in 1941 when the house was new.

For the dining room we chose paintings from the New York Historical Society depicting our home city of New York. For the living room we selected landscapes from some of our favorite places in America, among them New Hampshire, New Mexico, and Long Island by such artists as Helen Farr, John Sloan, and John F. Kensett. Contemporary art went into the adjoining music room: an early figurative Rothko watercolor lent us by the National Gallery, two de Koonings from the de Kooning Foundation, an Al Held watercolor, an abstract Hans Hoffmann, and a Philip Guston painting from private dealers.

When people learned that Donald and I have an art collection at home in New York, they often asked whether we were going to buy Hungarian art. Art dealers attempted to interest us in buying, as did the newly opened auction houses. The primary reason we did not acquire art while serving in Budapest was that our collection focuses on American art, mainly abstract expressionism. Another concern was that too many invaders had looted Hungarian treasures over the years, and Donald and I did not want to be among them.

Small moments during the refurbishing of the residence provided glimpses into the isolation and slipshod attitudes of the Communist era. When the garden room's worn-out linoleum was being replaced by beautiful Italian terra-cotta floor tiles I located in Vienna, a tradesman hired by G.S.O. proudly told me they had a new method of laying them. The "new method" turned out to be grout, which Americans had used for decades. On another occasion, looking out the dining room window I noticed that the last row of roof tiles was missing from the porte-cochere I had designed to replace a variegated plastic one hastily constructed for the visit of the first President Bush in 1989. In true Communist style, the workmen had run out of tiles before running out of roof and thought no one would ever notice the missing tiles.

Covering our terrace was a Soviet-style black-metal awning that looked more like an instrument of torture than a design feature. We removed it along with the terrace's searchlight-bright, Soviet-style lighting fixtures. Lampposts with more subtle lighting were installed in their place and along the driveway. Stonework in the sadly neglected garden was repaired and cleaned, and best of all, new groundcover, bushes, flowers, and trees were planted. This was never going to be an appropriate ambassadorial residence for the new post-Cold War era, but at least I tried to make it user-friendly.

The success of our renovations became apparent to me during a visit from a Congressional delegation, or CODEL. I was always guarded with CODELS, anxious not to say or do anything that might result in a negative comment about Donald or the embassy. One summer afternoon, however, when we were hosting a CODEL, and our garden was looking particularly beautiful with new furniture, awnings, umbrellas, and plantings, I strayed from my resolve. Donald and I were on the receiving line as a senator shook my hand and said, "Well, my dear, you don't look like you're suffering. This is a beautiful place."

Before I could catch myself, I replied, "I didn't realize that we were sent here to suffer, Senator."

Donald stepped in and tactfully asked me to get the photographs I had taken when we arrived. As he turned the album's pages, Donald pointed out the scruffy garden, the Soviet-style black iron awning and searchlights, the white plastic chairs, and the before-and-after improvements of the interior. Then he said, "This is what Vera has worked so hard to improve, so that visitors will find the American ambassador's residence as welcoming as you just did, Senator."

UNDER ONE ROOF

An ambassador's residence is run by a residence manager who knows the local scene and is an expert in protocol. Ambassadors leave, but residence managers stay on, so there is a continuity of experience. Residence managers are the institutional memory.

During the Cold War, when visitors behind the Iron Curtain were few and far between, the residence in Budapest was run by a live-in housekeeper and daily help. Arriving four years after the Cold War ended, we found that despite the embassy's greatly increased activity and, consequently, its increased level of entertaining, organization was haphazard. The staff had been expanded by only one person, a butler who oversaw receptions and dinners, but whose previous experience was as a doorman at a hotel.

For a long time, the live-in housekeeper at the residence had been a Hungarian woman named Iren. A small woman with gray hair in pigtails to the middle of her back, she was quite stooped over, absolutely silent, and had big eyes that took in everything. As it turned out, she had big ears as well. During the Communist era, Hungary's Ministry of Internal Affairs presented the embassy with a list of candidates from which to select employees for the residence. Ostensibly this was done for the ambassador's safety; in reality, the candidates were chosen because they were spies. Two former American ambassadors told us they had been informed that Iren was a colonel in the Soviet KGB and reported to Moscow via satellite from her room at the residence. This room was locked, and no one was allowed to enter.

Despite her background we were advised not to fire Iren because domestic help was hard to find in a post-Communist country, and she was now harmless since there was no longer a KGB to which she could report. Just looking at her, however, made me uncomfortable, and knowing that old habits die hard, we ignored the advice and insisted that she retire before our arrival. When the embassy's security swept the residence for possible eavesdropping equipment, they found cut wires that ran from the former spy-in-residence's ground-floor room to the attic, where an antenna had presumably been located. Replacing her with an experienced housekeeper turned out to be as difficult as I had been told it would be. After six frustrating and time-consuming attempts, I finally found an excellent woman from a very small pool of newly available domestic help.

Whenever we visited a well-run, usually Western European, residence, I sought out the residence manager. In Brussels, for example, I sat down with the highly efficient Maryanne Phillips, who kindly gave me copies of all her forms, directives, and State Department manuals for how to set a table, work with each other, keep accounts, and so on. The London residence manager was equally forthcoming and even gave me several toques, the high white hats that distinguish professional chefs from mere cooks. (Later, I instituted London's practice of inviting our chef, in his toque, to take a bow at the end of a dinner.) At these and other long-established residences, I often noticed other procedures we needed to follow as well as items we lacked, such as official place cards. We were using placecards that I had brought from New York, but I learned that we could order them with the Seal of the United States from the State Department. What should have been standard equipment and standard procedures were finally introduced in Budapest.

I also learned that the State Department had an official procedures manual that was available for each residence. I requested one.
Because so little entertaining had been done during the Cold War,
the State Department may have thought that the Budapest residence
didn't need a procedures manual; or, maybe it was lost after decades
of disuse; or—our favorite explanation—our former spy *extraordinaire*
Iren pilfered it in the hope that improper entertaining would undermine America's image.

When we arrived in Budapest, the staff wore baggy Soviet-style uniforms and sandals. I took everyone's measurements and I ordered
easy-care cotton uniforms from New York, another item not yet
available in Hungary. I even bought deodorant and mouthwash for
certain members of the staff and delicately informed them that its
use was necessary.

The most important change I instituted, however, regarded the
staff's demeanor toward our guests. I was told that under Communism
politeness and good manners were considered bourgeois traits and,
thus, undesirable. Rudeness in stores, for example, was not unusual
because consumer goods were in such short supply; buyers gratefully
took whatever they could get and sales clerks saw no need to be pleasant or helpful. I was concerned that the same attitude might extend
to our residence staff. They must have thought I had some sort of
neurotic fixation because I was continually urging everyone to smile.
"Americans are an open, friendly people, and we should reflect that.
So, smile!" I would also remind them, "This house is the United
States of America. When visitors come here, it is often their one and
only opportunity to see America. So, we must always be hospitable
and gracious."

Our hospitality to guests included a souvenir for them; I wrote
a booklet about the history of the residence. I was told that the
American government had "acquired" the residence, which made

me uncomfortable because it sounded too much like the property confiscated from my family. Wanting visitors to know that America respected property rights and Hungary's heritage, I asked an archivist to research the history of the building and how the American government "acquired" it. Happily, among the documents we discovered was a close-up of the bill of sale that displayed the price, $48,000, dated November 1948.

AN AMERICAN HOSTESS IN BUDAPEST

Entertaining is an important part, actually a tool, of diplomacy, and I was looking forward to it. However, the residence staff, brought up under Communism, retained a Cold War perspective on the role of women, including that of the wife of the Ambassador. You can imagine how surprised I was when Steve, the butler, assured me upon our arrival that he would bring a tray to me upstairs with exactly the same dinner my husband and his guests were having downstairs. What? I had come to Budapest to dine alone, hidden from our visitors? Donald changed that scenario immediately and included me in all representational functions he hosted at the residence.

Our first dinner party was for Carol Bellamy, the new director of the Peace Corps and an old friend from New York. I told both the chef and the butler to set the table and to prepare the food the way they always did, as if I were not there. The result shocked me. The tablecloth had holes from cigarette burns, and our spare tablecloths were ragged from too many washings and ironings. To prevent damage to the tabletop, a heavy felt cloth had been placed under the tablecloth, but it was so large it stuck out into the guests' laps. Our official State Department china was composed of pieces that came in slightly different sizes and tints. Over the years, it seemed, broken dishes had been replaced by different suppliers. To make matters worse, the gold seal and rim had worn off the older plates.

The table was set with stainless steel flatware although the residence inventory indicated that we possessed silver flatware. I asked the butler what had happened to the silver and was told that it had been stored in the attic because silver polish was unavailable in Hungary. He could use that excuse with our predecessors, who did not speak Hungarian, but I was sure that, despite decades of Communism, many Hungarians still had silver, so there must be silver polish in the stores. "I'm going to get you silver polish," I told him. "Just watch me."

And I did. He would have to rub harder than with a Western product, which was undoubtedly why the silverware had been stored away. Nevertheless, we polished every last piece, including a very attractive tea and coffee set, which got a lot of use during our stay. Later, on a trip to London, I bought a carton of excellent English silver polish, providing the residence with a long-lasting supply.

Learning from those enlightening State Department manuals that we were entitled to new china, including twelve more place settings than our dining room table could seat, I ordered a new set which arrived several months later. To my delight, contemporary culinary tastes had added pasta bowls with the Seal of the United States. We also ordered new tablecloths, but the State Department took six months to send us two tablecloths so flimsy that they would have disintegrated after a couple of washings, so I went to a shop in the village of St. Endre, where talented artisans produce linens, and bought embroidered place mats and napkins. From then on, we used only those for our entertaining, replacing items as they wore out.

Steve the butler had always bought the flower arrangements for the dinners. For the first dinner we gave, he appeared with an arrangement of multicolored flowers on a mirror base. To remedy that situation, I bought six cut-crystal hurricane lamps in New York, which I used instead of flowers, lining them up along the center of the table with votive candles between them. The softer lighting elicited many compliments from our guests, and this design element saved a lot of money for the residence's entertainment budget. I ended up taking many orders for those hurricane lamps from Hungarian friends.

Another of Steve's practices that I eliminated after our first dinner was wrapping a paper towel around the mouth of a wine bottle. The only paper coming out of the kitchen was to be our cocktail napkins imprinted with the Seal of the United States of America. We were delighted that guests often took one as a souvenir of their visit. That symbol never failed to touch me, as well. Whenever I set a glass on one of those napkins, I looked at the Seal of the United States of America and thought of the long journey I had made since running through the woods and trying to catch a train to freedom.

For several months after our arrival, although we invited Hungarian officials and businessmen to bring their spouses or partners to our dinners, the women, even though they had accepted the invitation, frequently did not come. At first I thought that I might be doing something wrong as a hostess, causing them to stay away. As it turned out, there were two reasons women did not attend: shyness over not speaking English and even more often the lingering shadow still cast by the old Soviet system, in which diplomatic dinners were usually all-male events that were strictly business. Gradually, the spouses started to show up, and I like to think the reason was that word had been passed that the American residence was now a welcoming, enjoyable place, where the ambassador's wife spoke Hungarian and would make sure that women guests hesitant about conversing in English would be seated next to a Hungarian speaker.

There are several little-known aspects of an ambassadorial assignment. For example, very few people outside State Department circles know that the official residence of the ambassador is available for rent, although not for fundraisers. To reserve the space for an event, whether requested by an American company or organization, the head of an embassy section would send the ambassador a memo specifying the date, event, and the people to be invited.

Once an event was approved, the section involved appointed a control officer to organize it, look after the VIPs for whom it was being given, finalize the guest lists, and send them to the Protocol Department. Protocol sends out invitations, follows up to determine who is coming, and most importantly, sees to it that the embassy receives a check for the cost of the event afterwards. We always knew ahead of time what the cost per person would be, but we never knew how many intended to come because most Hungarians did not consider it necessary to respond to invitations. People just arrived—or didn't. For example, the sponsors of an event would tell us one hundred people were coming, but only fifty might show up.

Because I always felt bad about wasting food, doubtless because I could still remember being hungry as a child during wartime, I adopted a rule of thumb: Prepare for half the number of guests invited, especially if the schedule called for dinner afterwards. Most of the time, my guess was right on target, no one left hungry, and, most importantly, large amounts of food were not thrown out.

The amount of food to order for dinners was easier to determine than for receptions because the table seated a specific number of guests, twenty-two. Nevertheless, I preferred buffets because they offered a more casual atmosphere and required less time on follow-up calls to confirm who was coming. To keep track of the sections' event planning, the embassy maintained short-range entertainment plans (one to six months away) and long-range plans (more than six months away), copies of which were sent to me by Donald's secretary. At a weekly calendar meeting, I went over these plans with the butler to see what was new and what might have changed.

PROTOCOL

When we arrived in Budapest, a woman named Saci worked as Protocol Officer at the embassy. She had held this position for the previous twenty years, and she worked alone. During the Communist era, Saci's job was an easy one because there was very little entertaining at the residence and official functions were few and far between. All that changed when we arrived, and Saci's workload became heavier because we were entertaining frequently at the residence, hosting a steady stream of visiting dignitaries, businesspeople, and Hungarians from all walks of life. The heightened responsibilities triggered a mysterious illness in Saci because she soon informed us that she was sick and, according to Hungarian law, entitled to one full year of paid medical leave. Furthermore, State Department rules stipulated that we could not hire anyone in her place because Saci technically continued to fill the position even though she would not be there.

I needed to find a solution to this dilemma as soon as possible. Donald assigned a daily rotation of assistants to fill in for Saci, but there was no continuity or follow-through. Finally, I stepped in and for several months spent long hours each day at the embassy supervising the writing of invitations, confirming guest lists, arranging seating charts, and overseeing all protocol activities.

Fortunately, Saci's luck ran out on her bogus illness. One day, we received a call from the Thai embassy to inform us that Saci had applied for a travel visa to go to Thailand on vacation. She was breaking a Hungarian law that prevented her from traveling more than 100 kilometers from her doctor's office during her medical leave. We promptly called her and informed her that we were sending over a letter of resignation and strongly suggested that she sign it, which she did. We were then able to hire two young Hungarian women in their early twenties to fill the position of protocol officer. They were not trained in the requirements of diplomatic protocol, but, more important, they were eager to learn, possessed strong computer skills, and spoke English. Soon, under my supervision, they learned to perform all the embassy's protocol tasks with precision and skill, freeing me to return to projects that I had put aside.

The repressive rules and regulations that governed the lives of people in Budapest and their interactions with Americans under the Communist regime went far beyond matters of protocol. During the Cold War years, Hungarians had to get written permission from their workplaces to visit a Western embassy. The secret police surreptitiously photographed them entering and later questioned them. This intimidation was aimed at preventing a free exchange of views and a frank discussion between Hungarians and Americans. One of our guests, an antiques dealer, told me that in the late 1980s he had accepted an invitation to the American residence for a dinner and afterward was interrogated by the Ministry of the Interior. When he said he couldn't remember the specific topic of a conversation or the names of the guests, his interrogators became dissatisfied and said, "I guess you won't be needing your passport for the next ten years." If the price of a visit to the American Embassy during the Cold War had been the loss of my passport for ten years—when foreign trips were restricted to only one every three years—I probably would have stayed away, too. Not surprisingly, most people did.

Another friend told me about her first visit to the residence; having been alerted to where a secret camera was hidden, she smiled right into it as she walked up the driveway. "I knew I wasn't important," she laughingly told me, "when the Ministry didn't call me in for questioning after that."

During that period, the Protocol Department had a list of approved Hungarian guests; people the Hungarian authorities had cleared and who reported back to them afterward. That policy officially ended with the fall of the Wall, but for a number of years Hungarians remained understandably nervous about accepting invitations to a Western embassy. In the beginning, Donald and I started with the approved guest list, but we branched out quickly to include many of the new people we were meeting. We felt that in this new era the most direct way to promote American policies and values was to invite to the residence as many influential Hungarians as we could, so they could personally meet the ambassador, his wife, members of the embassy, and visitors from the United States. This was the accepted tradition at other American residences but was new in countries that had been imprisoned behind the Iron Curtain.

INTERNATIONAL DINING

The dinners we hosted at the residence were a reflection of our country, and I was determined to make them exceptional. Under the circumstances, that was no easy goal.

Once a week, I met with Tomas the chef to plan menus for the week, which usually included several official dinners and receptions. We had to plan each menu well in advance of the event because many food items were unavailable or in short supply. (Demand for many foods was very low among Hungarians who were long cut off from different cuisines and accustomed to hardship living.) We could always get chicken, for example, but if we wanted beef or veal for twenty-two guests, we had to order it far in advance because distributors allotted individual meat markets limited amounts. Our friendly butcher saved the hard-to-get cuts for us, and we put them in the freezer until we had accumulated enough. Fortunately, all that has changed in recent years.

Vegetable variety was also an issue because we could never be sure what produce would be available at the market on a given day. The menus for residence dinners therefore referred only to "seasonal vegetables," a nice catch-all that usually meant broccoli and carrots. Anything else required Tomas to visit several other markets for an alternative, and finding enough for a dinner was rare.

I never expected to be caught up in a vegetable controversy, but a newspaper article embarrassingly reported that in Budapest I missed fresh greens for salad, and especially basil. By this time, I had become close friends with Sissi Ago, the wife of Italian ambassador Pietro Ago, who was aptly named for this post because the Hungarians still revere more than a century after her death the beautiful and cultured Empress Elizabeth of the Austro-Hungarian Dual Monarchy known as Sissi. In any event, our contemporary and equally generous Sissi brought back seeds from Italy and grew salad greens unavailable locally, including basil, which she supplied to her friends who loved pesto sauce. I put jars of it in the freezer, and thus Donald and I enjoyed our spaghetti dinners on the rare occasion that the two of us dined at home alone.

Once a month, the commissary sent several trucks to the PX in Germany for supplies not available in Hungary, and at Donald's request, they returned with sorbet and frozen yogurt, as well as cranberry juice, which we served our American guests for cocktails, and they were always thrilled. During my occasional trips to the States, I purchased food items not available in Hungary, such as English muffins, peanut butter, and canned tuna, which I packed into a duffle bag for the return flight.

One Hungarian food in ample supply held special memories for us. When we visited the factory where the famous Pick salamis are made and shipped all over the world, Donald smilingly told our hosts that when he and I started dating, he looked into my refrigerator and saw only breakfast food and Hungarian salami!

The accounting system for the embassy entertainment budget is complex and bureaucratic. Each ambassador receives a certain sum from the State Department for the embassy's "representational expenses," according to established categories. Before our arrival, Donald had asked for an increase in the residence's entertainment funding and staffing in order to handle the anticipated increase in receptions, dinners, and other representational activities. The State Department refused the request, not being able to anticipate that the official functions during our stay would increase significantly.

The division between representational and private spending is carefully drawn but not easy to follow. Accounting for the former was a laborious task, given the extent of our entertaining and the State Department's cryptic regulations. One example was my purchase of a forty-dollar juicer. We could have paid for it ourselves, as we did for many items, but because it had been purchased for the kitchen, I submitted it as a reimbursable expense. Payment was refused because, as the State Department explained, all purchases of more than thirty-five dollars had to be previously approved in writing. That rule meant the entire forty dollars was disapproved, not just the five dollars above the limit. The time wasted in this process surely cost taxpayers more than five dollars, and I learned yet another lesson in bureaucracy.

The complexity of the State Department's accounting extends to household salaries as well. Both the ambassador and the deputy chief of mission are required to write a check each month for 3.5 percent of their gross salaries as a charge for food, lodging, and the services of staff members employed at their residence, a miniscule amount compared to the actual official residence expenses. Their staff members are contracted personally to the ambassador and the DCM, but the bimonthly salary payment envelopes come from the embassy.

One of my most embarrassing evenings during our posting occurred when we hosted an unofficial dinner for thirty people from the arts community. A few days before the dinner party, our chef happily told me that the produce market would be getting asparagus, a great rarity and delicacy in Hungary. So, we put asparagus soup on the menu, along with beef, salad, pear tart for dessert, and the usual "seasonal vegetables."

When all thirty guests were seated, the first course arrived: asparagus soup. I couldn't believe my eyes. It was so green, so neon-bright, that it verged on psychedelic. There was astonishment on the guests' faces as the bowls were set down in front of them. I took a hesitant spoonful. It tasted like asparagus, so I stood up and said, "This very green-looking liquid in front of you is asparagus soup. It may not look like asparagus soup, but it tastes like asparagus soup, and I highly recommend it."

We got through the meal, and after the guests left, I asked Tomas about the color of the soup. He was very apologetic. The market only had white asparagus, which he had never seen before. To replace the soup's missing pigment, he added bright green food coloring, usually reserved for cake icing. With no substitute first course available, he had to serve the very green soup. Fortunately, Tomas was an excellent chef, so the soup was delicious, and our guests were very good natured about this culinary mishap.

Smoking was another issue I grappled with at dinners and receptions. Neither Donald nor I are smokers, but Hungarians at that time still smoked a lot—and very strong cigarettes. Despite my desire to create a welcoming environment, I drew the line at smoking. I asked about the possibility of instituting a no-smoking policy and was delighted to learn that the United States had adopted a policy prohibiting smoking in the interior of all U.S. government owned, rented, and leased office buildings and facilities, effective August 1, 1993. The policy had already been instituted at the White House. What worked for Hillary was going to work for me! Contrary to the warnings I received that people would stay away from the residence if they couldn't smoke, none to my knowledge did.

Steve, the butler, presented a persistent problem: He lacked all discretion, but we had to put up with him because there were no professionals available to replace him. During dinners, he entered the dining room at stunningly inopportune moments, often interrupting important, even politically sensitive conversations, oblivious to the intrusion. When a course was finished and the next one due, I would catch his eye, but if he didn't feel like coming into the dining room, we had to sit and wait according to his personal timetable. That ended only after I imported from New York a battery-powered unit not yet available in Hungary that buzzed in the kitchen when I, not he, decided that his presence was required.

Steve's surly attitude nearly damaged Donald's effort to convey his own and the Clinton administration's views on Hungary to a highly influential reporter. A little over a month after we arrived, we gave a dinner at which the guest of honor was the *New York Times* correspondent Jane Perlez, who was in Hungary to report on the imminent national election. Seated beside her, Donald could share his thoughts on the country's present conditions and its future prospects. Perlez's article, which would also appear in the *International Herald Tribune*, would greatly influence the impressions of American political and business leaders about the upcoming elections.

All our guests arrived on time, except Jane, whom we knew was engaged in interviews for her article and would be arriving late. As the cocktail hour lengthened, the dinner's control officer from the press office made inquiries and informed us, "I spoke to Jane. She has been delayed, but she is coming." Because we could no longer keep our other guests waiting, we finally went into the dining room. I decided that the seat next to Donald could not be left empty and switched Jane's place card with someone else's. I instructed Steve to switch it back immediately if Jane arrived before we sat down.

Moments later she did arrive, and I reminded Steve to put her place card back next to Donald. As we walked into the dining room, I said to Jane, "Your place is right here." But another person's name was on the place card at Donald's right. Fortunately, I was able to switch the place cards before the other person noticed.

After dinner, I was upset and asked Steve, "Why did you not follow my instructions to put the guest of honor back beside my husband?"

"She was late," he replied. "We have to teach her a lesson."

Teach the *New York Times* a lesson?

A diplomat, it is said, is a person sent abroad to eat for his country. If so, I am a true patriot. Donald and I were invited by other ambassadors to their functions and in turn we invited them to ours—lunches, receptions, dinners, commemorative observances, farewell get-togethers for outgoing envoys, and the inevitable ribbon cuttings. The food served at these events was a peril of diplomatic life.

It was very hard to keep my weight under control. I would solemnly promise myself to be careful; then at a meeting I would come upon a plate of *pogacsa*, a delicious Hungarian biscuit, and my resolve melted. Also, in New York I walk everywhere, but in Budapest because of the distances I was always in a car. I gradually gained weight and when we left, I was ten pounds heavier than when we arrived. Actually, that wasn't too bad. "Hungary," I had been warned, "is a twenty-pound post."

Among the many dinners and receptions we gave, an official event Donald and I hosted six months after our arrival filled me with pride.

It was a dinner to say goodbye to Chuck English, the head of the
embassy's economic section, and his wife, Patricia. At the conclusion of
the meal, Chuck graciously thanked us for the party and then toasted
Donald with words that deeply touched us: "We career Foreign Service
officers worry when we hear that we're getting a political appointee
as ambassador. But Ambassador Blinken showed us that one did not
have to be a career Foreign Service officer to be a professional."

As the staff's appearance and performance improved, so did
their spirits. They wanted to do a good job and just needed to be
informed of what was expected of them. To maintain that higher
level of performance, I continued to check details, such as whether
the silver was well-polished and uniforms clean and pressed. Also,
after every reception and dinner, I made sure the public areas had
been cleaned and everything properly put back in place. Occasionally, I even phoned the residence to check on whether the greeting
on the other end was polite and welcoming. Residence managers at
larger embassies oversee these matters, but I wouldn't have traded the
personal satisfaction of creating an efficient and productive center of
our country's greatly expanded presence in Hungary for any more
glamorous post.

Hungary's invitation to join NATO in the summer of 1997 occasioned
the most important dinner we gave while in Hungary. Every important Hungarian official was invited, along with the NATO ambassadors, about fifty guests in all. That was far too many for our dining
room, so we set up tables throughout the public rooms. Because of
the importance of the occasion, I asked the embassy to work out
the seating, something I usually did myself. Even having taken this
precaution, we nearly caused a diplomatic gaffe.

The event began with cocktails in the garden, with dinner scheduled for 7:30 P.M. Foreign Minister Laszlo Kovacs was to be seated
on my right, and although we were assured he was coming, by 8:00
P.M. he had not arrived. I explained to my friend George Habsburg

that we were waiting for the foreign minister because we could not start dinner with an empty place on my right.

"The foreign minister is sitting on your right?" George asked. "That is not correct. The speaker of Parliament should be seated on your right."

George is a very attractive and interesting person who at that time was Hungary's ambassador-at-large to the European Union or, more precisely, Ambassador Extraordinary and Plenipotentiary for European Integration from the Office of the Prime Minister. George is also the grandson of the last emperor, Charles, who ruled the Dual Monarchy of Austria-Hungary. George grew up in Germany, and his family was allowed to return to Hungary only after the regime change in 1989. He moved to Budapest in 1993 and made it his home.

Given his background, advice from George about the etiquette of table seating was not to be disregarded. Still, I thought, I'd better get a second opinion and consulted with the other person whose opinion on protocol I trusted, the Ambassador from Spain. He confirmed that indeed the speaker of Parliament should be seated to my right.

I immediately hurried inside to rearrange the place cards. Thank goodness I did. When the foreign minister arrived, he never even looked in my direction as he sought his seat for dinner. The speaker, on the other hand, walked straight to my table. Doubtless he would have been rightly offended on his own part and on behalf of his branch of government if I had lowered his status at the dinner by failing to place him beside the hostess. He would have assumed that the ambassador was deliberately slighting him to send a harsh message to Parliament.

America is an informal nation, and we do not take protocol as seriously as do older nations with a royal and aristocratic heritage. As a result, we may unintentionally insult their officials or their citizens. All our embassies should follow protocol correctly and flawlessly. Just as the State Department provided us with trained military, commercial, and political attachés, they should have sent us someone with knowledge of, and training in, protocol. Because the observance of protocol was not customary in former communist societies, local expertise was not available.

We were invited to many official dinners in Budapest, but the most memorable one was at the Japanese ambassador's residence on a bitterly cold winter evening. The ambassador and his wife were a gracious host and hostess, and we were looking forward to a pleasant evening. On the morning of the dinner party, however, snow started to fall, and as the day progressed, the snow fell heavier, the temperature dropped, and the roads grew icier. When Donald arrived home from the office, he said, "I am sure they are going to cancel the dinner; people just cannot get there."

So, I phoned our hosts to check and was told, "The dinner is on."

The Japanese residence was quite near ours, on the other side of a steep hill. Under normal conditions, the fastest route would have gotten us there in five minutes. This night, instead, we traveled half an hour, all the way around to the other side of the hill and very slowly up a less steep, but extremely icy road.

At the Japanese residence, the long table was set for thirty. Places were continually removed, however, as guests called to say they could not make it. Eventually, we numbered only ten around the table.

At the end of a delicious Japanese meal, the Japanese ambassador rose to propose the customary toast. His words were anything but customary: "This is to the good health of the ambassador of the United States of America. The others could not make it, but even in a snowstorm the representative of the only superpower came to Japan." There was much applause.

Back in the car, I said to Donald, "If we don't get killed on our way back, tonight we have really earned our keep."

HIGH TIMES AND HOLIDAYS

Since we at the embassy considered ourselves a family away from home, Donald and I enjoyed giving holiday parties for members of the embassy. Holidays are also when Congressional delegates (CODELS) usually travel since Congress is in recess. Embassy staffs do not look forward to these official visits because they would rather spend holidays with their own families or perhaps travel as well. Therefore, to attend to the visitors, the embassy relies as much as possible on singles or those at post whose families are home in the United States.

Donald and I thought the singles on standby for CODEL duty would be lonely, so we always invited them to Thanksgiving dinner at the residence. The most conspicuously single group was the Marine guard, several with Hungarian girlfriends who had never been to a Thanksgiving dinner. We also invited other Americans and some friends from the diplomatic corps who had served in the United States and appreciated the meaning of Thanksgiving. We usually had about fifty guests.

Our first Thanksgiving required a lot of planning. I wanted American Butterball turkeys, which were not available in Hungary. Several months before the dinner, at the embassy's commissary, I placed Butterballs on a list of items to be purchased during the monthly truck run to the PX in Germany. Later, on one of my trips to the States, I brought back a case of cranberries. Then a local restaurant somehow found sweet potatoes for us, not a common vegetable in Hungary.

One traditional item we had to do without was pumpkins. Some months later, I happened to mention their absence to a gentleman with a family farm in southern Hungary. As our second Thanksgiving approached, I received a phone call from him. "Mrs. Blinken," he said, "I have a surprise for you. Would you please let the guards know I'll be driving my truck in?" A short while later, he drove up with several of the biggest pumpkins I had ever seen. His kindness not only allowed us to serve pumpkin pies, but also to decorate the residence with these festive symbols of the holiday.

Another year, as November approached, I was delighted that my friend, Florence Fabricant, a *New York Times* food writer, and her husband, Richard, would be staying with us over Thanksgiving. Florence brought cookies and chocolate in the shape of turkeys, a treat that reminded us all of home. To this naturalized American citizen, Thanksgiving is the most special holiday, a time for giving thanks for the blessings bestowed upon us as citizens of a country where we live in freedom under the rule of law.

Donald and I also enjoyed giving an annual Christmas party and making it as warm, as happy, and as inclusive as possible. We hosted an open house at the residence for all who had connections to the embassy and their families, whether they were Americans or Hungarian foreign service nationals working for the embassy, whether they were the highest-ranking DCM or the plumber who fixed the leaky sink.

I decorated the house with big Santa Claus balloons that I found in a new shop on Andrassy Street opened by an American woman of Hungarian descent. Hungary had never seen anything like her American-style shop; she sold balloons, scented candles, greeting cards, wrapping paper, and ribbons. Such items were not available elsewhere in Budapest, where Communists had stripped away the layer of consumer goods that makes life more enjoyable. Needless to say, her store became very popular, and now such items are widely available in Hungary.

One year as I planned the festivities, I phoned a friend at the Liszt Academy and asked if we could engage student musicians to perform at our Christmas party. Certainly I could have asked Protocol to make the inquiry, but they would have had to write a letter and then wait for an official response. Being both the American ambassador's wife and Hungarian-speaking "Vera," I received an affirmative answer immediately. My friend arranged for a pianist and a singer from the Academy to perform at the party. Another year we had students from the American School singing American Christmas carols. The year after that, our butler, Steve, arranged for a local boys choir to sing Hungarian Christmas carols.

Our Christmas celebration was always a happy way to end the year.

"Outside the box" events that provided new opportunities for entertaining at the American ambassador's residence intrigued me. St. Valentine's Day, for example, was unknown in Hungary, but I thought a party to celebrate it would provide Americans with a cheerful touch of home and Hungarians with a view of the lighter side of American life. Knowing that I could find huge hearts and red balloons at the U.S.-style card shop on Andrassy Street made decorating easy and fun. Tomas baked heart-shaped cookies, and everyone had a wonderful time. The party's success can be judged by the fact that St. Valentine's Day now has become a fixture of the Budapest social calendar, and even the American Chamber of Commerce gives an annual black-tie Valentine's Day Ball.

Although the power to make decisions rested with Donald, I was always pleased when he delegated certain tasks to me, such as the organization of our Fourth of July parties. Our first two Independence Day celebrations were held in the garden of the residence and were so well received that we decided that the third one should be even bigger. For that, we arranged for a performance by the United States Marine Band, one of several Marine bands based in Germany, and invited almost a thousand Hungarian guests to a concert in the outdoor stadium on Margit Island.

Donald and I thought it would be nice to serve drinks first and to start the concert at 7:30 P.M. Several embassy personnel, including the administrative officer and I, went to Margit Island to inspect the outdoor space and make arrangements with the manager of the stadium. As the manager showed us around, he told us that he didn't think the 7:30 P.M. start was a good idea because the setting sun would cast its glare directly into the eyes of those sitting in the VIP boxes. He thought 8 P.M. would be better.

"Eight o'clock it is," I agreed and was about to move on when the administrative officer objected, insisting that the approval for this change had to come from the ambassador.

"Trust me," I said, "it will be fine with him." My word, however, was irrelevant to him: He refused to make the change until Donald approved it. So, all the arrangements stopped until he got Donald's approval—in writing.

On July 3, 1996, the Marine Band began its spectacular concert at 8 P.M. We were able to invite many guests for whom space would have been lacking at the residence but to whom hospitality and thanks were due.

An annual event Donald and I enjoyed was the newly revived Opera Ball. Balls have long been a custom at the Opera House in Budapest dating back to 1866, only two years after the Miklos Ibl designed building was completed. At the turn of the century, the galas were monthly occurrences. Halted during the Communist era, the custom was reinstated during our first year in Budapest.

To those forced to live through the grim years of the Communist era, walking into the glittering Opera House must have felt like stepping onto the set of an opera. Along with paintings and frescoes, gilding adorns the lobby, the magnificent red-carpeted staircase, and the auditorium, where thirty pounds of gold leaf completed the building's one-hundredth anniversary restoration. Along with Hungarians, resplendent in medals, sashes, tiaras, and floor-length gowns, the diplomatic corps turned out in force to dance beneath

Karoly Lotz's famed circular ceiling painting of the Greek gods on Mount Olympus and the three-ton bronze chandelier at its center that illuminates the splendor.

Considering it both my pleasure and duty to publicize American designers, my evening wear was always by Adolfo. I kept to myself how much I enjoyed wearing daytime clothes by the Italian designer, Giorgio Armani. At formal events, whenever a reporter asked the inevitable question, "Whose design are you wearing?" I truthfully replied, "Adolfo." During the day, however, if Sissi Ago, the wife of the Italian ambassador, was within range, a knowing wink would be directed my way.

Another annual event we attended was the Marine Ball. Less formal than the Opera Ball, it gave us the opportunity to catch up with members of the American community. Held on November 11, it was a great way to celebrate the birthdays of both the United States Marine Corps and Donald!

If the Opera Ball was the grandest event we attended, an occasion at the former Soviet base at Taborfalva had to be the oddest. To demonstrate their renunciation of their Soviet-linked past, Hungarian military leaders invited the NATO diplomatic corps and a representative number of foreign generals and dignitaries to watch them demolish the last of their Soviet antiaircraft missile batteries. Our Defense Secretary, William Perry, was there, as were the head of the Joint Chiefs of Staff, General John Shalikashvili, and several American legislators, including Congresswoman Pat Schroeder of the House Armed Services Committee. As if it were performance theater, which in reality it was, we all sat and watched the missile battery blown sky-high in a kind of military fireworks. Not all the Hungarians, however, were in a celebratory mood. I spotted drawn expressions on the faces of several military officers, worried that they had just lost the last bulwark of their air-defense system. Now they would have no choice but to rely on the promised military support of an America that had failed to come to Hungary's aid in 1956.

MR. AND MRS. AMBASSADOR

Before taking up our post, while attending the ambassadorial seminar, we were told that there are two kinds of ambassadorial spouses, the traditional and the nontraditional. The traditional spouse does all the things wives had always been expected to do: keep a handsome, orderly home; entertain; and avoid potential criticism by being personally gracious, amiable, and at all times presentable. The nontraditional spouse, on the other hand, shuns much of this activity and says, in effect, "I am going to my studio to paint." Or, she says more and more frequently nowadays, "I am not going overseas at all because I am not giving up my career for yours."

Whatever their nationalities, traditional wives of Foreign Service officers perform a real service by organizing their embassies' social functions and attending those of other countries. They receive no salary, but there are expectations of performance. Wives are unrecognized as support staff, but reflect on the ability of their husbands to function. Because they rarely get to join their husbands in language school, they are often isolated by their inability to communicate in even the most basic situations, such as at the grocery store. (British ambassadors receive extra pay if their spouses speak the local language, but we Americans ignore the problem.)

Of course, the role of the spouse of a political appointee, such as I was, is a privileged position because the posting is usually very comfortable, typically to a developed country with an excellent infrastructure and a well-trained staff.

At the ambassadorial seminar, we were warned that our most difficult task would be to prioritize the myriad demands made on our time. Be sure to prioritize, we were urged. Being a traditional spouse, my number one priority was to make Donald's home life comfortable and to support his work; to make his tenure as successful as possible, so he could represent the United States to the best of his ability. In addition, performing my tasks as the wife of the American ambassador to Hungary offered me, a former Hungarian refugee, an opportunity to give something back for my good fortune.

My second obligation was to the American community in Hungary—both those associated with the embassy and private citizens. That meant being available to, accommodating, and looking after high-level Americans visiting Hungary, whether they were there for business, a cultural exchange, a government assignment, or tourism. Put another way, I was the official sightseeing guide, especially to the spouses of official visitors. When our lawmakers engage in foreign policy travel abroad, critics often deride these trips as "junkets" paid for by U.S. taxpayers. However, it is essential that lawmakers get out of Washington to see the rest of the world and gauge the effects of our tax-funded programs abroad, especially in countries in transition, such as Hungary and the rest of Central and Eastern Europe. How much more advantageous and cost-effective it is to understand the challenges, strengthen democratic institutions, and win friends for America than fight a war when a country falls into the grip of a hostile dictatorship!

My third obligation was to the local community, to Hungarians. How Hungarians were received at the residence reflected America, and Donald relied on me to focus on expanding and deepening our relations with our host country. This was especially meaningful for me because I was serving as a bridge between my two countries and cultures. I constantly attempted to present a favorable example of America to both the influential opinion makers and average Hungarians and to bring the people of Budapest together with American guests and embassy personnel in situations in which they would feel at ease and could form lasting relationships.

I considered my obligation to the diplomatic community, especially the events given by and for other ambassadorial spouses, to be less important than my other responsibilities. Not being able to speak Hungarian, the diplomatic wives spent a lot of time together.

Also, moving from post to post every three or four years, they were reluctant to put down any roots. Although I was on good terms with my diplomatic colleagues, I wanted to spend my time in Hungary more productively. However, to maintain good relations, I did go the monthly teas the spouses gave for each other, teas that rotated among the residences. Each country offered lavish hospitality, and the smallest countries often presented the most elaborate displays. When it was my turn to give the tea party, so as not to be perceived as showing off the wealth and power of the United States, I served simple loaves of carrot and banana cake with the tea and coffee.

At one of those diplomatic teas, I sat by chance next to the wife of the Russian ambassador. We began speaking in Hungarian, our common language, and I noticed the other women watching us. When I got up to get some more tea, I heard one of them say, "Look at the two superpowers, chatting in such a friendly way." Then she added, "Well, actually, one former superpower and one hyperpower." Looking back, I wonder if this was the height of America's prestige, having just won the Cold War.

Another diplomatic obligation was courtesy calls. During our time in Hungary, the United States did not have diplomatic relations with three countries: Iran, North Korea, and Cuba, but we were obliged to receive the representatives of any other country that requested a visit. The ritual introductory courtesy calls that new diplomatic couples made to other countries' residences were bound by rigid protocol and scrupulously precise timing. (The punctuality of these events suited Donald's personality.) On the dot of five o'clock, a car flying the country's flag arrived at our residence with the ambassador and his spouse. Donald and I would be waiting downstairs at the gate to greet them. We served tea, coffee, tea sandwiches, and cookies, and engaged in polite small talk. No serious topics were ever discussed. There were many diplomatic couples in Budapest, and although we might only see them again at large official functions, the American ambassador had to receive all those who requested a meeting. The country would feel slighted otherwise.

In the afternoon, I often joined Donald at receptions given by American companies or by other embassies. Donald likes substantive conversations, he likes to work, and he quickly grows impatient with wasted time. So receptions where he made only small talk were among his least favorite events. Still, because our absence would be noted, commented upon, and our motives analyzed, we attended innumerable receptions and ceremonial events, even the National Days to which *every* ambassador invited us *every* year.

One National Day that we always did enjoy was Great Britain's, which celebrates the Queen's birthday. The British are excellent gardeners, and their Budapest residence has a very beautiful garden in which the ambassadors' wives take great interest, each one improving on the efforts of her predecessor. There was such concern about possible damage to the lawn that the invitation always included a directive to the ladies: "Flat shoes only. No heels." How delightfully English!

From time to time Donald asked me to substitute for him at ceremonial events, and I was always flattered to do so. One such occasion was an airport celebration to inaugurate direct service between New York and Budapest through a partnership between the American airline Delta and the Hungarian airline Malev. Donald thought that I was an appropriate choice to represent the United States because, like the partnership I, too, was bilingual and bicontinental.

During Holy Week in mid-April 1995, Donald and I traveled to Seville at the invitation of the American ambassador to Spain and Donald's college classmate, Richard Gardner, and his wife, Danielle. Holy Week is a colorful time in Seville. The faithful wear peaked robes, flagellate themselves, and well into the early morning hours parade along the main avenues bearing heavy religious floats atop long poles on their shoulders. On our third night in Seville, we were having dinner at the consular residence when the butler came into the dining room. "Ambassador Blinken, you have a call from Washington, from Assistant Secretary of State Holbrooke."

Donald told me afterward that his first thoughts were, "Oh, why is Richard calling me here? It must be important. Something has gone wrong and there is a crisis. Has Romania declared war on Hungary? Here I am in Spain, and he is going to be very unhappy that I am not at post."

Donald picked up the phone in the next room and instead heard Richard say, "Kati and I are getting married, and we would like to have the wedding at your residence in Budapest on May 30 and have you marry us."

Richard Holbrooke and Kati Marton are old friends, so Donald and I could not have been happier to oblige. The residence is filled with memories for Kati, an American born in Hungary. When she was a child, her parents, journalists and friends of the American ambassador, were frequent guests at the residence. In 1955, first her father and then her mother were arrested, secretly tried, and convicted on trumped-up spying charges; their friendship with the American ambassador was considered to be proof. During their imprisonment, Kati lived with her aunt down the street from the residence. Released the following year, the Martons' reporting of the 1956 uprising to the outside world put them in danger once more. The entire family was given refuge in the American residence, and in 1957, the family was smuggled out of the country.

Having the wedding at the residence posed a series of challenges. The first was who would perform the ceremony. Because an embassy and a residence are United States territory and the ambassador represents the government of the United States, ambassadors in many countries are empowered to perform marriages. Richard had hoped Donald could do the honors, but Hungarian law did not permit it, so we had to look elsewhere for someone to officiate. A technicality barred Budapest's mayor Gabor Demszki, our next choice, so we settled on the registrar of the district court where the residence was located.

As with any event held on its property, the embassy would name a control officer to take overall responsibility for the event. Out of friendship I volunteered my services. I phoned Richard and said, "Guess what? I am the control officer for your wedding." He seemed to find that amusing.

According to Hungarian law, the bride and groom must visit a marriage counselor to make sure they are aware of marriage's many responsibilities. Both Kati and Richard had been married before, so they found that requirement a bit odd. With no way around it, several plans were formulated. One was to meet with a marriage counselor at the Hungarian Embassy in Washington. Then other complications began to accumulate around compliance with the requirement—such as who would have to be present to consider it an *official* counseling—that the couple finally said, "This is becoming too complicated. Forget it. We are not going to get married in Hungary."

When I informed the Hungarian authorities that their many requirements would force the wedding to take place elsewhere, the roadblocks instantly disappeared, including the required marriage counseling. The way was magically smoothed for the couple to take their vows in Budapest, and it was now all hands on deck and full steam ahead for we did not have much time.

Our chef, Tomas, was eager to make the wedding cake. Had he ever made a wedding cake before, I asked? He admitted that he had not. Had he ever made a tall, multi-tiered cake of any kind? "No" to that, too. Moreover, our refrigerators were not large enough to hold a four-tier cake. I suggested that having Gundel make the cake would be safer.

Tomas looked heartbroken. "Please, Mrs. Blinken," he pleaded, "I can do it. I will practice." Because he had always done everything that he said he could do—if occasionally with overly vivid coloring—I acquiesced.

We looked at cake-baking books together, and he pored over more cookbooks on his own. We ended up designing a cake that would resemble my favorite Herend porcelain pattern, Queen Victoria. The frosting would be white, and the sides would look like latticework with pink flowers. In the wonderful party shop on Andrassy Street, I found little bride-and-groom figures for the top of the cake. And I crossed my fingers.

A few days before the wedding, Tomas closed himself off in the kitchen. I grew worried and wanted to see the cake. He replied that the kitchen was so hot that the frosting would melt if he took it out of the refrigerator for even one minute to show it to me. I would have to take Tomas's assurance on faith. I kept my fingers crossed.

On Friday morning, May 26, two days before the wedding, Kati and Richard flew in to Budapest's Ferihegy Airport, where Donald and I met them. Because Richard was Assistant Secretary of State for Europe, we had a small press conference in the airport's V.I.P. lounge, as was customary for important incoming officials. Then, with an American flag flying and a blue light flashing, the four of us—Vera Blinken and Kati Marton, Hungarian refugees who had escaped from Communism, and their American diplomat husbands—drove into Budapest in the ambassador's car. Kati and I hugged each other and exchanged a few words in Hungarian, which our husbands could not understand, but the sentiment of which they surely guessed.

The wedding was scheduled to begin at 6 P.M. on Sunday. The happy couple arrived a half hour before the ceremony and sat alone in our living room, looking so romantic and holding hands. Kati, in a light-pink silk suit with pearls, was radiant.

The ceremony took place on the terrace in our garden. I had decorated it with large pots of white daisies, and while the guests were gathering, a harpist played in the background. After the ceremony, the harpist was joined by violinists roving among the guests as they were served champagne and hors d'oeuvres before dinner.

During the marriage ceremony Richard was called upon to say one Hungarian word, *igen*, meaning "yes" for "I do." Hungarian law insisted that he must understand what he was agreeing to, so Frank Katona, Donald's special assistant, volunteered to stand beside the groom and precisely translate the registrar's question. At the appropriate moment, Richard said *"igen,"* and just to show he knew what he was doing, said "yes" in English as well.

As expected, many requests had come from the press to cover the wedding. We did not want to turn it into a media event, but fifteen minutes (which stretched into half an hour) were set aside after the ceremony for interviews and picture-taking. Viewers watching TV coverage on the news that night saw a reporter ask Richard to say a few words. Characteristically, he launched into his observations of the international political scene. Kati immediately whispered to him, "I will handle the questions," and refocused the talk on the wedding.

Nevertheless, later at dinner, foreign affairs were a major topic of conversation among such guests as Hungary's President, Foreign Minister, Defense Minister, and a member of Parliament, Laszlo Rajk, whose father had been executed by the Communists. Pete Peterson, the investment banker who headed the Council on Foreign Relations, attended with his wife, Joan Ganz Cooney, founder of the Children's Television Workshop; Peter Galbraith, our ambassador to Croatia, was also there with his wife-to-be, Tone, and several members of their families. All of us were acutely troubled by the escalating violence and deaths in neighboring Croatia and in Bosnia, even as we had assembled to celebrate a wedding, a symbol of life.

As Tomas's wedding cake made its grand entrance at dinner, I held my breath, but I needn't have worried. The cake was a triumph—and in all the right colors!

Many guests made moving toasts to the new couple. I had never before seen Kati, an articulate woman and a professional writer, choked up. As she finished speaking, Kati turned to me and said in English what she had said earlier in Hungarian on the way from the airport.

"Vera, these are not the same circumstances under which you and I left Hungary." Both of us had come a long way, and we both knew and appreciated it.

As with all functions at the residence, what followed the wedding for the control officer—me—was the accounting. Once again, appearances were extremely important; Donald and I wanted to be certain for our sake and Richard's that no one could claim that we had charged any wedding expenses to the government. This was personal, *unofficial* entertaining. How could we show that? Cancelled checks would have been proof, but Hungary was a cash economy. So, I had the residence pay for everything in cash, collected all the receipts, and Donald wrote a check to the United States government for the total amount of the wedding's cost.

Another extraordinary wedding also highlighted our years in Budapest. On October 18, 1997, Donald and I had the pleasure of attending the wedding of our friend George Habsburg at the Basilica of St. Stephen, with a reception following at the Museum of Fine Arts.

George's bride was a princess from North Germany, Duchess Eilika von Oldenburg, daughter of the Duke and Duchess Johann von Oldenburg. Eilika's family brought a group of attractive North German aristocrats to Budapest for the wedding. Also there to celebrate Eilika and George were members of the extended Habsburg dynasty and most of the crowned heads of Europe. The wedding marked the return to Hungary of the elegance and style of the aristocracy, royalty, even imperial splendor.

HUNGARIAN SPOKEN HERE

Because I could speak the country's impenetrable language, my status among Hungarians was different from Donald's. People considered me approachable and instinctively called me Vera. Although Donald tried to be informal as well, Hungarians, with their history of foreign occupation, tended to see him as an authority figure.

Talking to me imposed no such reticence on Hungarians. I was one of their own, born in their city. I was, simply, Vera, and my approachability was useful in breaking down misconceptions and outdated attitudes about America.

My approachability also generated a lot of requests, some of which were rather strange. One odd query came from a lady seeking to sell her land at Lake Balaton. Might I have some friends in the United States interested in buying it? Not then, but now I might have some interested buyers, perhaps including myself.

When President Clinton injured his knee and a photo of him in a wheelchair appeared in Hungarian newspapers, a letter came to me from a physical therapist. She claimed to have a method of healing the President's knee. Could I help her reach Clinton?

During the armed takeover of the Japanese embassy in Peru, a letter came addressed to me that the sender wanted forwarded to the CIA. The writer claimed to have a way to release the hostages. Another letter from a would-be magician wanted my help in marketing a cream that could cure cancer.

I referred all the requests to the Embassy for the appropriate replies.

It must have been frustrating for Donald to be isolated from the local population because he did not speak Hungarian. Whether American or Hungarian, people tended to meet him at the embassy with his American staff, and everyone spoke English. Outside the embassy, where English speakers were fewer, the language barrier separated him to a degree from the populace, even when someone was available to translate. Also, he could not read the local newspapers or understand TV broadcasts.

I helped by translating from the morning newspaper at breakfast. Although he would be briefed soon in his office, he was eager to know what was happening and would ask me to translate at least the headlines. Often, he asked me to translate further. I was his personal in-house twenty-four/seven interpreter.

Sometimes I was able to interpret more than just words for Donald. I remember, for example, what Foreign Minister Geza Jeszenski said the first week of our arrival at a dinner given in our honor. After toasting Donald, welcoming him, wishing him success, and making all the appropriate diplomatic remarks about furthering friendship between our two countries, Jeszenski added, "Mr. Ambassador, on a personal note, I would like to thank you for bringing your Hungarian-born wife to us. She will help you to interpret not only our language, but also our soul."

My ability to speak Hungarian and to understand the thinking behind the words was helpful when Donald was invited to speak at the University of Pecs. This experience showed how important perceptions are in diplomacy, especially in a country like Hungary, where citizens had been accustomed to reading between the lines, rarely accepting what officials said at face value.

Keep in mind that after the regime change in 1989, Hungarians seemed to say, "All right, we got rid of the Communists. Now, what should we do? Tell us what the new rules are." Even university students, who should have been the least regimented thinkers, could not understand that it was time to think for themselves; instead they expected to be handed a new set of directions.

For many years, six professors from the University of Pecs had been invited by the University of Arizona to spend a semester at its campus, a valued perk paid for by the American school. This year, however, the invitation was not renewed. During the question-and-answer period that followed Donald's speech, the interpreter translated questions literally. He did not accurately convey, however, the students' impression that the U.S. government had cancelled the invitation to the Hungarian professors in retaliation for Hungary's recent election of a socialist government.

It was up to me to explain to Donald the real concern of the students. When I did, he explained that in all likelihood, the University of Arizona simply lacked the funds to offer the visits this year. The audience was astonished that the decision could actually have been made by the university itself without a government directive or a political motive. The incident demonstrated to us that the challenge for Hungary was to open those closed minds and get them to start thinking on their own.

Hearing Hungarian spoken around me all the time was unexpectedly disconcerting. In New York, only my family and their friends spoke Hungarian. Now, although reason told me this was a country filled with strangers, I had the confusing feeling at first that they were all family.

Although I had long ago resolved to be 200 percent American, living in Budapest and speaking Hungarian again brought me the realization that my feelings were also Hungarian; that this language was a passageway to the Hungarian within me. I came to understand that my dual perspective enables me to be a bridge between my two countries, that this duality can make a positive difference.

STAYING SAFE

Even before 9/11, when circumstances did not call for heightened security or bodyguards for all our ambassadors abroad, I worried that someone might harm Donald, who had no bodyguards. The concern began in Washington when ambassador designates were warned never to fall into the pattern of taking the same routes every day, never routinely stopping, for example, at the same newspaper stand. I knew however that no matter how much his routine and schedule might

vary, at some point every morning Donald would walk from the car
to the embassy front door without any security. My fear was that ter-
rorists linked to the war in the former Yugoslavia, just over Hungary's
border, might try to bring attention to their cause by targeting an
American ambassador.

I never feared that Donald might be in danger when the two
of us were alone at a concert, at the opera, or even out for a walk,
because our private schedule was known only internally at the embassy.
As for our safety at the residence, an incident there dispelled much
of my concern.

Two Hungarian police officers provided security for us outside
the residence gates. Inside were two additional Hungarian guards
employed by the embassy, and at night they were accompanied by
two very fierce Rottweilers. I found out exactly how good those dogs
and guards were the night when, with dinner guests, we went outside
to view Haley's comet, forgetting to notify the guards that we were
leaving the house.

As we climbed up the hill behind the house to get a better view,
we suddenly heard barking dogs and a guard speaking to us on his
walkie-talkie. He said the dogs were getting nervous; although they
could neither hear nor see us, they felt slight tremors in the ground
from our footsteps and knew someone was on the hill. The dogs'
acuity eased my mind, at least at the house.

For the first time in our marriage, in his capacity as ambassador to
Hungary, Donald was obliged to keep secrets from me. A red folder
on his desk contained intelligence reports, and it was allowed to be
there only when he was alone in his office. When someone came in,
he immediately slipped it into a drawer. At night, after everyone had
left the building, the Marines made rounds, checking all desktops and
making sure no documents were left exposed.

Donald told me that the substance of the reports in the folder would very likely appear in the *International Herald Tribune*; the information itself was not as important as how it had been obtained. What disturbed me more than curiosity about the contents of the red folder was not being able to share this part of Donald's life.

Being a wonderful husband, Donald applied for and obtained a security clearance for me from the State Department. Now, when I was with him escorting officials on diplomatic missions, I could accompany them into the "The Bubble," the secure enclosure in the Embassy where sensitive information was discussed. I didn't do it often but was pleased that I could.

FAUX PAS

My most embarrassing faux pas during all our time in Hungary happened when Donald and I visited Hungary's neighbor Slovakia, and Ambassador Ted Russell invited us to dinner at his residence in Slovakia's capitol, Bratislava. Ted and Donald had been working to forge a treaty that would resolve disputes stemming from the presence in Slovakia of 600,000 ethnic Hungarians among the country's overall population of five million. Some of them still referred to Bratislava by its Hungarian name *Pozsony*, and they clung to their ethnicity, even though the 1920 Treaty of Trianon established new borders granting sovereignty over this former part of Hungary to Slovakia.

Eduard Kukan, Slovakia's foreign minister, was seated directly across the table from me, and keeping up a conversation was difficult at times. As I would at any dinner party, I started chatting with those around me, in this case mentioning that I had just voted by absentee ballot in an upcoming local New York election. I also mentioned that the ballot was not only in English, but also in Spanish, something I had not noticed when voting in person. "I don't approve of that," I added. "I think that at the very least people who become citizens should learn enough of the country's language to be able to vote in that language."

As I went on, Minister Kukan kept nodding and said, "That is very interesting, Mrs. Blinken, please continue." So I did, expressing my strong belief that it is important to speak the language of the country where one lives. When the foreign minister again said, "Please continue, Mrs. Blinken," I began to get the very uncomfortable feeling that maybe I was saying something inappropriate.

At last, the Foreign Minister asked, "Mrs. Blinken, does your husband share your opinion?" Instantly, I realized just how deeply I had put my foot into it. In Slovakia, the Hungarian language, spoken by 600,000 ethnic Hungarians, poses some very serious problems.

After some quick thinking, I replied, "I don't know whether my husband agrees with me or not, but let me explain why I think this way. People who come to the United States from other countries do so of their own free will; they want to come and live in the United States and be American citizens. It is very different in a country like Slovakia, where the minorities did not decide to move but stayed in the same place while the borders were changed by a higher authority with the Treaty of Trianon. These minorities only want to speak the language of their ancestors."

All the Foreign Minister said was, "I see," and we turned to another topic.

In April 24, 1999, Donald and I attended a White House dinner given in honor of the heads of state of the newly admitted countries to NATO: Hungary, the Czech Republic, and Poland, as well as prospective countries, members of "Partnership for Peace," such as Slovakia. I was seated next to Foreign Minister Kukan, and he asked if I remembered our very interesting talk in Bratislava. That almost five years later he also remembered that conversation was proof, if any was needed, that my embarrassment had been well-founded.

The conversation with Foreign Minister Kukan taught me an important lesson early on: chatting casually at a diplomatic dinner was out of the question. Everything I said in public would be scrutinized because I might be expressing my husband's opinions, which in turn were assumed to be the official policies of the United States. From then on, I always kept my remarks general, and my conversation was well-informed about the weather, interesting sights in Hungary, the flowers in our garden, and the china in the residence. I talked about the household, about children, the movies, concerts, shopping, where to find the best cheese, and how exciting it was that we had a new source for Norwegian salmon. It was not scintillating conversation, but for an ambassador's wife, these were safe topics and free of potential controversy. Although I chafed under my self-imposed censorship, I reminded myself that it was not nearly as constricting as that forced on Hungarians under the communist regime.

My second faux pas, another outspoken incident, occurred close to the time of our departure from Hungary at a reception with business leaders that Donald and I attended. While chatting with ambassadors from several countries, a representative of Coca-Cola told us about the great Christmas gift his company was planning for Hungarians: Coke intended to wrap the famous Chain Bridge in fabrics of red and green. Despite the presence of so many experienced diplomats, I frankly told the gentleman that his plan was not desirable.

The Chain Bridge was built between 1839 and 1849, the first permanent stone bridge across the Danube linking Buda with Pest. Destroyed by the Germans during World War II, it reopened on November 21, 1949, on its one hundredth anniversary. Atop its majestic middle arch, the official seal of Hungary had been replaced by the communist hammer and sickle. As soon as the Soviets left in 1991, the Hungarians covered the Soviet insignia with cloth until they had the time and funds to replace it once again with the seal of their national pride.

"The Hungarians are going to love it," the Coke executive insisted. "It will bring the spirit of Christmas to everyone who crosses the bridge."

I did not think so. "Maybe you ought to talk to Hungarians who have no connection to Coca-Cola—and *in* Hungarian, if possible—so they are free to give you an honest opinion. They will tell you the Chain Bridge is almost sacred to them, and they don't want anyone fooling around with it."

The Coca-Cola executive became rather upset and implied that I must be echoing my husband's opinion, which must be the point of view of the American government. I had to make clear that I was giving only my personal opinion and had no idea what my husband's or the American government's official position was regarding the wrapping of bridges. Donald supported me. "Vera is absolutely right to speak her mind and express her private opinion."

As I suspected, the Budapest authorities refused to allow the plan to be implemented.

There is a post-script to the Coke and Chain Bridge incident. Several years later, I met the Coca-Cola executive and he told me that Budapest had been his first foreign assignment; therefore, he did not fully appreciate cultural sensitivities. Only later did he realize that the Chain Bridge was a powerful symbol for Hungarians, an icon on the order of the Eiffel Tower for the French or Big Ben for the English. In hindsight, he conceded that his plan to wrap the Chain Bridge in Christmas colors as a Coca-Cola promotion was misguided.

OUT AND ABOUT

Despite my many visits to Hungary since 1987, I had failed to anticipate the instant celebrity that came with being the wife of the American ambassador in a new democracy. After a few months, I was recognized everywhere I went, and reporters were curious about the Hungarian-born representative of the United States. In a pre-9/11 world, we had no bodyguards and moved around freely, often just the two of us. Because we were frequently featured in the media, people would walk up to us—on the street, at a concert, anywhere—to say hello. The greetings were friendly and we welcomed them, but they created a new situation for us, a pressure to be "on" at all times. Even a simple walk down the street could turn into a photo-op. While this notoriety can be flattering and even fun, it would be a mistake to get too used to it and develop a chronic case of ambassadoritis.

Although we traveled to official functions in Donald's ambassadorial automobile, we had purchased a personal car for me. It was a navy-blue Opel, manufactured by a subsidiary of General Motors, so we were "buying American."

At that time, the streets of Budapest were still full of Soviet-era vehicles, such as the East German Trabant, a vivid example of why communism had collapsed. Looking more like a child's soapbox racer than an adult's automobile, the Trabant was made of unlikely materials: some steel, some plastic, and an outer shell of pressed cardboard. The fragile "Trabi" frame could only support a 26-horsepower engine, which gave it its characteristic cough. It could achieve a top speed of around 55 mph, had a poor safety record, and got only 17 miles to a gallon of gas while spewing pollutants. Then again, it was never intended to go very far because travel was restricted under communism. Despite all those drawbacks, Trabants had been treasured in Hungary, and all of them were spoken for before being built due to the difficulty of obtaining any car at all.

To buy a car during the communist era, you went with cash to an office to order the car. (Doing everything in person and in cash was typical of transactions under the old regime.) You put down a deposit, from 50 percent to 80 percent of the car's price, but were given no specifics about your purchase. You were glad to take whatever came, in whatever color, after a five to ten year wait for its arrival!

With the fall of the Iron Curtain and the opening of the border to competing automobiles, the Trabant was doomed, and it soon became a collector's item. In a sense it was the stepparent of our car, for when Trabant production ceased in 1992, its East German factory was transformed into a modern Opel plant. A few years later, Budapest opened a Rolls Royce showroom, and now the traffic congestion there is caused by a variety of imported cars.

Donald kindly hired a driver for me. Budapest traffic was dangerous at the time because the new Western cars could go fast, which their drivers weren't used to, and the cars could also stop on a dime, which caused frequent rear-end collisions by older Eastern European cars. We had been told that any accident with the ambassador's wife at the wheel could produce troublesome repercussions, so we were lucky to find an excellent driver named Imre. And there lies a very Hungarian story.

Imre had originally driven for the American embassy and was obviously well thought of because he had been given a promotion another driver wanted. This rival then began an effective but totally false whispering campaign attacking Imre's loyalty, which Imre learned about only after he had been summarily dismissed. Consequently, the Cuban embassy hired him, perhaps because the Americans had fired him. Imre worked there during the Cold War, retiring in the early 1990s. When I told our embassy I was hiring him, the reply was that his work for the Cubans had "tainted" him, and he couldn't be trusted. I countered that the days of such thinking were behind us, and we hired him. When Imre received his ID tag allowing him access to the U.S. embassy, he had tears in his eyes and said it was his reward for having suffered through the many years with the Cubans.

I have no idea how many sightseeing tours I conducted during our time in Budapest, either official or unofficial, but my car and Imre were essential to my role as tour guide. We were happy that many of our friends from home came to visit, and for many of our visitors, it was their first time in Hungary, which after so many years behind the Iron Curtain had not yet become a popular tourist destination. Certain sights were a must, and I made sure our visitors saw them:

the Castle District with its winding medieval streets and grand buildings, St. Stephen's Basilica, Parliament, the Opera House, and the Liszt
Academy of Music. I tried to tailor my tours to the specific interests
of our guests. If a visitor had an interest in film, we went to movie
studios and locations where films had been shot in Budapest. If the
travelers were interested in art, we chose among the Museum of Fine
Arts, the National Gallery, and the Ludwig Museum of Contemporary
Art, as well as the newly emerging art galleries.

The obsessive Hungarian focus on the past has produced a
bounty of museums for visitors. No matter what the interest, Budapest probably has a museum to explore it. Over a hundred in all,
these museums showcase ethnography (Hungarian culture and folk
art); arts and crafts; fire fighting; the postal service; banknotes and
coins; sports; telephones; transportation; underground transportation
(Budapest boasts the first subway built in mainland Europe); the Bible;
the Holocaust; Jewish life; aviation; agriculture; electrical technology;
stamps; commerce and catering; crime; terror; medical history; military
history; natural history, and medieval history; Budapest history; music
history; the composers Bela Bartok, Franz Liszt, and Zoltan Kodaly;
the artists Victor Vasarely, Max Ernst, and Imre Varga; and several
Hungarian writers. One might think that at the Palace of Miracles
at least Hungarians could have tried to reverse history and create a
glorious, happy past for their country, but that building is actually
a large, interactive children's science museum.

Shopping was also a favorite activity for visitors. A popular destination was the Herend porcelain factory near Lake Balaton, or, more
conveniently, one of the shops in Budapest where Herend products
were sold.

Even though I had led numerous visitor sightseeing tours to the key
sights in and around Budapest, I wanted to learn more about the

city that I had left as a young girl. Being an architecture buff and an interior designer, I signed up at Elte University to audit a weekly architectural course consisting of lectures and walking tours.

After the changeover from communism to democracy in 1989, and a subsequent infusion of private capital, attention finally turned to restoring Budapest's decaying buildings, most of which had been nationalized after the World War II and then ignored. Very quickly, as restoration efforts got underway, their hidden beauty began to re-emerge, revealing the city's rich variety of architectural styles, which reflect its long history, its occupiers, the tastes of its Habsburg rulers, and the creativity of its citizens.

The classes increased my knowledge of the city's architecture, and they also revealed how Hungarians both relate to their architecture and reflect it. For one thing, the people feel quite comfortable with the *appearance* of antiquity and do not require authenticity. For instance, architectural styles derived from earlier centuries can be designed into structures that may be fairly new, and the more symbolism enhancing the references the better. Thus, the neo-Gothic Parliament building, completed in 1904, incorporates 365 towers to signify the number of days in a year, and its 96-meter-high domes refers to 896, the year of the Magyars' conquest of the Carpathian Basin. Commissioned to open on the one hundredth anniversary of that event, its contentious nineteen years of construction overshot that date by eight years. Inside the building are seven hundred offices, great circular stairways, elaborate décor, and, in a perfect expression of Hungarian history, a dozen huge murals depicting grand castles that were the scenes of significant events in Hungary's past, but due to the 1920 Treaty of Trianon are now located in other countries.

Symbolism was also important to the architect of the ancient-looking Fisherman's Bastion, which overlooks the Danube on the Buda side.

Also built for the 1896 millennium, the Bastion displays in one building all of Hungary's architectural styles and is topped by seven turrets, the number of the original Magyar tribes.

Just up the hill is the Castle District's largest structure, Buda Castle, known as the Palace and recognizable from a distance by its great width and high green dome. Invaders have destroyed it many times, and the kings who rebuilt it, as I learned, usually expanded and altered the design. The most notable were Matthias, who enlarged it in the Renaissance style and made it a center of art and learning, and later the Habsburgs. The commanding mid-eighteenth century Empress Maria Theresa ordered an expansion that would reflect the Habsburgs' power. Known as the Mother of Europe for solidifying her family's alliances by marrying off her many children to other monarchies, she died a decade before the French beheaded her daughter, Marie Antoinette. A century later, Emperor Franz Jozsef had the now-Baroque structure remodeled with neo-Baroque embellishments.

The Habsburgs however, much preferred life in Vienna to Budapest, and except for Empress Sissi, they rarely visited the Hungarian side of their Dual Monarchy. Sadly, the Palace was largely destroyed during the Siege of Budapest in World War II. Rebuilt after the war, it now houses government offices, the National Library, the National Gallery, and the Hungarian History Museum.

Andrassy Avenue, Budapest's most elegant boulevard, was named after an extraordinary figure, Count Gyula Andrassy. A revolutionary in the struggle for independence, Andrassy was sentenced to death in absentia by Emperor Franz Jozsef after the Habsburgs regained control of Hungary in 1848. He escaped to Paris and lived a pleasant life, waiting for the time when Vienna would seek to negotiate with its restive Hungarian subjects. In 1867, Andrassy returned to Hungary as prime minister and placed a crown on the head of his would-be executioner, Franz Jozsef, to initiate the Dual Monarchy. Also crowned in Matthias Church was his Empress Sissi, who had played a large behind-the-scenes role in fashioning the political solution. The occasion was marked by the *Hungarian Coronation Mass* composed and conducted by Franz Liszt.

A product of nineteenth-century urban renewal, Andrassy Avenue was originally called Main Street and changed to its present name after the statesman's death in 1890. The thoroughfare was renamed in 1947 to honor Stalin, then changed to *Nepkozstarsasag*, or "the People's Republic," in 1957, and finally reverted to Andrassy Avenue in 1990.

The municipality of Buda had recently restored and made accessible to the public a chain of caves beneath Buda Castle. These caves soon became another sightseeing attraction to which I could take visiting Americans, and the caves also provided me with another insight into the Hungarian psyche.

In 1242, after the Mongol invasion, King Bela IV ordered the construction of high defensive walls around the village that sat atop a hill on the west side of the Danube. Placing his residence within the fortifications, the king more or less founded Budapest. The castle could be defended as long as food remained because water wells and natural caves existed beneath many of the surrounding houses. Over the millennia, water trickling through the limestone substrata had produced the numerous caves; over the centuries, humans had enlarged the caves and, in some cases, linked them together. This network of caves served as a chilly storage place for food, and a hiding place for valuables and people, including troops defending the castle.

The Turks, who occupied Hungary between 1526 and 1699, widened and joined many of the caves until they formed an underground chain. People entered or escaped the caves at several hidden openings that also brought fresh air into the tunnels. During World War II, bomb shelters with toilets and baths and a "Rock Hospital" extended the chain. Four thousand people took refuge in the chain during the bombings and often found solace in the Cave Church.

The communists extended the tunnel to its present length of two-and-a-half miles, closed the church, and further developed the hospital. What had been a hiding place for the citizenry became a hiding place for the ruling elite. Top communists were treated and operated on in the hidden hospital, so the public would never know when ill health threatened one of their leaders.

For me the Castle Cave was a perfect geographic analogy for the clandestine interior life that centuries of occupation had forced upon Hungarians.

AMONG OUR GUESTS

During our years in Budapest, Donald and I were pleased to host many well-known guests. One such visitor was New York Governor George Pataki who arrived with his family and a friend, Charles Gargano, a businessman and former ambassador whom the governor had appointed to head the state's Economic Development Agency. Governor Pataki was reciprocating Prime Minister Horn's visit to New York and continuing their exploration of trade and investment possibilities. The governor was proud of his Hungarian heritage and spoke some Hungarian; he planned to travel to the Debrecen region in eastern Hungary to research his ancestry and look up relatives.

Donald set up numerous meetings and dinners for the governor and his group, while I entertained his wife, Libby, their son, Teddy, and the governor's mother, Peggy. The four of us had a good time, even though members of the media pushed microphones at Libby everywhere we went. Despite these intrusions, she was always a gracious and articulate representative of the United States and the State of New York.

When our friend Florence Fabricant and her husband Richard visited us for Thanksgiving, *The New York Times* profited from her visit. Florence and I made the rounds of Budapest's renowned coffee houses researching an article she later wrote for the *New York Times*. Today's young people, sipping lattes and cappuccinos at Starbucks around the world, may think of their hangouts as innovative; coffee houses, however, have been gathering places for writers, artists, politicians, intellectuals, and just about everybody else in Budapest for centuries. Coffee houses existed in Budapest far earlier than in other European capitals because of the long Turkish occupation and the Turks' obsession with coffee. Florence and I went to the Café Ruszwurm, founded in 1827 in the Castle district, where we sampled their *rigo jancsi*, a rich, dark chocolate cake, and downtown to Gerbaud, where my grandmother met her friends for coffee and *dobos torta*, or drum cake, a mocha layer cake with a caramelized top—my favorite.

The citizens of Budapest are addicted to spending time sipping coffee, perhaps with a pastry, at these convivial establishments, usually conversing with friends, reading the newspapers supplied for customers, or, more recently, typing away on laptops. Much of the planning for Hungary's 1848 revolution is said to have taken place at a Budapest café, and on the night the New York Café opened, playwright Ferenc Molnar was said to have thrown the front-door key into the Danube, so the place would never close. Recently renovated, it remains a favorite meeting place.

Our friend Ronald Lauder found ways to effect change in Hungary, a country where he has roots through his mother, Estee. Donald and I were invited to the groundbreaking of his Javne Jewish Community School in the Buda hills. Ronald had conceived and founded this K-12 community school for eight to nine hundred students to replace a pre-World War II Jewish school system obliterated by the Holocaust.

As part of the groundbreaking ceremonies, a time capsule was buried with items and artifacts from the present time. At the top of the list was that day's newspaper. To represent an aspect of contemporary design, Ronald suggested I include my Estee Lauder compact because it bore a beautiful rhinestone rendition of the American flag. I declined because I treasured it since his mother, Estee, had personally given it to me before we left New York.

Once completed, the school's architecture proved to be modern, open, colorful, and cheerful. It quickly became a beacon of fine education and attracted non-Jewish students, as well. By recognizing and meeting a need, Ronald had made a valuable contribution, and I could see that the new school provided strong gratification to him. I hoped that I too might find a way to give back for my life's good fortune.

The groundbreaking festivities ended with a joyful dinner that Ronald gave at Budapest's most famous restaurant, Gundel. Founded in 1894 and situated in City Park, next to the zoo and near a 150-year-old amusement park, the restaurant was purchased in 1910 by the chef Karoly Gundel, who turned it into one of Europe's most renowned dining places. Having fallen in love with the restaurant during his days as a student in Austria, Ronald purchased the then rundown establishment in 1992 and restored it to its earlier elegance. Donald and I also had the pleasure of hosting Ronald's brother, our friend Leonard Lauder, chairman of Estee Lauder, and his charming wife Evelyn, who visited us early in our posting, as did Donald's brother Robert and his lovely wife Allison.

From time to time Donald and I found ourselves hosting visitors through requests from friends. Liz Robbins, who had introduced us to the Clintons, asked us to look after her friend who was coming to Budapest and was likely to be lonely because her husband was working on the film, *Evita*. The friend was Melanie Griffith, and her husband was Antonio Banderas.

Uncharacteristically, and one of the few times he had ever involved himself in our social arrangements, Donald immediately offered to phone "poor lonely Melanie" and invite her and Antonio to join us for dinner.

We had been told that Melanie was registered at her hotel under a false name for privacy. When Donald gave the alias to the telephone operator and identified himself, he was immediately put through to her.

Our friend and Donald's former partner, Lionel Pincus, was with us, and we took our guests to Gundel for dinner. Melanie was warm and sweet and insisted on sitting next to Antonio, so they could hold hands under the table. Antonio was a real surprise. Rather than being just a good-looking actor, he is highly intelligent and showed an active interest in Hungarian culture, languages, and history. Lionel and we had a enjoyable evening with the Banderases.

THE HOLY FATHER

How thrilling to learn that I was to have the honor of meeting Pope John Paul II! The Pope was coming to Hungary, and the ambassadors with their spouses were invited to greet him at the airport. Protocol required that we line up on a receiving line in order of tenure. The Albanian ambassador, who had been posted the longest, would be the first ambassador to shake the hand of the Pope. If Donald had been the most recent ambassador to present his credentials, we would have brought up the end of the line, regardless of our country's size and prominence.

I had been told that church protocol required that I wear a hat. As the Pope slowly made his way down the receiving line and reached me, the wind flipped down the brim of my hat, totally covering my face. So my souvenir photo shows Pope John Paul II greeting a hat. Although seeing Vera Blinken's face would not have mattered to him, I would have liked to have seen the Pope's face while shaking his hand. At least Donald has a perfect photo of this special occasion.

FLOTUS

In July, 1996, we were preparing for the first visit by FLOTUS, First Lady of the United States. The President of the United States, or

POTUS, had already visited Hungary twice since we had been posted there. An advance team, seemingly as large and thorough as her husband's, had arrived a week ahead of the first lady's visit to work out her schedule and security. Hillary had indicated that her special interests were women, children, and minorities, and we knew that she wanted to meet and have meaningful exchanges with as many people as possible. We worked with her advance team and her chief-of-staff Melanne Verveer, who was to accompany the first lady on her visit, to set up the kinds of activities she requested.

At 6 p.m. on a warm and sunny summer evening, I stood with Donald on the tarmac at Ferihegyi Airport watching Hillary's plane land. She emerged looking radiant in a two-piece blue dress and the famous headband. I was amazed to see her so fresh knowing that she had already visited two other Eastern European capitals that day, Prague and Bratislava.

Hillary gave us a big hug, and then we drove with her in her car to lay a wreath at a newly installed monument to Imre Nagy, the prime minister during the 1956 uprising who was later executed by the communists. In 1989, only a short time after the border with Austria was opened and a few months before the Berlin Wall fell, Nagy's remains were reburied in a very public ceremony to demonstrate the new spirit of reform awakening throughout Hungary.

From the monument, we proceeded across the square to Parliament, where Donald took Hillary to meet with Prime Minister Gyula Horn. As they emerged from the meeting, I heard Donald say, "Hillary, if you ever get tired of being first lady, you might consider becoming secretary of state." In retrospect, it was a very prescient call.

That evening the Hungarian government gave the first lady a lavish dinner in Parliament's spectacular Hunt Room, decorated with frescoes of twelve magnificent "Hungarian" castles no longer in Hungary. The following morning, we accompanied Hillary to her first scheduled meeting at a community center with representatives of the Roma, or Gypsy, community. A large and very poor minority in Hungary, the Roma live for the most part under difficult conditions.

The first lady was very knowledgeable about their problems and, as always, asked astute questions.

Our next stop was Central European University, a George Soros-founded and funded institution that had opened the previous year. Hillary had been eager to meet with Hungarian women, so I had arranged a round table discussion with fifteen women based on their mastery of English and their various professions; two were members of Parliament.

I introduced Hillary, who made some brief remarks, and then the participants around the table introduced themselves. Speaking on their own and in answer to Hillary's questions, my Hungarian friends accounted themselves extremely well. I think Hillary was a bit surprised by how articulate and accomplished they were, by how many languages they spoke, and by how successful they were in their fields. At one point, Hillary asked how they had managed to raise their children while pursuing their careers. Surprising to her and to me was that most had relied on their mothers to help with child care, rather than on government provided daycare.

After a buffet lunch, we moved on to a neighboring building, the new Bank Center, where Donald and the first lady cut the ribbon for the commercial section's new offices, a great photo-op.

Dinner was scheduled for seven o'clock at Gundel, and we were planning to meet Hillary there. The restaurant had been checked out by the Secret Service, who told us that for security reasons we were to dine in the dining room instead of the beautiful garden. At about five o'clock, the advance team called us to announce a change of plans: The first lady would like to walk across Heroes Square with us to the restaurant, a distance of a couple of blocks, and then have dinner in the garden because it was such a glorious day. Would we please meet her at her hotel at six thirty?

After a scramble to arrive on time, we found her ready to leave, punctual as usual. Exiting the car at Heroes Square, we began our stroll, with Hungarians, tourists, and a sizable entourage of reporters traveling with the first lady following us to our dinner in the garden.

After a delicious meal, Hillary turned to me at dessert and said, "Vera, why don't you tell us the story of how you left Hungary?"

So, I did. As I finished, Jill Dougherty, a reporter for CNN said, "This is a book and a miniseries."

The last morning's schedule began with a breakfast meeting with President and Mrs. Göncz at their official residence in the Buda hills. Hillary and President Göncz had met previously, and this was going to be a half-hour courtesy call. Instead of sitting opposite each other in the big chairs according to custom, the warm and grandfatherly president said, "Hillary, come sit next to me on the sofa"; meanwhile Donald and I and the other participants were seated around a low coffee table.

Suddenly, disaster struck. As refreshments were being served, I was talking with my hands and knocked over a glass of orange juice, spilling most of it on my beige skirt. With photographers waiting outside to take pictures of us saying goodbye to the Gönczes and then of Hillary's departure at the airport, I would look conspicuously awful. I knew I did not have time to return to the residence to change, so I was quite upset but tried not to show it.

Zsuzsa, the president's wife, came to my rescue and said, "Come with me." Applying some water with a towel, she cleaned off the stain, dried the wet spot with a hair dryer, and saved the day. When we rejoined the others, the conversation was still flowing; fortunately for me, a "courtesy call" that was supposed to last half an hour had lasted an hour and a half, giving me time to be camera ready.

A NEW ATTITUDE

The Hungarian predisposition to pessimism is understandable for a people used to foreign occupations and drained of hope that their lives would improve. One manifestation of this pessimism was the highest suicide rate in continental Europe. Another was the typical Hungarian reluctance to speak up or take individual action and to make only surreptitious attempts to manipulate the monolithic political system under which they lived. Out of necessity, Hungarians had spent their lives looking for an angle, for a hidden agenda in the government or an individual, while always concealing their own motives. Hungarians liked to work things out through the *kiskapu*, which means "the small gate," or, as we say in English, "through the back door." Such a strategy was calculating but necessary for survival in the difficult times Hungarians had endured.

The sudden transition to democracy and freedom of speech was arduous for Hungarians. Their way of thinking had been shaped by half a century of communism and four prior centuries of Turkish occupation and Austrian rule. About the present situation, Hungarians say, "It took five days to change the government, five years to change the economy, but it will take fifty years to change the mindset." That may be overly pessimistic, but the transformation is indeed a slow process.

During the Soviet occupation there was another saying: "Everything is forbidden, but what is not forbidden is compulsory." People were conditioned to behave like captives, to be sheepishly timid, to swallow their words. Survival of a Western-oriented people in a country occupied by an alien Eastern dictatorship depended on it; those who did otherwise were imprisoned, or worse. The system stifled initiative, repressed individuality, and resented creativity, even punished it. As Tom Friedman of the *New York Times* astutely observed, "Under communism, you don't do well by doing better. You do well by keeping your head down, by not making waves, by not challenging the status quo, by not calling attention to yourself. This, of course, results in inefficiency, a terrible sense of being powerless, which leads to a population filled with inner rage. And it also leads to corruption."

Citizens had to wheel and deal to find a way through the cracks of the unresponsive command economy. Barter was important because no one had money; friendship and connections were important because, with so many restraints and so little available to buy, people were always trading services. Hungary became a giant web of interconnections and IOU's, of people who owed something to someone who owed something to someone else, who would then collect it from a fourth or fifth person down the line. The Hungarian word *protekcio* sounds like it means "protection," but it's a totally different concept: It is the art of getting things done through connections, by calling in IOU's, by doing favors, and repaying. If you knew someone you could deal with at an embassy, you got a visa to travel. If you knew someone in the right place, you got an apartment, an automobile, theater tickets, opera tickets, doctors' appointments, veal from the butcher, and sometimes even a telephone.

Another saying that exemplifies that era was, "If you are not cheating the state, you are cheating your family." A citizenry that has wheeling and dealing down to a science must necessarily be suspicious and distrustful of authority and of each other. During many phone conversations, I had been told, "No, this is not for a telephone conversation. I will tell you about it when I see you." Old habits die hard.

Under communism, Hungarians also lived by an eleventh commandment: "Thou shall not get caught." Of the four state security branches, one was run by the so-called counterreactionary secret police, who recruited informers and spies from the general population. If they caught you for something, in order to avoid imprisonment or Siberia, you turned informer on your friends, the only people you knew well enough to inform on. To avoid trouble, parents admonished their children to abide by the three N's, which in English would be: "Never tell Nothing to Nobody." It was an awful way to live, but just to be able to live was what mattered!

Despite the pessimism of the Hungarian mindset, which was still recovering from long years of communism, Donald and I tried to foster positive developments in the country. At the end of its six year plan in 1997, the Peace Corps was closing down its operations in Hungary because English courses were now openly available in public schools and private institutes throughout the country. The

Director of the Peace Corps, Mark Gearan, asked Donald to make remarks at the closing ceremony, but Donald suggested that it would be more appropriate for me to do so because of my original funding of the 1989 conference that brought the Peace Corps to Hungary. I happily accepted. Because we were to leave at the end of the year, every event was now imbued with extra meaning for me, and none more so than this one. The closing ceremony was held in the very grand Ethnographic Museum, formerly the Supreme Court Building. My remarks centered on the success of the English language program and how intertwined my own history was with the Peace Corps in Hungary. The circle closed on a happy note.

The spirit of volunteerism to help others that so enriches Americans and our society still separates us from much of the world. My European mother, for example, did not understand why, when I was working so hard at my interior design business, I added volunteer work to my load. Since volunteerism is so important, I was pleased when Donald designated me to represent him as Hungary's chair of Junior Achievement, an American volunteer program that teaches business practices to children from kindergarten through high school age. In the program, each child is assigned a particular business project to get off the ground—exactly the entrepreneurial spirit we were trying to promote in Hungary. These projects were especially challenging for Hungarian children because the adults in their lives had always depended on the government to take responsibility for everything.

Previous ambassadors had been honorary chairpersons, but my involvement in Junior Achievement was active. I helped organize events such as cook-outs and fundraising runs, visited local school programs, presented awards, and gave receptions for potential supporters at the residence. It was gratifying to support a program that introduced effective business practices to young people who would become Hungary's future entrepreneurs and volunteers.

In keeping with the spirit of volunteerism, in March 1996, I joined a small delegation of fellow members of the board of the International Rescue Committee (IRC) on a trip to Bosnia and Croatia to observe the devastation and refugee displacement. With the United States providing a large portion of the funding, the IRC had been among the first voluntary agencies to arrive when the conflict started, and it rapidly expanded its role until it was the leading voluntary agency providing food, clothing, shelter, materials and repairs, agricultural needs, sanitation, medical and psychosocial assistance to refugees in need. The IRC field staff often worked under extremely dangerous conditions, such as when our engineers and construction crews rebuilt the Sarajevo gas and water systems under Bosnian Serb fire.

Our group met in Zagreb, Croatia, and traveled to Banja Luca in the Bosnian Serb Republic, Tuzla and Sarajevo in the Muslim-controlled section of Bosnia-Herzegovina, and to Split in southern Croatia. In several places we were warned that snipers remained a danger. Nevertheless, we toured hospitals and rehabilitation centers, visited with refugees, and observed attempts to aid women and children who had lost husbands, brothers, and parents. We spoke with people who remembered the time when Muslims and Croatians lived together peacefully, many in mixed marriages. Later, my photographs of bombed-out buildings and the ruins of the famous medieval bridge at Mostar appeared in a Hungarian magazine along with an interview about the refugee problems I had witnessed.

Finally, during our time in Hungary, I also established an office for the International Rescue Committee in Budapest, as well as assisted in setting up a presence for the IRC in London.

TASZAR

On a cold and foggy day in early December 1995, with the leaves already off the trees and a dusting of snow on the ground, Philip Reeker, the embassy's deputy press attaché, and I drove down to Taszar, the newly established NATO base and a staging area for peacekeeping forces headed to Bosnia. Our task was to welcome the press corps, on its way to view the arrival of the first American soldiers.

As our van approached the sprawling former Soviet airbase, I was struck by how quiet, how barren, how forbidding it was. A high metal fence topped by barbed wire surrounded the base, and guard towers kept people from coming too close. We faced the same bleak barrenness inside the gates. The barracks and other buildings had a bare, stripped-down look; whatever the Soviets could not take with them, they had sold to the locals. Lighting, plumbing, and bathroom and kitchen fixtures were all gone. Even the pipes and wiring had been ripped from the walls, and the buildings had been deteriorating for the five years since the Soviets had left.

For the Hungarians invited to the event, this was the first time they had ever been allowed inside the base. Under Soviet control the base had been top secret and off limits. Residents of Taszar and the neighboring city of Koposvar, where my mother was born, were aware of the base's presence, but were never allowed inside. Piercing the secrecy surrounding this uninviting place was part of the press conference's allure. More significantly, I think, were two other factors: First, people were relieved to see that the U.S. was finally taking steps to assert its presence on the warring factions only a few miles away in Bosnia; second, people were gratified to see Hungary, after its long imprisonment behind the Iron Curtain, finally moving onto the world stage while acting in concert with other democratic nations. Furthermore, businesspeople and officials looked forward to the economic benefits, the demand for supplies and services and the increase in jobs, that the revitalized base would bring.

Not everyone was pleased by the new development. Some people in the Taszar-Kaposvar region wondered whether their government had opened the door to a new occupation force. Indeed a major reason for the early press conference was to emphasize America's openness and to assure the Hungarians that we had no secret imperialistic agenda.

After waiting a while, we learned that the two C-130 Hercules transport planes coming from Germany had been delayed and would not be arriving that day. Many reporters had come from far away—a CNN correspondent had traveled from Moscow—and they wanted to see something they could write about or broadcast. The problem of finding a story for the press corps rested on Philip's shoulders.

Thinking quickly, our clever press attaché led a tour of the base and, with the aid of a flip chart, outlined construction plans and sketched out the dramatic changes to come. That makeshift tour of the base that the Soviets had kept off limits for so long satisfied the reporters and astonished the Hungarians, many of whom were still flabbergasted at their invitations.

I spent a good deal of time speaking to the Hungarians who had been invited to the event and who were very surprised that the wife of the American ambassador spoke their language. Often, they appeared daunted from encountering so many foreigners and by their limited knowledge of English. "We speak English, but we still don't understand it," they complained. "We look words up in the dictionary, but can't find them."

As it turned out, the Hungarians were baffled by words like IFOR and USAREUR and ISB, the acronyms our military uses, which are like a private code. The first two acronyms I happened to know, but ISB required a translation, and I was informed it meant "Intermediate Staging Base" or, more simply in our case, Taszar.

Philip and I returned to Budapest after a long day.

More than a year after NATO peacekeeping troops convened in Taszar, bound for Bosnia, American officials were still traveling to Hungary to evaluate conditions. The highest-ranking official was the new Secretary of Defense, William Cohen, who brought along his charming wife, Janet Langhorn. Donald and I flew to Taszar with them aboard the Secretary's plane, a military jet with blacked-out windows, which impart a very strange feeling on takeoff and landing. Seated beside me was a member of the Hungarian government. He and the Hungarian ambassador to the United States had just flown back on a United States Air Force plane from the conference in Madrid where Hungary had been officially invited to join NATO. The official confessed that if anyone had told him ten years ago that Hungary would be given such an invitation and that he would return to Hungary on a U.S. Air Force plane, he would have considered them absolutely crazy.

This same official explained that he had been brought up in a loyal communist family and had been a true believer. A trip abroad in his mid-twenties, however, had changed his life. Travel had opened his eyes to personal freedom, to freedom of choice, and to having options in life, causing a disillusionment that led to his rejection of communism. We agreed that despite the progress being made, the residue of nearly half a century of communism would not disappear overnight. More time was needed for the Hungarian mindset to adjust to democracy.

By now, Taszar had taken on the look of an American town, with a supermarket, a movie theater, ice cream stands, and a K-Mart. Although our permanently stationed military personnel enjoyed traveling around Hungary, being able to live the rest of the time much as they would in the United States made the stay of many easier. Donald and I both felt a surge of pride whenever we spent time with our military; whether they were career soldiers or members of our National Guard, they invariably were great people and selfless professionals dedicated to the security of our country.

EARLY MEMORIES

Although I did my best to submerge painful childhood memories, unexpected sights and sounds caused deeply buried recollections to surface. It became impossible to deny any longer that in my effort to become 200 percent American, I had erected an "iron curtain" in my mind, pushing behind it early memories of war, of want, of turmoil, of pain, and of loss. Now as an adult, I could no longer deny the existence of that frightened child still within me. Somehow I would have to make peace with her and confront those memories.

During our posting, Donald worked hard to open Hungary to outside commercial interests; one feature of the resulting economic development was that shopping malls came to Budapest. One of the malls included an ice rink, and one day I was watching the skaters, when I heard a little girl on the ice suddenly call out, *"Anyukam!"* That term of endearment, meaning "My Mommy," is what I called my mother. Suddenly childhood memories of Mother taking me skating in Varosliget in Budapest and later at Rockefeller Center in New York came rushing back.

Only moments after I returned to the residence that day, I received a phone call from a Budapest relative of my wartime governess, Mitzi. She was passing through on her way back home to Montreal, and she was hoping to see me. I rushed right over.

Mitzi and I had not seen each other for years, and we had a very emotional reunion. I sensed her pride in me as we reminisced about those cold days in the bomb shelter during the winter of 1944–45. A good deal of my character was formed in that period and, surely, much of it by her. Mitzi died a few days after returning home to Canada. I am sure that she, like my father and mother earlier, had come to say goodbye.

I had often walked past our old apartment building on Hollan Street, but had never summoned the courage to ring the bell in order to enter. Perhaps I wanted to believe that those doors had shut behind me forever when we left for America, for inside was loss, fear, and pain. Soon after seeing Mitzi, however I was again drawn to the building and was walking by when someone emerged, leaving the front door to close very slowly. On an impulse, I dashed into the lobby.

As I looked around, not knowing what I was looking for, an old woman appeared and asked if she could help me. I took a deep breath. "I used to live in this building."

The old woman was surprised. "All the families are still here." I could see her searching her memory. "Oh, there was a widow on the top floor who left Hungary with her child," she added. Then she paused and took a closer look at me. "It's you!"

I froze, unable to utter a word. Yet, as she said it, it felt as if we were standing there in 1950. She did not offer and I did not ask to visit our old apartment.

It had been a routine day driving with Imre. When he stopped the car for a red light on a wide boulevard, the locale seemed familiar, but I did not know why. When I asked Imre where we were, he named several nearby buildings and then added, "And right over there is the Children's Hospital."

Suddenly the bright, sunny Sunday morning of March 19, 1944, swirled up around me. Mother was trying to push through the crowd to get me back to the hospital to stop the bleeding behind my ear caused by a recent operation. Flowing endlessly past us was a river of uniformed Nazi soldiers and menacing vehicles. Even now I was feeling the fear I had sensed as a small child fifty years ago.

Some time later, Donald and I were invited to the opening of a new wing of the same Children's Hospital. While waiting for the ceremony to begin, I glanced into a display case filled with memorabilia and was stunned to see a photo of my stepfather, Paul. I did not know that the hospital was founded by his uncle Armin, and that Paul had interned there.

When Paul died, my mother kept the medical bag that had accompanied him everywhere, and when Mother died, I kept the bag, not knowing what to do with it. Now, I offered it to the director of the hospital, who was pleased to receive it. I was happy to find such an appropriate home and believe Paul would be too.

Another time, while riding with Imre, I was reading in the back seat when again we stopped for a light. I looked out and saw the name of the street and the number on a building. Those, too, seemed familiar. Later, I telephoned my cousin Peter in Toronto and asked if he recognized the address. He instantly replied, "Your father's office was there."

PRIMAVERA

Women initially did not show up when we invited couples for official functions. I was curious to know who these women were and why they were reluctant to come. I knew Hungary had many accomplished professional women, and I was eager to meet them. Utilizing the contacts of my Hungarian and American women friends, I organized a series of lunches, each one for women in a specific profession. We had no agenda, just open conversation and an opportunity to get to know each other; the challenges facing women in a society in transition were certain to generate compelling exchanges.

I held ten lunches in all, with twenty women at each. My guests behaved similarly at every lunch: The first few to arrive would take a glass of orange juice or mineral water and stand around in a circle, first sizing up each other and then looking me up and down while wondering what this was all about. Incredible to me was how few of these women in the same professions even knew each other; this sort of networking had never been done before in Hungary. The country's history of secrecy and fear had kept people to themselves, hoarding their knowledge and contacts for fear of sharing information that might help advance someone else's career. There was a long way to go in turning around this mindset.

I was not sure how to seat my guests who were mostly unknown to me. To make sure no one felt slighted, I asked everyone to pick a slip of paper from a bowl. Each slip bore the name of one of our states; the guest then sat at the place with the same state name on the place card at the table. As I did at all residence functions, I started off each lunch by saying, "Welcome to America." Continuing in Hungarian, I said that I had no agenda, no ulterior motive; my only desire was that we get to know each other and that they feel welcome at the American residence. We went around the table, each woman introducing herself, and inevitably, interesting conversations ensued. I felt excitement grow as the women became acquainted and found common ground. At the end of each lunch, many women came up to me and said, "Vera, this was really wonderful. We would like to continue to meet."

I always replied, "So would I. When all the lunches are over, let us see what we can do together."

I enjoyed meeting these interesting women and seeing how exposure to other dynamic women empowered them. Although I did not know what it might be, I vaguely sensed that something important might develop within these get-togethers.

After all ten lunches had been held, I invited the approximately two hundred women to a reception. There I passed out a questionnaire asking whether they wanted to continue regular meetings for networking or to take on a project we could work on as volunteers. About half chose to network, and half wanted to get involved with a project. I continued giving two receptions a year for those who wished to network, and I scheduled meetings once a month for those interested, as I was, in finding a worthy cause.

The project group started out with about one hundred women. Searching for a name, and because it was springtime, someone suggested PRIMAVERA, which was unanimously accepted. PRIMAVERA means springtime in Italian and represents rebirth. It also contains my name, Vera, a gesture I truly appreciated.

Finding a name was easier than finding a cause everyone could agree on. I was getting discouraged when on the plane returning to Hungary from what would be my last visit back to New York, I sat next to an American businessman who owned a factory in Hungary that manufactured T-shirts. He told me how excited he was by his recent participation in a charity event in New York, "The Fashion Industry Targets Breast Cancer," a sale of designer clothes to raise money to fight breast cancer. At the request of the event's organizers, he had produced Ralph Lauren-designed T-shirts with the target insignia. Energized by the experience, he hoped to replicate the event in Hungary, but it would take a group of committed women to make it happen.

I happily told him that I had just such a group. I felt sure that the members of PRIMAVERA would be as enthusiastic as I was about this possibility.

At our next meeting, I presented the proposal to launch a campaign to make women aware of the dangers of breast cancer and the need for regular mammograms to detect the disease at an early stage. All members, except the doctors, were in favor. The doctors were fearful that we would create a demand that could not be satisfied. At that time in Hungary, the National Health Service would reimburse a woman for a mammogram only with a doctor's prescription and only if she had a complaint. Women in Budapest and in larger cities who could afford it, got mammograms privately; poor women and many in small towns and rural areas had no access to mammography. The great danger was that our campaign for early detection would create a demand that the Hungarian healthcare system could not meet. Then the idea came to me. "If women cannot get to a facility for screening, we have to bring the facility to them," I said. No woman should ever fail to receive a diagnostic mammogram simply because the equipment is not available. We have to create a mobile mammography program."

At last we had our project: The PRIMAVERA Mobile Mammography Program.

How could we get it done? I am not a doctor, and Donald and I would shortly be leaving Hungary to go home. Knowing that I would be far away and not in daily contact, I recognized that our project would have to be professionally managed by a trustworthy person or organization. So I arranged a meeting with Eva Bakonyi, then the executive director of the Soros Foundation in Hungary. I asked Eva to manage the project through the Soros Foundation. She liked the concept but wisely pointed out that neither she nor I knew how to operate a mammography screening program. Clearly the program should be managed by a professional in the field.

Eva arranged a meeting with Szilvia Madai, the founder of MaMMa Klinika in Budapest, a private mammography center established two years earlier. After a feasibility study proved the viability of a mobile mammography program, we agreed that Szilvia would be the operating partner of PRIMAVERA. In her, we found a woman who was energetic, knowledgeable, competent, compassionate, and eager to move forward.

Eva offered to have the Soros Foundation provide the first year's operating costs, enough to screen twelve thousand women, provided that PRIMAVERA raised the funds to buy the equipment. Although philanthropy was not yet a common practice in post-communist Hungary, we raised all the money in Hungary from Hungarian companies, multi-national corporations, foundations, and private individuals.

Real volunteerism was dormant in Hungary during communism because citizens were forced to volunteer for parades and other events; a "volunteer" event was really compulsory. Now, not only were the women who raised money and helped organize PRIMAVERA providing a much needed health service; by their example, they were also spreading the spirit of volunteerism. What had started out as informal lunches had evolved into a mission!

On May 1, 1999, the PRIMAVERA Mobile Mammography Program opened its doors at the Victoria Rehabilitation Center for the disabled in Szekesfehervar. By popular demand we twice extended our stay, screening women who had no previous access to mammography facilities, such as women in wheel chairs.

We introduced the PRIMAVERA Mobile Mammography Unit to the public at a press conference on June 23, 1999, the fifteenth anniversary of the Soros Foundation. This provided us the opportunity to acknowledge the major contribution of the Soros Foundation and to thank George Soros personally for his generous support. At that point our equipment, the screening unit and the computers, still had to be plugged into electrical outlets at the location that was donating space for the screenings. We were still raising funds for a generator and a trailer that would make the bus a self-contained unit.

On March 2, 2000, Aniko Levai, the wife of the prime minister, cut the ribbon to launch our completed unit. The red-and-green trailer now fully furnished with the mobile screening unit and all the necessary support equipment is completely self-sufficient and, at last, truly mobile. As the screening unit rolls into the countryside, women at all levels of society are made aware of its availability. Local doctors, nurse practitioners, and regional administrators give the names of their women patients to the local representatives of the National Health Service. The representatives then send out letters informing the women of the dates that PRIMAVERA will be in their areas and urging them to make an appointment for a free screening. Sadly, less than 50 percent accept the invitation. As of December 2007, PRIMAVERA has screened 110,419 women.

Acknowledging the success of PRIMAVERA programs, the Hungarian National Health Insurance has been financing a substantial portion of the cost of the screenings since January 1, 2001. The following year, PRIMAVERA became a participant in the "Program for a Healthy Nation," funded by the Ministry of Health. This effort established over forty permanent mammography centers throughout Hungary and guarantees free biannual mammograms for every woman between the ages of 45 and 65. No more need for a doctor's prescription; just a routine, possibly lifesaving, check-up.

To ensure a high degree of competence in both diagnostics and therapy at these centers, PRIMAVERA has also organized interdisciplinary conferences for radiologists, pathologists, oncologists, surgeons, and other healthcare professionals. Instructors have included Dr. Laszlo Tabar of Falun University in Sweden, a country that has an excellent national screening program. PRIMAVERA continues to offer periodic training sessions. I continue my involvement with PRIMAVERA as we develop new programs, and I hope that our life-saving work pays at least some of the rent for the space I occupy on Earth.

After a round of farewell receptions and dinners given in our honor, on the day of the NATO vote, November 16, 1997, Donald was invited to President Göncz's office, where he became the first American ambassador to be awarded the Middle Cross of the Order of Merit of the Republic of Hungary, the nation's highest civilian honor. Asked to prepare a list of guests to be invited to the ceremony, Donald, in typical fashion, asked that only the top members of the embassy staff be invited because without their support he would not be receiving the award. Donald and the president toasted each other and their countries with a glass of Hungary's famed sweet wine, Tokaj.

President Göncz then turned to me and said in Hungarian, "I wish I had two of these to give. You deserve it. Ask Donald to let you wear it half the time."

"When?" I asked. "At night on my nightgown?"

On the twentieth of November 1997, three years, seven months and twenty days after Donald signed the book at the Embassy in Budapest to take up his duties in Hungary, we flew back home to New York.

On November 5, 2002, I was awarded the Middle Cross of the Order of Merit of the Republic of Hungary. It was presented to me in New York by the Prime Minister of Hungary, Peter Medgyessy, for my work with PRIMAVERA.

PART IV

DONALD

Flag outside the residence in Budapest

With Senator Daniel Patrick Moynihan at Donald's confirmation hearing, Washington, D.C., March 1994

Vice president Al Gore presiding as Donald takes oath of office, Washington, D.C., March 29, 1994

Presenting credentials to President Árpád Göncz, April 1994

Greeting President Clinton at the steps of Air Force One, December 1994

Vera guiding President Clinton at the Basilica of St. Stephen, December 1994

President Clinton addressing embassy staff, December 1994

Seeing off Air Force One, Budapest, December 1994

Vera with Governor George Pataki, Libby, Teddy, and the governor's mother, Budapest, September 1995

Vera with Bosnian child at a refugee camp in Hungary, Spring 1995

Wedding party for Kati Marton and Richard Holbrooke at the ambassador's residence, May 28, 1995

Opening of the Clinique Boutique, Budapest, October 1995

Vera and Estée Lauder, Budapest, 1989

Presentation of the colors

Fourth of July National Day celebration at the ambassador's residence

Taszar Airport with President Göncz, Richard Holbrooke, Dan Rather, and Bill Siefkin, January 13, 1996

Vera and Antony, Taszar, January 13, 1996

With the troops at Taszar, January 13, 1996

President Clinton greeting U.S. forces at Taszar, January 13, 1996

With Secretary of Defense William J. Perry, General John Shalikashvili, Hungarian Minister of Defense Keleti, January 1996

With Secretary of Defense William J. Perry and the Marine Guard

Christmas with Santa and Congressman Tom Lantos, Budapest, 1996

With President Jimmy Carter at Habitat, summer 1996

Lunch with Bill Gates

Drinks with George Soros

Donald with President Arpád Göncz, Ronald Lauder, and the mayor of Budapest Gábor Demszky, at the opening of the Lauder Javne School, February 1996

Donald greeting Pope John Paul II, Budapest 1996

With Attorney General Janet Reno and FBI Director Louis Freeh, April 22, 1996

U.S. Ambassadors at the Regional Meeting, Budapest, 1995

The Marine Corps and Donald share a birthday, November 11

Vera and Donald with Hillary Clinton at Hero's Square, July 1996

With Janet Langhart Cohen, and the wife of Hungarian Minister of Defense Keleti, Budapest, July 1997

Farewell visit to Taszar with Secretary of Defense William Cohen and his wife
Janet Langhart Cohen, July 1997

PRIMAVERA Mobile Mammography Unit

Vera delivering closing remarks for the Peace Corps, Budapest, May 1997

Receiving the Middle Cross of the Republic of Hungary, Vera with Ambassador
András Simonyi and Consul General Gábor Horváth, New York

Donald receiving the Middle Cross of the Republic of Hungary, Budapest, November 1997

Vera and Donald in New York

GETTING THINGS DONE

"At this critical moment in Hungary's history, I believed the U.S. ambassador needed to speak out unequivocally on issues facing Hungary and America."

POLITICS AND MONEY

It was easy to become distracted by daily demands; we had far more pressing matters confronting us. Hungary's national election was held on May 8, 1994, and the result was as expected. As polls had predicted, a coalition led by the Socialist Party won in a landslide, collecting 72 percent of the vote and taking two-thirds of the seats in the National Assembly. In an alliance of strange bedfellows, the Socialists' governing partners would be their former anti-communist opponents, the Alliance of Free Democrats. After just four years of freedom, Hungarians appeared to be rushing back, at a rate of three to one, into the arms of a party filled with their former oppressors.

On election night, my aides in the political section of the embassy accompanied me on a visit to the campaign quarters of all six parties in the national election. Only the Socialists had cameras at the ready, and they took pictures of me as I entered and sent those images to Hungarian TV and newspapers. A right-wing journalist with an anti-American agenda wrote that I was already showing my favoritism by going only to the Socialist Party headquarters. I fired back a response to his newspaper, which they printed, explaining that had I visited all six party headquarters on election night—but only the Socialists had the wit to position a photographer at the entrance.

Jane Perlez summarized the national election in her *New York Times* article. "The sharp swing to the Socialists, who got only 11 percent of the vote in 1990, reflected disenchantment with economic conditions across a broad section of society. Hungary's gross domestic product has fallen 20 percent in the last four years as exports of agricultural and other goods collapsed and factories cut production. But while many Hungarians became poorer, a few became conspicuously richer, causing considerable resentment in a society that had become accustomed to a sort of egalitarianism under forty years of Communism."

I felt certain, and Perlez quoted me as such, that the Socialists would not squander the momentum gained over the past four years of democracy and were fully committed to upholding Hungary's constitution and democratic principles. The seemingly backward slippage did not erase the larger victory: this former totalitarian state had staged honest national elections for the 386 members of the National Assembly for the second time in just four years as a free nation. Still, I had concerns about the state of certain democratic pillars, including a rather feeble press and an economy that had not yet found its free-market footing.

My goals as President Clinton's ambassador did not change. Our priority was to help Hungary grow its economy while solidifying its democratic institutions. That would help stabilize Hungary, increase trade with America, and, in turn, provide unique investment opportunities for U.S. companies and individuals. Conversely, a breakdown in its democratic foundation could send the country spiraling back into repression and tyranny.

My biggest concern was to gauge the intentions of Gyula Horn, the Socialists' leader, who won the election despite a black mark against him for helping the militia put down the 1956 populist uprising. He had been coy about his personal intentions during the campaign and finally revealed that he would head the new government shortly before it was to take office in July.

I scheduled a full, formal meeting with the soon-to-be prime minister emphasizing the importance of transparency and straight talk. One of the worst remnants of communism was a latent fear of being reported to the police and imprisoned, which led people to dissemble. So at this critical moment in Hungary's history, I believed the U.S. ambassador needed to speak out unequivocally on issues facing Hungary and America. Straight talk might seem both startling and suspicious to a deeply distrustful people, but I felt strongly that honesty would build trust over the long run.

Far more than my predecessors, I gave many public speeches and was quoted in newspapers and interviewed on TV (with simultaneous translation). Vera and I made a special effort to travel to outlying areas of the country, where 80 percent of Hungarians lived. In these small towns and rural villages, the main attraction was not the ambassador, but his Hungarian-born, Hungarian-speaking wife. Once again, Vera proved invaluable and truly seemed like a co-ambassador.

I began my meeting with the newly elected prime minister by reiterating the hard choices required to put Hungary on a solid economic footing. We then moved on to the subject of Hungary's aspirations and where I thought its energies could be best applied. I suggested to Horn that his remarks in the press about wanting Hungary to join the European Union were a bit premature. Setting his sights on NATO membership was a much more attainable goal in the short term. The bar was set quite high for EU membership, but the criteria for becoming a member of NATO were achievable and would lead to EU membership a few years down the road.

Horn listened to me with his usual poker face, and I left the meeting with no indication of his intentions. He maintained that same enigmatic manner over the years that I knew him. The prime minister was guarded, impersonal, and businesslike, and made no effort at a relationship of personal trust. What he lacked in personality, he made up for with a sharp intellect and a very pragmatic sensibility when it came to advancing Hungary's interests. I tried to keep pressure on him by making frequent public statements in the Hungarian media about the need to change the government's economic policies. I realized that this was a marathon, not a sprint, and tried to ensure that the prime minister would embrace change before Hungary faced a dire economic crisis.

Much of my time was devoted to boosting American business and investment in Hungary. Trade ties with the United States could never rival Hungary's long and deep relationship with Germany, its principal trading partner, but I made it my goal to increase the volume between the United States and Hungary. Even more important, I believed, was increasing American investment in Hungary by establishing new ventures, buying into existing Hungarian companies, or expanding the facilities and workforces of American companies already located in Hungary. These included, among others, Motorola, IBM, Ford, GM, GE Capital, and El Paso Energy. I encouraged American investors by showing them that Hungary offered great investment opportunities.

My team and I spent considerable time behind the scenes with Hungarian ministries advocating on behalf of American companies to facilitate trade and clarify and help eliminate regulations that applied unfair or counterproductive taxes, import quotas, and other restrictive mechanisms. Such negotiations were often difficult because the Hungarian government used those regulations to siphon off private sector revenue and create administrative obstacles that shielded outmoded and uncompetitive state-owned industries.

American business interest in Hungary did grow rapidly during my time as ambassador and, as a result, I could have attended an American reception or cocktail party every night of the week. I was under no illusions and understood that my presence was simply a trophy to show that the company and its executives were important enough to corral the American ambassador. When those same executives wanted to talk business, they came to my office. In all my efforts on behalf of American business, I was ably advised and supported by commercial attaché John Fogarasi.

Another option for American companies wishing to gain prestige was to have an event at the ambassador's residence. In effect, they rented the residence and its staff and received Vera's organizational skills in the bargain. They paid for the food and drink, but they were mostly interested in the presence of the ambassadorial couple, which lent cachet to their event. Fortunately, Vera and I had a short commute upstairs to our private quarters when such receptions were our final commitment of the day.

One of the first business-related events Vera and I attended was the opening of a large carbon-black manufacturing plant in Tisza, about ninety minutes outside Budapest. This was a technologically advanced plant that manufactured a product—known as soot in a less public-relations minded era—vital to the rubber, plastics, and chemical industries. The new plant was designed not to release any carbon pollution into the air. That environmental consideration was particularly significant in Hungary, where the Communists had paid little attention and committed few resources to the safe disposal of the waste products of manufacturing. For decades, soft coal-burning power plants, numerous factories, and Soviet-bloc trucks and cars had spewed pollutants into the air unchecked, and chemicals had routinely been dumped into lakes and streams.

President Göncz attended the plant's opening because of its importance to the Hungarian economy and the clout of its American parent company, Columbian Chemicals. He invited me to share the ride to Tisza in his car so that we might get better acquainted. I was happy to accept the invitation, and we rode in the presidential limousine with his driver and a colonel in charge of his personal security; meanwhile Vera traveled to the plant opening with an aide from the Hungarian Foreign Ministry. The president had a warm personality, a keen interest in U.S. diplomatic objectives, and a firm belief in the importance of a strong U.S.-Hungarian relationship. It was a pleasant drive, a useful introduction to the president, and an excellent overview of the Hungarian perspective.

President Göncz and I made some remarks after we toured the plant. I focused on the value of this kind of investment to Hungary's economy. Then Vera and I joined the guests for a buffet lunch and prepared to return to Budapest, a trip we will not soon forget.

My predecessor, Charles Thomas, had warned me never to accept a ride in a Soviet-made helicopter. Vera and I were scheduled to fly back to Budapest in a Hungarian government helicopter. I had asked ahead of time and the Hungarians had assured me that it would be an American-made aircraft. At the landing pad next to the chemical factory, however, we were greeted by the less than reassuring sight of a Soviet-made helicopter. It was a huge museum piece, resembling a 1920s-vintage streetcar, with fins on its sides and a propeller on top.

With no other choice at that point, Vera and I climbed aboard. It was roomy inside, but as soon as the engine started up, the noise was overwhelming and the helicopter shook vigorously, an ominous development. All we could do was hope that the law of averages would hold long enough for us to cover the distance to Ferihegyi Airport. After landing safely in Budapest, we reminded ourselves never to ignore Charles Thomas's advice again!

Sadly, my concern about Soviet helicopters was not unfounded, and a number of them did crash subsequent to our adventure. We were fortunate most of the time to have access to American-made helicopters and the embassy's twin-engine Beechcraft airplane. No commercial flights were available within Hungary at that time, and having access to an airplane that could land at small, local airports and even on grass fields often saved me and others on embassy business a great deal of time.

The holdover Soviet helicopters were simply a factor of the high cost of buying American or European replacements. The desire among Hungarians to shed the visible signs of Soviet domination was intense. On streets throughout Budapest and beyond, signs were soon being changed back to traditional Hungarian names. At first, the Soviet names were simply crossed out and the Hungarian names written over them. Later, as money became available, the old signs were taken down and replaced by new ones.

Another example of the Hungarian purge of its Soviet past was the disappearance of the statues of "hero" workers and soldiers that the Communists had erected around Budapest and the countryside. Other former Soviet satellite nations melted their statues down for the raw metals. With typical pragmatism, the Hungarians created a tourist attraction called Sculpture Park, placing over forty of the statues on a large field just outside Budapest. Tourists and other visitors can see for themselves what Soviet socialist realism looked like.

Two monuments honoring the Soviets remain in Budapest. Both memorialize heroic actions during World War II. The Liberation Monument is a column topped by a forty-foot tall bronze statue of a young man holding aloft a palm leaf that symbolizes the city's liberation from the Germans. (A Red Army soldier that was part of the original monument has been removed to Sculpture Park.) The second monument is the Soviet War Memorial. An obelisk on Szabadsag, or Liberty, Square, it honors the sacrifices made by Red Army troops who died while liberating Budapest in World War II. Paradoxically the American embassy looks out onto Liberty Square and this monument, an appropriately symbolic setting.

By the time of our arrival, an independent judiciary was in place to protect the rights of Hungarians. Still, much of the law-enforcement establishment, which is an integral part of any democratic government and its system of justice, continued to operate on the level imposed during the Soviet era. A good sign that the Hungarian government was eager to upgrade its police force was its positive response to an offer to place an FBI police-training center in Budapest. Unfortunately, the project got off on the wrong foot and could have easily become an embarrassing turf clash within the Clinton Administration.

FBI Director Louis Freeh proposed an initiative to increase professionalism among mid-level police officers from former Iron Curtain countries by establishing an FBI-run regional training center to teach better law-enforcement methods and to increase cooperation in cases of international crimes, including the drug trade, money laundering, and car theft. At that time, terrorism had not yet reached the top of the list.

Freeh thought Budapest would make an excellent central location for his training program. Unfortunately, FBI officials contacted their Hungarian counterparts without informing the embassy, thus ignoring the State Department's responsibility for the U.S. government's foreign initiatives. Freeh thought he could manage the project alone, which was a critical mistake because the FBI did not know the Hungarian players. Being left out of the loop by Freeh also could have marginalized me in the eyes of Hungarian government leaders. Obviously I had to explain the problem to the FBI director immediately.

"The academy's a great idea, and we'll help you get it done," I said. "But you have to do it through us and not around us." Freeh did not disagree.

On an evening in late June 1994, Vera and I picked up Director Freeh at the airport and took him to a dinner in his honor hosted by President Göncz. I made the case to the president in favor of locating the academy in Budapest. In the days and weeks that followed, I pushed the plan with the new Minister of the Interior and the new Foreign Minister, both of whom promised me their support. We at the embassy managed to negotiate a very attractive arrangement: the Hungarian government donated a former military academy in Budapest. It included a nice campus, but the complex was rundown and outdated. The FBI, in turn, agreed to renovate the buildings and campus, to supply the faculty and teaching materials, and to develop the curriculum.

An agreement on this important U.S.-Hungary collaboration on law enforcement training was reached quickly and with few glitches due to the work of my talented team. The embassy had people with expertise in many areas, enabling the FBI to focus on its work of training Hungarian and other former Soviet bloc police officers in the latest methods of law enforcement.

My DCM soon set me straight about attending every country's national day celebration. There are so many embassies in Budapest that this practice could become a full-time job. We pared down the list of countries that rated a high priority with the United States. Every week, it seemed, I had a country's national day festivities to attend, even with the shortened list. Each July our turn came to host a celebration for our national day, the Fourth of July. All American embassies celebrate Independence Day, and we planned a large gathering, an enjoyable event that would create goodwill for America.

The spending limit set by the State Department for a Fourth of July party is modest, but fortunately that is the one event for which ambassadors are permitted to seek outside local financial support. We contacted all the American companies in Hungary and requested a small financial contribution to defray the cost of food, drinks, and music for the hundreds of guests we had invited. To give them credit for their donations, the company names would appear on a billboard at the entrance to the embassy.

At our first Independence Day celebration in 1994, Esther Vescey, a reporter with the *Budapest Sun*, wrote about our festivities and focused on Vera, who told Vecsey that although she cherishes her Hungarian heritage, "I am a proud American, patriotic to an extent that perhaps only a naturalized American can be." Vera added, "I am honored to have the privilege, together with my husband, of serving my country."

Vera immersed herself in the detailed arrangements for these receptions, and I was grateful to her for taking on those duties. She is very good at planning a large event and, unlike me, actually enjoys it!

Vera and I and a few senior members of the embassy formed a receiving line on the terrace at the top of the lawn and shook hands with some five hundred people before they descended the steps to the garden for refreshments. By the end of all that hand-shaking, my arm was sore, but I was comforted by knowing that our successful and well-attended celebrations reflected positive feelings towards the United States.

After the French celebration of their national day, Bastille Day, on July 14, the Hungarian government essentially shuts down for five weeks, from mid-July until August 20, the Hungarian national day.

The political situation in Hungary was much on our minds when we hosted a dinner at the residence for Abe Rosenthal, the distinguished former managing editor of the *New York Times*, a position that made him one of the most influential newspapermen in America. At the time, he was writing a biweekly column for the paper's Op-Ed page, for which he was on a fact-finding tour around Central Europe. Rosenthal's experiences as the *Times* correspondent in Poland four decades earlier had left him deeply pessimistic about the region and convinced him that the Socialists' return to power in Hungary was the first step toward reimposing communist tyranny.

Convinced that Rosenthal was wrong, I mounted a campaign to change his thinking. The Hungarians are an intelligent and pragmatic people, I told him, and they were eager to lift themselves out of the poverty to which communism had reduced them. They craved the prosperity they saw throughout Western Europe, thanks to capitalism and democracy. As part of my plan to influence his thinking, I introduced Rosenthal to several Hungarian government officials and to other Americans in order to persuade him that Hungarians were strongly committed to freedom and private enterprise. Despite my best efforts, he returned to New York and wrote a misguided column predicting terrible consequences for countries electing Socialist governments.

I took small pleasure in the I-told-you-so aftermath. Rosenthal's predictions turned out to be wrong. He should have had more faith in the power of democracy to seize people's hearts and minds and change them for good.

Vera and I enjoyed our time away together. Budapest's central location in Europe allowed us to have breakfast at the residence and sip a cappuccino in Milan by afternoon. London, Paris, Barcelona, and even St. Petersburg were within easy reach. I had to eat my words when it came to St. Petersburg. I had vowed to Vera that I would only visit that Russian city when its name was changed from Leningrad; the fall of the Berlin Wall took care of that, and St. Petersburg turned out to be an enjoyable destination for both of us.

Leaving Budapest was helpful in other ways. Time and distance allowed me to assess how I was doing. Vera became my sounding board, my indispensable advisor, and, as always, my best friend. I relied on her constructive criticism of my speeches and the positions I had taken, and her point of view was invaluable. Time and again, Vera was my secret weapon, particularly when it came to understanding social context, the underlying psychology and attitudes of the Hungarian people.

For her part, Vera went about her work for the embassy quietly and with an intense focus. Already, she had managed to renovate the residence, shedding its grim and depressing Cold War ambiance. Slowly but surely, she instilled a renewed commitment to quality service among the residence staff, whose communistic holdover attitudes gradually withered away. I did my best to listen to Vera's concerns and frustrations, as well, and I knew for certain that I couldn't do my job in Hungary without Vera as my partner on every level. We were two sides of the same coin. Her contributions to our posting in Budapest became inseparable from my own.

One of the issues important to me from my first days in Budapest was restitution to Hungary's aging Jewish Holocaust survivors for their suffering and loss. This was an important moral issue just entering into the public consciousness when we arrived in Budapest, one that had been festering in Hungary since the end of World War II. A Hungarian Jewish population that once approached 700,000 was now estimated at between 125,000 and 150,000, including about 20,000 aging Holocaust survivors. Restitution was an issue that had to be addressed immediately and directly, and I was committed to making clear how seriously both the U.S. government and I considered this issue.

Soon after our arrival, I attended a Sabbath evening service at the orthodox synagogue on Kiraly Street in the company of Frank Katona, my special adviser on cultural, religious, and other issues. Frank's father was the former chief rabbi of Budapest. A few weeks later, Vera and I attended a service at the great central synagogue on Dohany Street, a Byzantine-Moorish architectural marvel and the largest synagogue in all of Europe. It had undergone only sporadic restoration since World War II. To send a strong signal that the United States government was aware of the Jewish community's issues and was sympathetic to their cause, I had my driver fly the American flag on the car while parked outside the Dohany Street Synagogue.

So that Hungarians would know we played no favorites in religious matters, Vera and I attended a Roman Catholic mass commemorating the anniversary of the death of Joszef Cardinal Mindszenty. It was held at the impressive Cathedral at Esztergom, about ninety minutes outside Budapest. The green-domed edifice on a low cliff overlooking the Danube had been the seat of Hungary's Catholicism since the investiture of Stephen I in 1000 A.D.

I soon met with leaders of two international Jewish organizations, B'nai B'rith and the Joint Distribution Committee, and with two Americans, Sam Keller and Israel Singer, of the World Jewish Congress. These organizations and others were seeking our help in resolving Hungary's moral obligation to provide compensation and to restore property to Hungarian Jews who had suffered during the Holocaust. The Hungarian government pleaded that it was a poor country with limited resources and no responsibility to pay for crimes that had occurred under a different regime in totally different circumstances. Yet Roman Catholics who had lost property under the Communist regime had already been compensated while Jews had received nothing. On their behalf, I made it my goal to press for restitution.

Joszef Cardinal Mindszenty remains a courageous figure to Hungarians. He spoke out publicly against the Germans' deportation of Jews in June 1944, and he went so far as to hide Jews himself and he urged others to save their fellow countrymen. Mindszenty condemned the savage tactics of the fascist Arrow Cross Party and its leader, Ferenc Szalasi, who had the cardinal arrested along with other resisting prelates. Later, Mindszenty also protested the Soviet occupation that followed World War II and the rigged elections that brought the Communists to power in 1947. The following year, as he became more vocal in his opposition, Communist authorities arrested him on Christmas Day, 1948. He was tortured, drugged, and forced to sign a contrived confession before being moved to an isolated castle where he could not organize his followers.

During the 1956 uprising, freedom fighters freed Mindszenty and led him in triumph back to Budapest. When the rebellion was crushed by the Soviets, the cardinal took refuge in the American embassy. I felt a strong personal connection to the cardinal because for fifteen years, until arrangements were made for him to leave the country, he lived in the space that would later become the ambassador's office. The cardinal died in exile in 1971 and was temporarily buried in a church in eastern Austria, awaiting the day when his wish to be buried in a free and democratic Hungary could be realized. On May 4, 1991, his remains were re-interred in the Esztergom Cathedral.

LEAVING COMMUNISM BEHIND

American envoys planning to visit another country during their ambassadorships are required to request permission to enter the country on a specific date. This requirement stems from an incident in which a visiting ambassador spoke at a news conference and expressed views different from those of the resident U.S. ambassador. To avoid such embarrassments, the protocol of an advance notice was instituted, and although a bit cumbersome, it makes a lot of sense.

Prior to traveling to Paris one weekend with Vera, I cabled our ambassador to France, Pamela Harriman. "Permission granted, provided you stay with me," she replied. Vera and I had no complaint with that arrangement.

The U.S. ambassador's palatial residence in Paris is located in a private park on Rue du Faubourg St. Honoré, one of the city's most elegant and vital streets. Situated next to the Elysee Palace, the French version of our White House, the ambassador's residence contains enormous rooms, great art, and important antiques. Built by a New Orleans heiress who survived three bullets in the chest from her father-in-law's gun in a dispute over her considerable fortune, the mansion was also once the residence of the Rothschilds. It is very grand.

Pamela Harriman seemed right at home there. A British aristocrat by birth, at nineteen she married but soon divorced Randolph Churchill, son of the British wartime Prime Minister. Her second husband was the Broadway producer Leland Hayward. Her third and last husband was W. Averell Harriman nearly three decades her senior. Scion to a railroad and investment banking fortune, a former New York state governor and former ambassador to the Soviet Union, Harriman once said that his only mistake in marrying Pamela was that he hadn't done so a lot sooner.

President Bill Clinton appointed Pamela ambassador to France, and even the cynical French were captivated by her. She was fluent in their language, which always impresses the French, and she also proved to be an excellent mediator on sensitive issues between their country and the United States.

On our first visit, we were disappointed to learn that Pamela had been called away that weekend on business. Alone in the sprawling

French ambassadorial residence, aside from a maid and butler, we felt as if we were wandering through a great museum after closing time. Fortunately, we were the beneficiaries of Pamela's legendary charm on subsequent occasions.

I soon learned that U.S. ambassadors to large countries, such as France and the United Kingdom, often have less authority than U.S. ambassadors to smaller ones. In fact, the ambassador to a large country is sometimes expected to be a ceremonial figure in a well-organized and well-run embassy. A Clinton administration ambassador to one major Western European country told me that President Clinton often bypassed the ambassador and spoke directly by telephone to the prime minister with whom he had established a personal relationship.

Even in countries where top officials deal directly with the U.S. president or the president's top-ranking aides, an irreplaceable role remains for the ambassador. As recently as September 2005, a London *Times* editorial criticized an outgoing U.S. ambassador: "His apparent allergy to microphones, let alone his reluctance to engage with the British people outside London, did not serve the best interests of either the United States or the United Kingdom. More importantly, it left Washington without a spokesman in London during a contentious conflict in which Britain was playing a prominent part." That conflict was the Iraq War.

Even in the twenty-first century, a time of instant communication, the role of the ambassador remains critical. He or she is the human face and, as the personal representative of the president, establishes meaningful personal contacts with foreign leaders, opinion-makers, and the public of the host countries. E-mails and faxes are no substitute for sitting down across a table. Public diplomacy, in which the ambassador is the key player, has become more essential when so many people abroad question U.S. policies.

A president's casual disregard of an ambassador's position can undermine the diplomat's authority, even if the matter has nothing to do with the ambassador's responsibilities. In early 2005, President Bush gave a small dinner for French President Jacques Chirac at the residence of the U.S. Ambassador to Belgium, Tom C. Korologos, a political appointee. Korologos was not invited to the dinner and had to leave soon after seating the presidents in his living room. Reporters mentioned that Korologos, banished from the residence, dined at a restaurant with the White House deputy chief of staff and members of the White House advance team. Although the meeting of Bush and Chirac presumably didn't concern Belgium, the barbed reporting made the ambassador look like an irrelevant figure and undoubtedly undermined his authority and prestige among Belgians. Months later, in an effort to put a more positive spin on the slight, Korologos made reference in his speeches to welcoming Chirac and Bush to his Brussels residence.

My mandate as ambassador was to nurture and stabilize the emerging democracy in Hungary. My role could be more influential than that of some ambassadors to larger countries because Hungary was just emerging from behind the Iron Curtain. Personal relationships between Americans and local leaders were not yet in place, as they were in Western Europe. Except among academics who were considered experts on Eastern and Central Europe, Hungary did not attract much attention from Washington. These circumstances allowed me to speak clearly, firmly, and authoritatively in a newly emerging democracy, eager for American understanding and support.

As the newly elected coalition government of Socialists and Free Democrats took office, I wanted to make the rounds of the new ministers as soon as possible. An early guest from Washington at this time was Ambassador Richard Schifter, who was in charge of human rights issues at the State Department, particularly in the former Communist countries. He accompanied me to several of the meetings with the new ministers and, as a pair, we sent an unequivocal signal about the importance a democracy must place on individual and minority rights.

A short time later, we were pleased to welcome another visitor from the State Department, my son, Antony. He was working as assistant to Steve Oxman, the Assistant Secretary of State for Europe and the official to whom I reported. Oxman's counterpart in the White House was Dan Fried, the National Security Council Assistant in charge of Europe. I was proud of Antony, and we had a lot to discuss, personally and professionally.

Richard Holbrooke, our next visitor, was about to leave his ambassadorship to Germany to assume Oxman's post. An old friend and an extraordinarily accomplished and experienced diplomat, Richard had also served as Assistant Secretary of State for East Asian and Pacific Affairs under President Jimmy Carter. Despite having returned to private life when the Republicans regained the White House, Richard had traveled to the former Yugoslavia and urged the first Bush administration, without success, to launch air strikes that would have quickly halted Serb aggression and atrocities in the breakaway provinces of Croatia and Bosnia-Herzegovina.

Holbrooke and I agreed that Hungary's location at the geographical heart of Central Europe made it a natural hub for regional industrial and distribution facilities, but that its present economic policies were ruinous. After a long discussion about my work in Budapest, Richard suggested that my staff was failing to give me all the support it should, a problem to which he was particularly sensitive since he himself had once faced a similar situation.

Richard and I both demand a great deal from those reporting to us; my own day-in and day-out analysis, however, told me that he was mistaken about my staff. One of the things I learned early on as ambassador was that the people working in the embassy, whether in traditional State Department positions or in USAID, USIS, the Commercial section, and the military, were excellent and always helpful. Also, I kept in mind the military adage, "Take care of your troops, and your troops will take care of you."

In the end, I respectfully disagreed with Richard and told him that I felt certain that the imminent arrival of Jim Gadsden as deputy chief of mission, would eliminate any concerns. Gadsden turned out to be an ideal DCM. As a longtime State Department veteran, Jim knew the State Department's workings inside and out and was skilled at operating within its culture. Having previously served as a junior officer in Hungary, he was fluent in Hungarian. His deep reservoir of State Department knowledge was particularly important to a politically-appointed ambassador.

Jim was also calm, patient, and very good at handling personnel. I was responsible for about four hundred people, both Americans and Hungarian nationals, and I considered it absolutely essential to understand their concerns and defuse potentially troublesome issues. Jim and I made it a point to get out of the office for a weekly lunch, where we could quietly discuss issues without interruptions. I think many ambassadors would agree that their success was facilitated by an excellent DCM. I was fortunate to have Jim Gadsden. He was later named ambassador to Iceland. On subsequent visits, Holbrooke agreed with me about the excellence of my team and was very positive about my performance as ambassador.

Holbrooke and I had serious discussions about the challenge of negotiating restitution for Jewish Holocaust survivors in Hungary. He told me that our envoys in many European countries were facing this complex issue and promised to lend me whatever support he could. He called a few weeks later to recommend that Stuart Eizenstat, our ambassador to the European Union, meet with me, the Jewish community, and the Hungarian government. Holbrooke had given Eizenstat the added assignment of serving as a special ambassador to deal with restitution issues throughout Europe.

I questioned the wisdom of Eizenstat's involvement, especially if it stemmed from Holbrooke's doubts about whether our embassy could handle the issue. Richard made a strong pitch for Eizenstat, however, and asked me to give him a try. I grudgingly agreed and later realized that I had been wrong to resist his involvement. His low-

key manner concealed a tenacity that turned out to be a great asset
to our mission. Only years later did I learn that all the ambassadors
whom Holbrooke had asked to involve Eizenstat in resolving their
Jewish restitution issues had initially expressed the same reluctance
that I had voiced.

I continued to try to forge consensus among Jewish leaders and
convince the Hungarian government of its moral responsibility regarding
restitution. Our efforts began to bear fruit when Hungarian officials
came to realize that restitution was an important human-rights priority of not only the United States, but many other Western governments, and that it was clearly a prerequisite for acceptance into the
European Union. Foreign Minister Laszlo Kovacs chose a meeting of
the World Jewish Congress in New York to make a public admission
in his speech. He said the time had come "for the Hungarian nation
to face itself bravely and honestly" and that "it was wrong to shift
responsibility for the genocide in Hungary solely and exclusively to
Nazi Germany."

Many U.S. companies were arriving in Hungary, and I was frequently
asked to cut a ribbon for the opening of an American business. My
first such occasion was the opening of the Marriott Hotel, which
meant Hungary's commercial prospects were taken seriously by a major
American hotel chain. Vera joined me in this ceremonial activity when
she cut the ribbon to open Estee Lauder's new Clinique boutique.
Later, I particularly enjoyed opening a new Ace hardware store since
I've always enjoyed poking around amid rows of tools and gadgets.

It was an amusing occasion when I presided at the opening of
New York Bagels, a food then unknown in Hungary. Something of an
expert in this culinary pleasure, I explained to the crowd at the opening that a bagel was more than a stale doughnut with a hole punched
through it. I ventured that such a description was like calling the
Parthenon a shed with columns. I went on to note that for true New

Yorkers a day without a bagel was like a day without sunshine. The Americans in the audience were cheering my bagel exhortations until I disclosed that I enjoyed watching TV Sunday evenings while eating a toasted bagel with peanut butter and jelly. The sustained groans that arose from those who considered anything other than cream cheese on a bagel a form of sacrilege left the Hungarians mystified. Later, I did my part to help this brainchild of two young Harvard Business School graduates prosper by starting monthly brown bag bagel lunches for the younger members of the embassy This was a forum to raise any issue they wished to discuss. Although a free bagel lunch was an inducement, the opportunity for sharing views with the ambassador was obviously appealing.

Helping American companies do business in Hungary was one of my most challenging tasks as ambassador. U.S. firms were very aggressive and well-managed on their home turf, but their executives typically dropped into Hungary, spent a few days making an offer or presenting a proposal for a tender, and then quickly left. They often ignored our advice that a more nuanced, gradual effort at wooing Hungarians would be more effective in achieving long-term success. Their rushed approach to making deals sometimes frustrated me because they had the instincts to seek out great opportunities but lacked the ongoing commitment necessary to gain a foothold in the Hungarian market. Doing business in Hungary, a former command economy society, presented many bureaucratic obstacles. Here was a peculiar culture that took time to learn to navigate. Also, the Hungarian legal system was murky, and much of the economy remained in the hands of the Hungarian government.

Americans were unlike their counterparts in Germany, Austria, Italy, and the United Kingdom, who took the time to have representatives live in Hungary, to get to know the ministers, and to cultivate relationships with the local business community and the media. The

Europeans worked over the long haul at making a favorable impression and building solid connections with the decision makers. The drive-through style of American companies put them at a competitive disadvantage that no ambassador, no matter how engaged, could overcome. Furthermore, the European companies held a marked edge in being able to leverage direct and indirect subsidies, and thus beat out American companies time and again in winning contracts and making acquisitions. An example was a Canadian group that won the right to build Budapest's new airport at Ferihegy over an American bidder whose plan was technically superior. The deciding factor was that Canadian banks were prepared to put up almost all the money at a low interest rate, and the Americans could not come close to matching the Canadian financial package.

In order to eliminate barriers between the American business community and Hungarian officials, I began a series of what came to be called fireside chats at the residence. We brought together a dozen to fifteen Americans involved in various industries in Hungary to talk over problems or air complaints in a relaxed setting with the appropriate Hungarian officials and members of our embassy. We served drinks and hors d'oeuvres; the bimonthly chats ran from 5 to 7 P.M. The gatherings were successful because the comments were candid and usually led to a better appreciation by both sides of the prevailing business, political, and logistical challenges. Vera was always present, and aside from being a lively and knowledgeable conversationalist, she viewed the proceedings objectively and gave me useful suggestions on how to improve the process and get more substance out of the meetings.

In a similar vein, Vera suggested hosting a weekly Sunday brunch at the residence as a way for us to reach out in a more personal way to the Americans who were living and working in Hungary for small companies or as local managers of large corporations. Three or four couples joined us in the garden room and enjoyed bloody marys,

English muffins, scrambled eggs, smoked salmon—and, of course, bagels. The relaxed and informal setting fostered a friendly, open spirit and gave our American compatriots a boost knowing that their embassy was there for them and cared about their lives and how they were adapting to life in Hungary.

While the majority of Hungarians whom we got to know well were government officials, a notable addition to our circle of friends was Sándor Demján, his wife Lidia, and associate Ildiko Takács. From a childhood of rural poverty he rose to become the premier builder/owner of office and retail facilities in Hungary and throughout the region. The embodiment of the spirit of entrepreneurship and a leading symbol of the new Hungary, Sandor has built a tangible legacy, on a par with those of the region's post-Cold War political leaders.

Receptions at the residence also gave us the opportunity to meet notable visiting Americans. We hosted the U.S. Junior Figure Skating team that included a confident and lively twelve-year-old, Tara Lipinski, who would go on to win an Olympic gold medal. A dinner we gave for pianist Murray Perahia and his wife, Ninette, after we heard him play so impressively at the concert hall in the Liszt Music Academy, grew into a friendship. Murray played for our guests on the residence's fine Hubay piano. Another world-renowned musician who dined with us on several occasions was Isaac Stern, who was frequently in Budapest to record with the Liszt Academy Orchestra. Isaac regaled us with amusing stories about his musical career and revealed an unknown skill: he could put away two or three martinis before dinner without blinking an eye.

One of my ongoing challenges was to explain to audiences in Budapest, who were used to authoritarian government, how U.S. and free-world institutions work. This was underscored during a question-and-answer period at the Hungarian Press Club. "Mr. Ambassador," asked a journalist, "why does the American government tolerate the very unattractive McDonald's restaurants popping up all over Budapest, including some very big, disturbing illuminated signs? Are you putting your best values forward by exporting commerce, rather than serious culture?"

I carefully explained that, unlike in a command economy, neither the American government nor its ambassador has anything to do with the opening of restaurants or the placement of electric signs in Budapest or any other foreign city. Admitting I did not personally appreciate the garish signs or restaurants she complained about, I noted that citizens should bring up their concerns with local authorities, who decide what is appropriate. In a free market and open society, I continued, people vote with their pocket books, and they are obviously voting in favor of McDonald's because the restaurants are popular. Also, I added, the embassy is promoting American cultural values by sponsoring exhibits, concerts, and lectures by American intellectuals. The journalist did not have a follow-up question.

In a speech at the Budapest Collegium, I laid out the democratic principles binding Hungary and the United States I began by suggesting that as democracies, the United States and Western Europe share a common vision for Hungary and Central Europe. I said the fundamental question is not what criteria Hungary must fulfill for membership in NATO and the European Union, but whether Hungary shares our common vision of a vast Euro-Atlantic region of peaceful, democratic, free-market states that observe international norms both internally and externally, that get along with their neighbors, and that work together for a peaceful and prosperous future.

My reference to Hungary needing to get along with its neighbors was planned and pointed; independence from Soviet domination had many benefits, but it also reignited Hungary's disagreements with Romania and Slovakia that dated back to 1920 and the Treaty of Trianon. Some two million ethnic Hungarians had been impacted by the shift in borders in Romania and six hundred thousand in the newly re-drawn Slovakia (formerly part of Czechoslovakia). Unlike Americans, who might live in six or more states during their lifetimes,

Hungarians are loath to leave the places where their families have lived for hundreds of years. They cling to their unique cultural identity, which stems from a shared language unlike any other in the world. They desired to retain the option to teach their children to speak Hungarian, Romanian, or Slovakian—or all three. They wanted street signs in Hungarian as well as the national language, and they wanted to celebrate important cultural and historical Hungarian anniversaries freely and openly. Many of the demands of ethnic Hungarians upset the countries in which they lived, and this created conflict between Hungary and its neighbors.

In my speeches and in meetings with Hungarian leaders, I made it clear that if Hungary wished to join NATO, it had to settle its problems with Romania and Slovakia and achieve a long-standing peace. Encouraging such a settlement as a forerunner to NATO membership became one of my priorities.

I framed my discussions and recommendations from the vantage point of a U.S. ambassador and businessman striving to help Hungary enter the late-twentieth-century global economy. Vera complemented my approach by responding to the challenges facing us in our diplomatic post from a more personal perspective and her own nuanced understanding of Hungarians, Hungary's tormented past, and precarious present.

WELCOMING PRESIDENT CLINTON

A presidential visit is a special occasion, one that does not befall every ambassador. Vera and I were honored that President Clinton visited Hungary twice during my posting. When it happens it is the highlight of an ambassadorial assignment. It is also a stressful and challenging time. When an ambassador receives word of a pending visit by POTUS (the acronym for President of the United States), he and the entire embassy shift into high gear. When President Clinton decided at the last minute to attend the December 1994 summit meeting of the Conference for Security and Cooperation in Europe (CSCE), Vera and I found ourselves leading an all-out effort.

The CSCE dates back to the early 1970s and was envisioned as a multinational forum for dialogue between East and West, a way to prevent conflicts and manage crises. It was the forum for the Helsinki Final Act of 1975, an attempt to improve relations between the Communist bloc and the West. As a function of the historic changes following the end of the Cold War, the institution's name was changed from CSCE to OSCE (the Organization for Security and Cooperation in Europe) by the Heads of State at the December 1994 Budapest Summit hosted by Hungary's foreign minister Laszlo Kovacs.

Although President Clinton would pay only a brief visit to the CSCE summit—he would be in Budapest for about seven hours because he was due back in Washington to host the annual White House Christmas reception for members of Congress—the preparations presented us with an enormous task. One error among the scores of logistics, security, and protocol details could spell a State Department career setback or an international incident.

Security is extremely thorough and intense for a presidential visit to a foreign country, and nothing is left to chance. The presidential limousine is flown in ahead of time and kept under around-the-clock armed guard. We worked closely with the Secret Service and President Clinton's advance team.

The POTUS communications center was set up, quite fittingly, in the presidential suite at the American-owned Marriott Hotel. The equipment filled the space and spilled out onto the large, covered terrace where satellite dishes were installed. It was essential that even during a seven-hour visit the President have all the communications options he needed to operate as fully and as seamlessly as if he were in the Oval Office.

The focal point for the POTUS team was Budapest's Congress Hall. In the days leading up to President Clinton's arrival, we made several visits to Congress Hall to help with the planning for the

U.S. delegation, the largest among the seventy-three countries present. Of those CSCE member countries, fifty-three Heads of State were confirmed to attend for some or all of the two-day conference. Security required streets to be blocked and traffic to be rerouted, an enormous disruption to Hungary's already congested traffic; furthermore, the city's limited hotel accommodations would be pushed to the limit and beyond. Local authorities kept busy towing more than seven hundred cars that had been parked too close to embassies or on roadways that would be closed during the conference. The two thousand delegates would fill eight hotels, as well as their countries' embassies and residences.

The first member of the U.S. delegation to arrive at the CSCE summit was Secretary of State Warren Christopher, who came in the day before Air Force One was scheduled to land. I met the Secretary at the airport in our backup Cadillac limousine, a more appropriate vehicle than my more modest Ford. Secretary Christopher was a considerate, polite, and highly intelligent man whose style was to listen to all sides of an issue before slowly and deliberately forming an opinion. As we traveled from the airport to downtown Budapest, we had a good, substantive discussion on Hungary-related issues, including its progress toward NATO membership.

Our first meeting was with Sam Brown, the U.S. envoy assigned to the CSCE and based in Vienna; I had first met Sam during ambassadorial training and had continued to confer with him on a regular basis. I sat in as he briefed Secretary Christopher on the pending summit. At the top of the agenda was the ongoing ethnic bloodshed in the Balkans. Later on in his visit, I would head our embassy team's briefing of the secretary on conditions in Hungary in more detail.

Next I accompanied Secretary Christopher to our meeting with Hungary's Foreign Minister Laszlo Kovacs and confirmed our later appointment with Prime Minister Horn. Both Hungarian officials were well schooled in the Warsaw Pact version of diplomatic hardball, and both said essentially the same thing to Christopher: only the threat of military force made credible by the staunch support of the highest level of the American government would impress the Serbs in Belgrade and Zagreb enough for them to heed calls to end their aggression against other ethnic groups. Anything less would be ignored, they assured us. I joined the Hungarians in reiterating that hard truth and hoped that Secretary Christopher would keep that assessment uppermost in his mind as he discussed the situation with President Clinton as they considered various alternatives for forcing an end to the fighting in Bosnia and Croatia.

Standing on the tarmac at the airport the following day, waiting to welcome President Clinton, protocol placed me as ambassador at the head of the receiving line. Second in line was Vera, followed by Secretary Christopher, Hungarian officials, and my DCM, Jim Gadsden, and his wife, Sally. Since this was not an official state visit and President Clinton's purpose was to attend the CSCE conference, neither the Hungarian president nor the prime minister was there to greet him.

In the frigid December early-morning air, Vera shivered in a thin black coat (she didn't think fur would have been appropriate) and began feeling uncomfortable about standing second in line, in front of the Secretary of State. "Shouldn't you be ahead of us when the President comes down the steps?" she asked Christopher.

"No, Vera," he explained. "In a foreign country, the American ambassador outranks the Secretary of State. He's the president's personal representative and always the senior American official in that country. In Hungary, your husband outranks me." Vera said nothing, but I could detect a slight smile.

President Clinton waited until his security and personal bodyguard walked down the steps of Air Force One and then quickly followed. He first shook hands with me, gave Vera a kiss, and then shook hands with Secretary Christopher and the Gadsdens. The entourage that followed was an impressive group, including Madeleine Albright, the U.S. Ambassador to the United Nations, who wore one of the large hats that had become her signature. She was on hand because it was a chance to meet with so many heads of state in one place. National

Security Council Director Tony Lake stepped out of the plane next, followed by Senator Dennis DeConcini of Arizona, Congressman Tom Lantos and his wife, Annette, Congressman Steny Hoyer of Maryland, and President Clinton's chief of staff, Erskine Bowles.

Then to my great surprise, directly behind these powerful officials, I was delighted to see my son, Antony, emerge from the front door of *Air Force One,* rather than as was customary from the back of the plane with the other staffers. Antony was part of the delegation as a foreign-policy speech writer for the president. It was a proud moment for this father!

The Secret Service and advance team did not waste a moment. As soon as President Clinton had finished shaking the last hand in the receiving line, there was a rush to the cars, which would travel in assigned positions in the motorcade to Congress Hall in the heart of the city. We had been warned that if we missed our place, the motorcade would not wait. So, Vera and I hurried to our car, which should have been immediately behind the presidential limousine, but instead was further back.

My driver, a middle-aged man who had been driving American ambassadors for nearly thirty years, had failed to note a last-minute change and, consequently, missed his place in the convoy. He was deeply apologetic and felt that he had let me down. Concerned about making a more serious mistake in the future, he decided to retire a few months later. He conceded to me that the airport blunder had convinced him that he was no longer up to the job and that a younger person was needed.

At the convention center, we went to a private area set aside for the U.S. delegation, and I attended a briefing for the president. Because he was on Hungarian soil, before going into the main conference hall, he also held a short bilateral meeting with the Hungarian leadership.

The CSCE proceedings started promptly at 10 A.M., despite Bosnian President Alias Izetbegovic's two unsuccessful attempts to delay the proceedings in a gambit to force the assembled leaders to focus on Serbian aggression and the invasion of his country. He forcefully condemned European leaders for failing to honor their commitments to come to the aid of his country. "The result shall be a discredited United Nations, a ruined NATO, a different, worse world," President Izetbegovic warned. Sadly, his entreaties failed to move the conference attendees. The rest of the world, it seemed, was not yet ready to focus on the harrowing, deadly brutalities underway in his country.

According to the format of the CSCE conference, each head of state spoke in turn. President Clinton was the center of attention at all times, even when he wasn't speaking. A good deal of his charisma has to do with his powerful physical presence. He seemed larger than life even among fifty-two other heads of state. Clinton greeted others with a warm smile, a hint of humility, and even shyness that adds an engaging dimension to his appearance. That was my impression, anyway, after spending several hours in his company and observing how he interacted with other leaders.

Despite the careful planning and although the previously agreed-upon CSCE treaty was duly signed by all heads of state, an irritating incident occurred after President Clinton delivered his remarks that no one in the American delegation had foreseen. Russian President Boris Yeltsin surprised everyone by turning his speech into an attack on U.S. plans to bring Hungary and several other former Russian allies into NATO, portraying this collaborative effort as a hostile act toward his country. President Clinton seethed at Yeltsin's ambush, but because he had already spoken and each head of state only got one speaking opportunity, he had no way to rebut Yeltsin in front of the other heads of state at the conference.

Upon departing Congress Hall in the early afternoon, President Clinton summed up the purpose of his trip for the media. "I came here to reaffirm our nation's commitment to a secure and united Europe," he said. "We put the START I nuclear reduction treaty into effect today, and Ukraine has joined Belarus and Kazakhstan in acceding to the nonproliferation treaty. We strengthened the CSCE to help prevent ethnic and regional conflicts. So, as a result of what has happened today, this world is a safer place." What that statement so carefully sidestepped, of course, was the warfare raging so near to Budapest in neighboring Bosnia and Croatia.

The CSCE conference would be deemed a success, and the U.S. delegation would be praised for its role in the meeting. As I joined the president in his limousine for the trip back to the airport that afternoon, however, I could see that being blindsided by Yeltsin had both angered and depressed him. He would write about the incident in his memoirs.

In the car with President Clinton, I felt the excitement that comes from playing an integral role in the center of an internationally important gathering. I had a sense of what it feels like to be within that small influential sphere where powerful leaders push and jostle for position as they shape world events.

On our way to the airport for the president's return flight to Washington, we were slightly ahead of schedule. As we passed a coffee house and saw people talking and relaxing inside, the president looked wistfully at his own travel food supplies—a couple of bottles of water and a bunch of bananas. He had spent more hours getting here than he had on the ground, and I empathized with his desire to hit the pause button and enjoy a brief, relaxing respite. So I suggested a break from the tightly planned itinerary. "Mr. President, do you have time for just a little tour and perhaps one stop?"

The president said he would enjoy that. So I quickly instructed our driver to turn in the opposite direction, not toward the airport, which confused and worried the drivers in the motorcade behind us. We stopped in front of the city's impressive St. Stephen's Basilica. Having foreseen this possibility, I had asked that the basilica's authorities turn on all the lights inside, and to prepare for an unexpected visitor.

As President Clinton stepped out of the car, followed by Warren Christopher, Madeleine Albright, Tom and Annette Lantos, myself and several flustered Secret Service agents, I sent an aide to find Vera. She would be the perfect guide as she had been bringing official visitors and guests to St. Stephen's regularly.

Vera caught up with us and, at the president's side, proved to be a very knowledgeable guide. She described the basilica's history and attributes as our group walked through the spacious, opulently decorated interior. She paused with the president in front of the 315-foot cupola and the marble statue of St. Stephen on the main altar. Inside St. Dexter's Chapel, we all looked closely as Vera described the history of the most precious object in the basilica, the hand that is believed to have been St. Stephen's. On the August holiday honoring him, this relic is paraded throughout the city in a sacred ceremony revered by the faithful.

Flanked by President Clinton and Madeleine Albright, I was filled with pride at how confidently and competently Vera had stepped in and performed her impromptu assignment. Her self-assured tour and commentary demonstrated for these most powerful VIPs what I had stressed when I sought the Hungary post: Vera's value as my partner in the work of the ambassador would be immeasurable. We were truly a team and her contributions were critical.

As we left the basilica, Tom Lantos suggested to the president that he ought to have a look at the extraordinary Parliament building in Budapest, the eye-catching structure that combines a neo-Gothic façade with traditional Eastern European and Turkish architecture into a splendid whole that purposely paid homage to the British Parliament building in London. Our motorcade made another detour through central Pest, which also gave me a chance to point out our embassy building and other sights. We made a loop in order to see the Parliament building's beauty from all sides before getting back on the itinerary and proceeding to Ferihegy Airport.

On the way, the President and I turned our discussion to the progress the Hungarians were making, the issues facing them, and some of the positive developments taking place in this country. Despite Yeltsin's sneak attack, the president was again in good spirits and had recovered his famously engaging personality. At one point, he paused in the conversation and asked what I considered to be a rather odd question. At first, it caught me off-guard, so he repeated it. "Are you having fun?" he asked, looking straight into my eyes.

"Yes, Mr. President," I said. "I am enjoying it very much, but of course what Vera and I really enjoy is the chance to be of service, to make a difference."

I detected a look in his eyes that my answer may have disappointed him for being too diplomatic. I sensed he wanted me to blurt out with great enthusiasm," I'm having a ball being ambassador!" That was not my style, though, and Vera and I truly had sought the ambassadorship because we wanted to make a difference for Hungary and America, however trite that may sound. Perhaps if I had taken a moment more to consider my response, or if it wasn't the POTUS posing the question, my answer would not have sounded quite so proper. What I found appealing in this unguarded moment was the president's interest in the human feelings behind a person serving at the president's pleasure in public service.

My outstanding embassy team had worked so hard preparing for the presidential visit that I thought they would feel cheated if they did not have an opportunity to spend a few minutes with the president. At the airport, therefore, we had set up a podium and sound system on a platform in the hangar we used to house the embassy's twin-engine Beechcraft. We had decorated the drab space with cheerful banners, bunting, and American flags.

As Vera and I stepped up onto the platform alongside President Clinton, the sight and applause of three hundred and fifty people who had gathered created an energetic scene that seemed to invigorate him. I offered a few words of introduction for the president, whose comments were kind and generous. He told the embassy staff what a great job they were doing and then walked around the periphery of the crowd as he shook hands, signed autographs, and posed for photos, obviously loving what seemed to come naturally for him. The event was very good for morale, and I think it went a long way to restoring President Clinton's good mood after the Yeltsin incident. He seemed to get more enjoyment out of this brief meet-and-greet than anything else he had done the entire day. He truly was a man of the people.

Vera and I said our goodbyes to the president and the rest of the entourage, as well as an emotional farewell to Antony, grateful to have even a short time with him. Then it was wheels up at 3:30 P.M. as *Air Force One* lifted off with a thunderous roar and disappeared into the sky. In flight, a gastronomic treat awaited POTUS and his entourage. One of the president's wishes had been to "taste Hungary," but his visit was too short for a stop at a restaurant. So, Vera and I had arranged for the cuisine to come to him. We had coordinated with the chef of the celebrated Gundel Restaurant to deliver a typical Hungarian lunch to *Air Force One*: an appetizer of goose liver and baked apple, a main course of chicken *paprikas* with dumplings, and dessert of sour cherry and cheese strudel. It was not a small order. The restaurant sent enough food to feed sixty people.

As we watched the plane take off, I felt a knot in my throat. Vera waved, dabbing at her eyes until the giant plane was only a speck in the December sky. Finally, I put an arm around her and said, "Time to go."

REGIME CHANGE

I began the New Year of 1995 with a sense of alarm. Hungary's economy was in a dangerous free fall. Its foreign debt, about which Hungary had taken the high road and refused to disown after the fall of communism, was approaching $30 billion, the highest per capita debt in all of Central and Eastern Europe. A quick look at a spreadsheet revealed that there was no solution in sight because the country's annual budget, bloated with social program spending, was $3 billion in the red; most of that would have to be borrowed, causing the debt load to balloon further, and at unfavorable rates. The balance of payments showed a $4 billion deficit, largely due to the long-deprived Hungarians' rush to buy luxury foreign goods. The really frightening number, however, was the rate of inflation. We grow concerned in the United States if inflation runs a few percent a year. In Hungary, the inflation rate had skyrocketed to 30 percent annually! That meant the average Hungarian could buy only two-thirds the groceries and household goods with his or her forints in December as in the previous January. That sharp decline in their currency's value was a catastrophe for consumers and prospective outside investors alike.

I met frequently with George Kopits, the International Monetary Fund's representative, and we concurred that Hungary's failure to redress its economic problems could result in a crash and perhaps necessitate a costly bailout by the United States. A similar economic disaster had developed in Mexico the year before, and our neighbor south of the border had turned to us for massive economic aid to avoid defaulting on its loans and going bankrupt.

I used the occasion of a speech at the Budapest Collegium to point out that Hungary's social support system was proportionately more generous than those of the richest EU members. My conclusion was both obvious and a harsh pill for Hungarians to swallow: Hungary was living beyond its means. As a result, despite heavy social spending by the government and its faltering attempt to transition to a free-market democracy, the typical Hungarian worker's income and benefits were no better than they had been in 1989 under communism. This was a distressing situation and a recipe for a slide back to its totalitarian past.

The numbers told the story. Nearly 70 percent of Hungary's economy was still controlled by the government. Although more than $10 billion had been invested in Hungary by foreign sources since the end of the Cold War, much more restructuring needed to be done. Selling state-owned industries to foreign entities that would pay dollars, marks, or yen to buy and upgrade Hungarian factories and facilities could transform Hungary's lagging economy and outmoded industrial sector and boost the country's financial position.

Hungary's Prime Minister Horn deserved credit for beginning the politically unpopular process of selling its most significant industrial companies to foreign corporations, the best economic strategy. The old communist guard and nationalist fringe, however, expressed its outrage and complained that Hungary was selling the country's "crown jewels." An even more unfortunate example of this post-communist thinking occurred in the Czech Republic, where Prime Minister Vaclav Klaus barred foreign investors from buying shares in privatized businesses, thus blocking fresh capital and progressive management from entering the country.

As Hungary's poor economic conditions were causing foreign investors to delay decisions and Gyula Horn was losing his political will to attack the country's financial problems, I met with the prime minister to impress upon him how critical the economic situation had become. In order to hammer home the seriousness of Hungary's position, I brought with me Richard Holbrooke, now Assistant Secretary of State for Europe, as well as the Treasury Department's David Lipton, a tough-minded and knowledgeable specialist in international economic and financial matters. The three of us told the prime minister in unequivocal terms that Hungary's political stability and its hope for a stable democracy were dependent on the government's ability to control its own economic future. Without that, neither NATO nor the European Union would admit Hungary to its membership. The assets Hungary had, including obsolete, failing nationalized factories and businesses, could be sold to spur an economic turnaround. We made it clear to him that the proceeds of the sales had to be used to repay the country's foreign debt and not be dumped back into the national budget to fund the Socialists' bloated roster of social programs.

In keeping with his secretive political style, Horn asked only a few questions and made even fewer comments as we gave our presentation. We left after about one hour without a sense of whether he accepted the necessity we described. Would he take tough economic measures, or would he continue to wait and hope events changed on their own?

Unfortunately, the first major action Horn took within a few days of our meeting caused an international uproar. He reneged on an already agreed-upon deal to sell HungarHotels, a state-owned hotel group, to an American entity for $57 million. He apparently had a quibble about the sale price at the last minute. Through USAID, we had all invested much time and effort in teaching Hungary's privatization officials how to write tender offers, seek buyers, evaluate bids, and structure and negotiate deals. After Horn cancelled the HungarHotels deal, Ferenc Bartha, the privatization minister, felt his only recourse was to resign. Peter Akos Bod, the National Bank head, accused Horn of political interference and also resigned.

This was hardly the chain of events we had hoped for after our meeting with Horn. At the time, I was in Cleveland for an investment conference, a Clinton Administration initiative to promote direct investment abroad that brought together American business executives and U.S. ambassadors from around the world. The HungarHotels incident raised such concern about backsliding toward old-style totalitarian methods that President Clinton specifically criticized it in his speech to the conference, calling Horn's action "a mistake which must be avoided in the future."

Shortly afterward, I gave an interview to an influential Hungarian weekly to voice my apprehensions about the Hungarian economy, knowing that Horn and his Cabinet ministers would read it. I expressed sympathy for workers worried about losing their jobs in the wake of any sales to foreign investors, but I also made it clear that if Prime Minster Horn and his government did not put a brake on overly generous social and medical expenditures, collect revenues more efficiently, and create a fair tax system that works in all sectors, Hungary would not even have a chance of improving its economic situation. I also stressed that the United States had helped Hungary in many ways during the past year, including a $60 million loan guarantee to bolster home construction. We had also made significant contributions to upgrade the country's air defenses and military forces. The total amount of U.S. economic aid to Hungary since the change from communism had reached $200 million and had grown to about $50 million a year.

The larger point I wanted to make with the publication's readers, as well as with government officials, was that haggling over a few million dollars for the hotel group was beside the point. The overarching concern was that Hungary was anxious to attract foreign visitors and needed sufficient, quality hotel space for that to happen. (At that time, the hotels outside Budapest were outmoded.) In short, the government had to attract foreign investment to raise the HungarHotels properties to world-class standards by bringing in top management with ready capital for renovation.

At the same time, outside forces were putting pressure on the Horn government. Standard & Poor's downgraded the outlook for Hungary's credit from stable to negative at this juncture, citing the budget deficit and the privatization squabble. The rating service warned that unless a more conservative financial policy was adopted, the country's debt rating could soon be downgraded. Hungary's economic troubles were on the agenda later in February 1995, when Richard Holbrooke arrived in Budapest for a two-day regional meeting that I had conceived and organized for U.S. ambassadors to former Soviet-bloc countries. I realized that many of us were dealing with similar issues, and the regional meetings became a regular event, giving ambassadors a chance to share ideas and strategies and to learn from each other's successes and failures. At the first meeting, I took the opportunity to air my concerns about Hungary's financial plight and several colleagues offered helpful opinions and insights.

Because Prime Minister Horn remained such an enigma to me, I set up two lunches with Dr. Laszlo Bekesi, the Minister of Finance, in an attempt to get his take on the hard-to-fathom Horn. These meetings revealed that Horn had not given Bekesi authority to deal with the economy in any broad sense; he was as much in the dark as we were about the inscrutable prime minister.

While the public face of Gyula Horn remained a glum, taciturn façade, we had begun to piece together a portrait of the man and his upbringing that revealed a fascinating and complex person. As a teenager, he worked in a factory during the day and attended school at night. As an enthusiastic and promising young communist, he was chosen by the party to study in the Russian city of Rostov. In stark contrast to the "workers' paradise" extolled in Soviet propaganda, the squalid conditions in Rostov appalled the young Horn. Although he had fought to put down the 1956 rebellion, he had also recently placed a wreath at the memorial to the victims of the uprising. Doing so, he stood beside the daughter of Prime Minister Imre Nagy, who helped lead the rebellion and was executed by the communists two years later. Paradoxically, Horn's brother, killed by an anti-communist mob, is buried nearby.

The *Wall Street Journal*'s Ernest Beck offered this telling sketch of Prime Minister Horn. "The brusque manner is part of Mr. Horn's well-honed sense of timing, a friend adds. He's a shrewd political animal—a true Machiavellian. He pounces when he knows it's right, and he knows what the public wants. He can be very calculating. He came out of HungarHotels a hero." Beck was right that Horn's last-minute reneging on the deal played well to a certain Hungarian constituency, but it had damaged his reputation among investors abroad.

Beck continued about Horn:

> At the same time there's a pragmatic and sensitive side to Mr. Horn. "He's clearly a selfless and honest person," says a Western diplomat who has, nevertheless, tangled with Mr. Horn on official matters. . . . Mr. Horn had no qualms about making an official public apology for Hungary's role in the Holocaust. He has offered neighboring countries concessions on old grievances—like acknowledging Hungary's current borders with Slovakia, rather than preaching to them about how to treat their ethnic-Hungarian minorities. When he's out meeting the people, Mr. Horn relaxes and feels at home, cracking deadpan jokes. Otherwise, the friend says, "Basically, he's a loner."

I was delighted when Horn made his crucial new economic decisions in early 1995 just a few days after our stern warnings were delivered to his minister of finance. He made a constructive move and did the right thing, yet it was another example of the duality his friends described. Horn replaced Laszlo Bekesi and the interim head of the central bank with two Western-trained bankers: Lajos Bokros as finance minister and Gyorgy Suranyi as president of the National Bank of Hungary. I knew both of them and was delighted at Horn's appointments. Both men were experienced, English-speaking economists who were highly regarded and well-known among their counterparts in many Western capitals. I dubbed them the "Dream Team," a term the press picked up on, and the new appointees didn't disappoint when they immediately stressed the necessity for reducing Hungary's large deficits.

I liked the way Lajos Bokros operated. He had a classic Hungarian profile and sported a thick handlebar mustache. With no use for political small talk, he quickly instituted a series of austerity measures. He cut back on imports by imposing a surcharge, he raised taxes in critical areas, and renegotiated Hungarian debt with foreign lenders, particularly Japanese banks and some German entities that were heavily invested. He offered the Hungarian people no promises other than his belief that an austerity budget would bring the economy under control. I admired his candor and decisiveness.

At a lunch with Bokros and several of our colleagues shortly after his appointment, I was pleased to hear that the finance minister intended to make the privatization of Hungarian industry a top priority. We all agreed that the infusion of capital to the Hungarian budget and of managerial experience to the privatized companies was the only way for Hungary to jump-start itself out of its present dilemma. From that point on, the pace of privatization accelerated. With our urging and consultation, the Hungarian privatization agency, given the green light in 1995, sold forty-two companies in its first four months, which brought in about $620 million of new capital to the Hungarian government. Much of that money went to repay the foreign debt and to put the country on a stronger financial footing.

The plan we had helped lay out and convinced Hungarian officials to adopt was beginning to bear fruit. At this time, I also developed deep respect for the skills of Bokros's fellow top-ranking economic leader, Gyorgy Suranyi, the new President of the Hungarian Central Bank. I appreciated his clear, direct style and especially the way he made judgments based purely on the economic merits or demerits of an issue and what he considered good or bad for Hungary. In my experience, his actions were never clouded by political motivations.

Another economic project I had been spearheading with our USAID team together with the Central Bank was bank-reform assistance. We were helping the Hungarians redesign their outmoded, inadequate banking system to make it more transparent, responsive, and better able to serve corporate and individual customers. Gyorgy Suranyi made it clear that Hungary would pursue these objectives of the overhaul and would not print additional currency or engage in other discredited methods to bolster the economy artificially to provide Hungarians with a false sense of prosperity. Suranyi immediately took a tough approach and announced that the Hungarian forint would be tied to the rate of inflation. At the start of each year, he would announce what the inflation decrease and currency devaluation would be so that everyone would know in advance exactly what the forint would be worth on December 31. That was a major step in reestablishing confidence in the Hungarian economy and in convincing foreigners to invest in the country and to purchase Hungarian assets.

Although economic commentators were not convinced that Horn could persuade hardliners in his Socialist Party and its trade-union allies to slash cherished social programs, such as free health care and university education, to help balance the budget, I was impressed with his initial actions. Despite his command-economy roots and an often noncommittal style, the prime minister was pragmatic and, above all, a patriot. It is my opinion that this disciplined and far-reaching initiative was his finest moment as Hungary's leader. He displayed courage in adopting a new economic policy that would bring more short-term hardship to the Hungarian people, thus undercutting his popularity and his chances of winning re-election.

Congressman Tom Lantos and I decided it would be helpful for Horn and his key ministers and advisors to visit the United States and to meet in person and cement relations with top American officials. The trip would reward Horn and his ministers for the course of action they were pursuing. We made arrangements for a June trip.

A month before our departure, a crisis erupted. It was the most unpleasant experience I faced during my entire term as ambassador in Hungary. The entire contretemps blindsided me because it occurred as a result of trying to do my job conscientiously.

Here is how it unfolded: Credit Suisse First Boston, a major international investment banking firm, was seeking to win a contract to advise the Hungarian government on privatizing an important segment of the Hungarian economy. The embassy cannot take sides among competing American companies, but any responsible U.S. firm should be able to count on its support. Although the CSFB executive in charge was an American citizen who lived in London, the firm itself was eighty percent controlled by Swiss investors and other Europeans. Nonetheless, the claim was made that the firm was an American company, and the executive insisted that it should be entitled to the same rights and privileges as other American investment banking firms seeking my support from the Hungarian government.

At the same time, a fully American investment bank, Salomon Brothers, was seeking our help as well to win the contract. I had had a long career in the investment banking field and felt I understood the ownership requirements that made Salomon Brothers our sole client in the privatization deal. So I supported the Salomon bid in a letter to the prime minister that urged him to give the firm high consideration. I wrote that Salomon Brothers were experts in the field, and that, as an American firm, favorable consideration of their bid would foster goodwill both for Hungary and the prime minister when he visited Washington a month later. Although what I wrote was perfectly proper by any interpretation of my role as ambassador, it turned out to be a mistake; not the statement itself, but rather my failure to realize how my words could be misperceived and twisted if the letter became public.

What I wrote in private to Horn became public after a staff member in the prime minister's office, whom we suspect may have been paid by CSFB or its German partner, Deutsche Bank, slipped the bank a copy of my letter. Someone in the prime minister's office then leaked the letter to the press with the claim that it was evidence that I favored Salomon Brothers over CSFB. The first mention in the press of this matter painted me as an ambassador with a private agenda.

Based on these events, the Hungarian government announced a delay of at least one week in its decision to appoint the financial advisor; on that same day, late at night, a CSFB executive phoned me from Washington, D.C. The CSFB executive began the conversation by claiming that he had traveled to Washington on personal business since he had a home in Alexandria, Virginia. He did not realize that I already knew that he had spoken to Under-Secretary Joan Spero about the matter earlier in the day. I told him I knew he had met with Spero. This seemed to catch him off-guard, but he acknowledged the meeting and then got down to the purpose of his call. The caller claimed that my letter implied that if Hungary failed to award the tender to Salomon Brothers, our government would cancel Prime Minister Horn's trip to the United States. I assured him that was not our intent and was an incorrect conclusion on the part of whomever was feeding him his information. I agreed to rectify that erroneous impression by phoning the three Hungarian officials involved to deny explicitly that a failure to choose Salomon would impact Horn's planned visit to the United States. The CSFB executive asked me to put that in writing.

Suddenly I felt as if I were in a high-stakes poker game where bluffing was encouraged, but I was in no mood to play any games. Having been burned by the leaking of my original letter, I told the caller that he had my word that I would phone the ministers the next morning to make that point clear. I added that I would also state that clarification immediately to Dr. Andrās Gobolyos, a personal advisor and confidant of Prime Minister Horn and a guest of ours that evening, and that I would restate it in the presence of Ambassador Stuart Eizenstat, who was staying with us.

I made the promised clarification to Dr. Gobolyos as soon as I hung up and made the promised phone calls the next day. After these accommodations on my part, I assumed the matter had been fully resolved.

That evening, Secretary Holbrooke called me and spoke of his deep concern. He had drafted a letter that put my verbal clarification of my original letter in writing. His reason for taking this extra step was to counter what the CSFB executive told him: his firm was soliciting support from Republican members of Congress and was about to unleash a "firestorm of protest" initiated by Senator Alphonse D'Amato, a Republican from New York, who was preparing to lodge a complaint on the floor of the Senate. If that were true, the charge that I had favored another American investment bank over his firm would make me a large target for partisan political attacks in both Hungary and the United States. Even if my actions were vindicated and proven correct beyond all doubt, it would be difficult for me to retain the stature of a U.S. ambassador and to remain effective in Hungary. I was beyond being upset. I was extremely angry!

Once more, my best friend and most trusted ally was Vera, who gave me reassurances during that difficult week and was a wonderful listener as I talked everything through with her. As I reviewed every conversation and document, I confirmed for myself that my support for Salomon Brothers had been totally proper. I had been placed in this position only because my statement had been leaked and distorted and CSFB's nationality misrepresented. If a firestorm came, Vera's calm support would allow me to proceed with a clear mind and a forceful attitude.

My written clarification was hand-delivered to the Hungarian officials the next morning. In the interest of transparency and fairness, I reported to Douglas Redicker of Salomon Brothers what I had decided to do and why I had felt compelled to do it. Redicker called me the next day to say that their representative in Washington, who was well-connected in Republican circles, had contacted Senator D'Amato to ask whether he had, in fact, been prepared to attack the State Department and our embassy for its stand in the matter. According to Redicker, the senator had never heard of the situation.

Redicker also told me that he had learned that in addition to the CSFB executive's personal call on Prime Minister Horn, Deutsche Bank had prevailed upon its high-level German connections to urge Horn to recommend the Credit Suisse First Boston/Deutsche Bank consortium as privatization advisor. Amazingly, CSFB was now a German entity! Could this be the same "American" CSFB? These nationality chameleons and economic opportunists clearly played whichever country card they thought suited the moment.

The outcome of this story, which was one of the most difficult and distasteful events of my long professional career, was that Credit Suisse First Boston won the contract—albeit after its manipulation of my letter, and only after German political pressure was applied and after a nudge from the bank's paid ally within the prime minister's office. Thankfully, my own reputation as a diplomat survived the onslaught, and I learned some hard lessons about international business dealings that were more aggressive and underhanded than any I had theretofore encountered.

Months later, when it sought to bid on a tender put out by the European Union, the chameleonic CSFB changed its color once more and claimed that its firm was European, not American. As for the CSFB executive who had treated me most foul, and who had been less than truthful at least five times by my count, he was rewarded with a major ambassadorship by President George W. Bush.

In keeping with my promise, I welcomed Prime Minister Horn and his entourage when they arrived in Washington, D.C., in June 1995 on their first stop of their U.S. tour. Horn was joined by his deputy chief of staff, Ferenc Somogyi, administrative State Secretary in the Foreign Ministry; Hungary's Ambassador to the United States, Gyorgy Banlaki; Istvan Kovacs, director of U.S. affairs; an official spokesperson; a chief of protocol; and two interpreters. Congressman Tom Lantos was part of our group, too. Hungarian television sent a crew, and several Hungarian newspapers assigned reporters to cover the visit. They started with a half-hour visit with President Clinton in the White House.

We traveled to other Washington stops on a Hungarian-made bus; a success story of Hungary's fledgling industrial sector, the buses were in use in public transit in several American and European cities. I acted as host and tour guide as we met with Bob Rubin, Secretary of the Treasury; Ron Brown, Secretary of Commerce; Dan Fried, National Security advisor for Eastern Europe; and officials at the State Department who could discuss in depth Slovakia, NATO membership requirements, and related issues.

The rapid transformation of Hungary's former communist politicians into capitalists drew some cynical reactions. Their attitude adjustment never bothered me, however, because I had seen them in action and knew them to be nationalists first, realists second, and ideologues a distant third. They were smart people and quick studies, who had learned very quickly that the way to succeed in the modern world was to embrace the best aspects of capitalism while utilizing the bureaucratic skills they had learned in the old Soviet days, skills which were carefully honed.

Hungarians have had to become shrewd diplomats, given their geographic location. They understood Europe and the Russians and Serbs because they had lived both under their rule and alongside them for generations. Horn's motives may have sometimes been difficult to read, but his firm grasp of foreign policy was obvious. In June 1995, he offered this assessment to the U.S. Secretary of State: "Above all, the Serbs, like the Russians, respect strength. Any sign of weakness by the West, particularly the United States, would be counterproductive; always be very firm with them and ready to use military force where it is absolutely essential, such as might be necessary in Bosnia."

During Horn's Washington visit, I was staying at the Watergate Hotel, where I ran into Henry Kissinger one morning. He knew that the Hungarian delegation was in town and promptly invited the group to come over from their hotel, the Marriott, to meet with him. We all gathered and discussed the current situation in Hungary and Central Europe, as Kissinger lent his considerable experience in foreign policy to the conversation.

New York was the second city on our itinerary, and the timing was in our favor. Budapest Mayor Gabor Demszki met with New York businesspeople, and the entire group met with New York Governor George Pataki at his World Trade Center office. Pataki had Hungarian ancestry on his father's side of the family, talked about his Hungarian heritage, and expressed a desire to travel to Budapest later that year. For the Hungarians, the Pataki meeting got great play on Hungarian TV and in newspapers back home, showing the delegation meeting with the governor of a powerful state with a large Hungarian population. The visitors also took the opportunity to make their case for investment from manufacturers and financial institutions in New York, a world center of finance and corporate headquarters.

The Hungarian delegation stayed at the Hungarian U.N. Mission and Consulate Building in Midtown Manhattan, which was convenient for me because it was just two blocks from the apartment where Vera and I live. We hosted a cocktail reception for the delegation at our apartment before a formal dinner at the River Club. This represented a very rare social engagement for Gyula Horn, who had never come either to the U.S. embassy or to our residence in Budapest. We did not feel slighted because we were told that he never went to any of the other embassies or residences, either. Business was business. Social life was another matter and something he apparently had little use for.

We next flew to Detroit and visited Dearborn Village and the Ford Motor Company Museum and met with various manufacturing officials, including the head of Guardian Industries, which had a major glass plate manufacturing facility in Hungary. We were hosted by Michigan Governor John Engler, an interesting and cordial politician.

Our final stop was San Francisco, which included Tom Lantos's Congressional district. Horn and his advisors met with California business leaders, particularly in the data communications and computer manufacturing sectors. Congressman Lantos also arranged for a trip that registered high on the wow scale: a tour around the harbor on the immense yacht owned by Larry Ellison, founder of Oracle. It was fun to observe the collective jaws of the Hungarians drop as they toured the luxury vessel. They walked from stem to stern and admired the best advertisement for open-market capitalism one could imagine. It was a wonderful exclamation point for a productive, successful visit.

PREPARING FOR PEACE

Six years after the fall of the Berlin Wall, Hungary continued to lurch, with frequent setbacks, from the old habits of communism to a democratic, free-market economy. In the middle of my second year as ambassador, I encountered a situation that demonstrated just how deeply cronyism and back-door dealing were ingrained in the mentality of Hungary's leaders when it came to privatization, direct investment, and awarding contracts. I have no way of knowing whether money or personal favors were exchanged; my perception was that corruption instead seemed based upon cronyism, and that created some of my deepest frustrations.

Hungary receives a disproportionately large share of its electricity, roughly 45 percent, from a single, enormous nuclear power plant at Paks. Unlike in the United States, where nuclear power plants provide about 10 percent of the country's electrical power, or in France, which has a dozen nuclear power plants, the Paks nuclear power plant was an anomaly. Soviet engineers built it a decade after they built Chernobyl, so the technology was at least second generation and far safer in providing clean energy. On a visit to Paks, I felt nothing short of profound awe as I stood on a catwalk above three huge silo-like cylinders that enclosed the enormously powerful and potentially very dangerous nuclear reactors. From that vantage point, there was no denying the power and importance these reactors hold for Hungary's well-being and economic future.

The reactors are operated by technicians seated at consoles lined with complex controls in instrumentation rooms. Although it had been upgraded once and was well-maintained, the instrumentation needed another upgrade. The Hungarian government agency that operated the nuclear power plant issued a tender with detailed specifications, requesting bids from qualified suppliers.

I met with Bert Hutchberg, a vice president of Westinghouse, who had enlisted our embassy's support in helping his company win the contract to supply the new instrumentation. Westinghouse's main competitor was Siemens, a well-regarded German company. As far as my colleagues and I could determine, the Westinghouse instrumentation was more technically advanced and better suited to the specifications laid out in the Hungarian government tender. Other forces, however, were coming into play.

Prime Minister Gyula Horn had earned the deep gratitude of Germany's chancellor, Helmut Kohl, by opening the border of Hungary to fleeing Germans in 1989, a decisive first step on the road to German reunification. Forever after that historic decision, Kohl proved very helpful whenever the Hungarian government sought German support on financial and military matters. In the case of the nuclear plant's call for instrumentation bids, the German government aided the Siemens bid by including partially used nuclear fuel rods to run the generators for several years at virtually no cost to the Hungarians. Nothing in the instrumentation tender called for nuclear fuel. Westinghouse would have had to charge for the nuclear fuel if they had included it in their bid. In the end, the American company simply could not match the huge free bonus in the German offer. This was a glaring example of how the playing field was not level when it came to competing for business in Hungary, and it became painfully obvious to me, again and again, that American companies operated under a considerable handicap because European companies and European governments often colluded in under-the-table deals.

Despite many complaints in the United States about the occasionally excessive and over-zealous methods of the American press, a free press that scrutinizes government actions is one of democracy's bulwarks against backroom dealing. While the media is proudly callled the fourth estate in the United States, Hungarian journalists had long been used as rubber stamps and photocopiers to publicize government pronouncements and policies without scrutiny. My own experience dealing with Hungarian journalists had demonstrated that they were either excessively docile, or, in one case, so biased that the actual facts were either never sought or ignored. We could not assume that the principles and techniques of a free press operated in Hungary; they needed to be learned. To its credit, the United States put money and resources into that effort, helping to educate journalists and create a Hungarian press that would be well-informed and critical when necessary.

Vera and I made it a point to attend the reopening of the International Media Centre in Budapest. This journalism school taught the rudiments of responsible journalism to working reporters and university students. Other International Media Centres, also with U.S. support, were being established in Prague, Bratislava and Bucharest.

Speakers at the opening of the Centre in Budapest included Al Neuharth, chairman of USA Today, and James L. Greenfield of the New York Times Foundation. Both of their organizations provided financial and professional support to the school, as did our USIS. Budapest Mayor Demszki and I spoke as well, which gave me personal satisfaction because I had resisted attempts to close a predecessor media center by people who complained that some of its teaching and courses were biased against the United States. I felt that the essential purpose of the Centre—to promote professional journalism—was far too valuable to abandon. Common sense prevailed, fortunately, and the Centre functioned very effectively in Budapest from then on.

My conviction that entrepreneurship was a powerful impulse in the minds of young Hungarians was confirmed in September 1995, with the arrival in Hungary of the second most celebrated American. Less than a year earlier, our number one celebrity, President Clinton, visited Budapest so briefly that the Hungarian people never got to see him. When Bill Gates came to Budapest, however, he received a rock star's welcome. Microsoft was doing business all over the world, and the ubiquitous Windows software, as well as Gates's wealth, had made him famous. Crowds of young Hungarians gathered everywhere Gates went during his visit.

One morning, I took Bill Gates to Prime Minister Horn's office. Each man naturally wanted to meet the other, and with the aid of an interpreter, they had a good exchange. Later that day, a huge crowd had gathered outside the Kempinski Hotel to get a glimpse of Gates when he arrived to speak to an American Chamber of Commerce luncheon. I sat next to him at lunch and found him to be modest, charming, and most agreeable and low-key in conversation. Naturally, his speech to the Chamber concerned the wonders of computers and modern communications. When asked if there was anything a computer couldn't do, he replied, "There are certain things it will never replace. It will never replace getting a love letter on scented pink paper."

Throughout my tenure as ambassador, I used my business background to improve the efficiency of the embassy's operation. In my second year at post, I started the quarterly review process, a management tool I borrowed from Warburg Pincus, the investment capital firm I co-founded with Lionel Pincus. There, we had gathered our executives for a two- or three-day meeting every quarter so that everybody could become informed and get up to speed on what everyone else was doing. The review served to eliminate artificial internal rivalries and turf battles; it also countered the isolation felt by people working on projects in specific niches.

I felt that the same management tool, revised slightly, would be useful at the embassy. Because we typically met to strategize, we rarely stood back in order to probe deeply or to discuss long-range plans, programs, and missions. Also, people operating in one section of the embassy's activities had little knowledge of what was happening in the other areas. This fragmentation was a hindrance to working as a unified whole, and I set out to remedy the situation.

To begin, I asked each department head to submit a short paper summarizing two essential areas: one, what progress, if any, had been made during the past three months in meeting our agreed-upon goal; and, two, what remained to be done; what changes needed to be made to attain that goal and what new initiatives had to begin in the next three months. I had these summary papers collected, printed in a brochure, and distributed to our personnel.

At the quarterly meeting, the heads of the various agencies and sections highlighted issues that had been raised in their segments of the brochure and answered questions from the others, the DCM, and myself. Everyone with a key position in the embassy learned what the others considered their priorities, whether they had succeeded or failed in meeting those priorities, and the initiatives in which they were engaged. The process imposed accountability and also increased embassy unity and a sense that we kept no secrets from each other.

Afterward, I sent the brochure and results of the meeting to Washington and strongly urged the State Department to institute the quarterly review process at other embassies. I don't know if that was ever done, but I found this very useful practice another instance of the value of my business experience.

Early in my tenure, I was asked what natural resources Hungary possessed that could generate revenue for the country, as oil did for Saudi Arabia and Venezuela. I replied that Hungary had something far more valuable than oil: brain power. Throughout history, Hungary has produced some of the great minds of Europe, and the country's future now depended on the education it provided to its young people and whether it supplied the opportunities for them to capitalize on that education, as the country had done in decades past.

This point was emphasized when Vera and I visited two universities that had experienced dramatically different fates. The university in Szeged, a city near the border where Hungary, Romania, and the former Yugoslavia meet, was renowned for language training. Szeged boasts an impressive synagogue and a beautiful cathedral. Many of our Foreign Service officers go there for a few months to learn Hungarian before taking up their posts. For that reason alone, it was important that I make an appearance. The institution seemed to be thriving and relevant to the students' futures. The handsome city, with an immense park-like square and wide boulevard, looks more welcoming than ever, having been lovingly rebuilt after disastrous flooding along the Tisza River.

We also flew to Miskolc in Eastern Hungary, where we met with local officials and visited the university and a regional labor retraining center. Miskolc was a sad case. The end of the Cold War had doomed its once thriving industries—iron and steel production and coal mining—and devastated its university, which educated engineers for those industries with an outdated and largely irrelevant curriculum.

The Miskolc visit made me think about the future direction of Hungary's technological and scientific education and what could be done to revive the sciences in Hungary. In the past, the country had produced renowned scientists in disproportionate numbers to Hungary's population. A short list would include these names: Ignaz Semmelweis, the great nineteenth-century pioneer in antiseptic medicine; John von Neumann, the central figure in the development of the electronic computer; Loránd Eötvös, a major contributor to the theory of relativity; Leo Szilard, the physicist who first recognized the need to study the wartime application of nuclear energy; Edward Teller, the developer of the thermonuclear bomb; Albert Szent-Györgyi, a Nobel Prize in Medicine winner for the discovery of Vitamin C; and Charles Simonyi, one of Microsoft's chief scientists.

In a speech I gave at a dinner for Israel's Weizmann Institute held at the Budapest Forum Hotel, I compared Hungary to Israel; both are small countries with traditions of great scientists and a mysterious but undeniable aptitude for theoretical and scientific exploration. Under communism, however, Hungary had stifled inquiry and repressed new ideas, forcing promising Hungarians to go abroad to succeed. This was precisely the case for two recent Nobel Prize laureates from America who had been born in Hungary, the chemist George Olah and economist John Harsanyi.

The advent of democracy had not slowed this brain drain. Hungary's financial difficulties led to drastic cuts in spending for scientific research and kept salaries too low to entice young people into careers in the sciences. I concluded my Weizmann Institute remarks by asserting that an act of faith, like a small country's founding or the funding of a world-class scientific enterprise, could attract great minds and support; the time to show this faith, I asserted, was now. A new Hungarian nation was taking shape, and a bold move could lead once more to scientific and technological excellence.

We were aware at all times of the bloody ethnic conflicts in the region. For centuries the majority of Orthodox Christian Serbs, Roman Catholic Croats, and Muslim Bosnians had lived together in relative harmony. Furthermore, after World War II, the independent Communist leader Marshal Tito, himself half-Slovene and half-Croat, helped bring the various regional factions together into the nation of Yugoslavia. Tito died in 1980, however, without naming a successor and with a communist party in decline. At his funeral, Henry Kissinger and Margaret Thatcher gave Yugoslavia five years before splitting apart. Their assessment wasn't off by much.

By the early 1990s, political leaders in the constituent provinces were agitating for separate sovereign nations. Slovenia, Yugoslavia's westernmost province, and Croatia, just to its east, seceded in 1991. Bosnia-Herzegovina, the next region to the east, followed suit in early 1992. The ethnic Serbs, who comprised nearly a third of Bosnia's population, resisted and began a civil war intended to expel or otherwise eliminate other ethnic groups and to widen the enclaves under their domination. The Serb insurgents were secretly backed by Serbia-controlled Yugoslavia, which was situated on Bosnia's long eastern border, and they broadcast viciously racist TV programs that whipped its population into a fury to gain support for Serbian expansion. Serbia had a smaller population than Bosnia, but it controlled Yugoslavia's arms manufacturing plants, so its onslaughts were abetted by the well-meaning but ignorant international ban on shipping weapons to participants in the Bosnian fighting.

By the end of 1992, Bosnian Serb forces controlled 70 percent of Bosnia and Croatia and had embarked on what the Serbs termed "ethnic cleansing," a ruthless euphemism for a policy of expulsions, secret massacres, and other atrocities—almost entirely committed by Serbs, according to independent press accounts. The conflict would eventually create some three million refugees, mainly non-Serbs.

Several of my colleagues believed, as I did, that the United States could not sit on the sidelines and watch the carnage any longer, that it was time to get involved. Agreeing with us were Richard Holbrooke, U.N. Secretary Madeleine Albright, Senator Joe Biden, and Congressman Tom Lantos. The United Nations' failure to retaliate against the

Bosnian Serb shelling of Sarajevo and Srebrenica, a region with European hopes and pretensions, was morally and politically unacceptable.

I was shocked and horrified by the escalating brutality, as were ordinary Hungarians reading newspapers and watching TV coverage. In addition, every morning I received an intelligence briefing with confidential material, and I was in continuous discussions with other diplomats, including those from the affected area, such as Bosnia-Herzegovina's Ambassador to Hungary, Bisera Turkovic. All of that made me painfully aware that, with our failure to step in and halt the fighting, U.S. prestige was noticeably ebbing away, not only in Hungary and the new democracies of Central Europe, but also in Western Europe.

Four years after President George H. W. Bush failed to use air power to put a stop to the Serb aggression when it first began, America was still hesitating. The aggressors felt that gave them carte blanche. Instead of air power, we had supported an ineffective U.N. effort that placed too few peacekeeping troops in the war zone and gave them no authority to halt conflicts or save lives. The United States had to face up to its responsibility by becoming part of a real NATO force that separated the sides in Bosnia and ended the violence. After all, with the Soviets no longer a threat and the Cold War concluded, what was the purpose of NATO except to maintain the established peace in Europe and to help resolve arguments peacefully?

For a long time, the Bosnian Serbs' military success gave them little reason to heed calls for a ceasefire. In August 1995, however, the tide began to turn against them. At the urging of the United States, the Croats and Bosnians had joined forces. Contrary to the advice of Western military experts, Croatia launched an offensive to push back Serb forces. Its surprising, decisive military victory was the first Serbian defeat in the four years of fighting.

Prompted by these events, the United States and other NATO nations finally recognized the necessity to end the conflict. President Clinton and Warren Christopher named Assistant Secretary Holbrooke to head a small group that would engage in shuttle diplomacy in an attempt to bring the warring factions together for a peace conference. A NATO meeting in London drew a line in the sand by warning Serb forces not to attack the city of Gorzade in eastern Bosnia. The meeting also declared that NATO, and not the ineffective United Nations, would make the decision to use air power if Gorzade was threatened.

Earlier, Sarajevo had suffered through a horrendous bombing by the Serbs during a siege of the capital city. Just as the American diplomatic team was about to meet with ethnic Serbian leaders to negotiate terms for a peace conference, news arrived that a mortar rocket fired from Serb positions on the city's outskirts had killed seventeen civilians in Sarajevo's marketplace. Richard Holbrooke later described this incident in his book, *To End A War*, a superb account of efforts to bring peace to the region: "The August 28 mortar attack was hardly the first challenge to Western policy, nor the worst incident of the war; it was only the latest. But it was different because of its timing: coming immediately after the launching of our diplomatic shuttle . . . it appeared not only as an act of terror against innocent people in Sarajevo, but as the first direct affront to the United States."

The timing of that mortar attack seemed to be a tipping point, and it went a long way toward convincing President Clinton and other NATO leaders that failure to retaliate would further embolden the Serbs and end any chance for a peace treaty. Hungary's leaders had warned them, and now Serb actions had removed any doubt. Only military force would coerce the Serbs into backing off from aggression and opting for peace.

In the early morning of August 30, 1995, American warplanes began massive sustained bombing of Bosnian Serb positions around Sarajevo. More intensive bombing elsewhere over the next few days made clear that the Serbs would pay a high price for continuing the civil war. The call for a peace conference now fell on more receptive ears.

Like Americans and Western Europeans, the Hungarians and their neighbors also watched CNN, and the Sarajevo footage too often reminded them of Budapest in 1944 and 1956. With Hungary separated from Bosnia-Herzegovina by only the abutting northern panhandles of Croatia and Serbia, the relief in Hungarian government circles when NATO finally bombed Serbian positions could be felt in the air. Our B-52 bombers had finally brought hope that the war next door might soon end.

With so much heating up in this ethnic conflict, America's highest-ranking military and defense officials began making regular visits to Hungary. September 20, 1995, was significant for two reasons. In the morning, we cut the ribbon to open a new entrance to the chancellery, an improvement that created a much larger and more efficient entryway for visa applicants, and a large, attractive space for interviews of Hungarians seeking visas. Sadly, the threat of terrorism after 9/11 narrowed that entrance, funneling visitors through a maze of concrete barriers complete with metal detectors similar to those used at airports.

The other significance of this date for Central Europe was the arrival of Defense Secretary William Perry that afternoon. Perry and I had met only briefly at the missile destruction ceremony at Tabor-falva. After a country team meeting to bring him up to speed on how well the modernization and training of the Hungarian defense forces were proceeding, we met with Hungarian Defense Minister Keleti and other officials from the Defense Ministry and attended their dinner in honor of Secretary Perry and his wife, Lee. In separate one-on-one meetings the next day, both Foreign Minister Kovacs and Prime Minister Horn—concerned that the Americans might lose their backbone and pull back—strongly reiterated to U.S. Defense Secretary Perry that only the continuing threat of force would deter the Serbs.

Our last stop of the day was the Kecskemet Air Base where Perry, our aides, and I were met by the head of the Hungarian Air Defense Forces, Major General Szegedi. The aim of the visit was to demonstrate our country's interest in modernizing the Hungarian Air Force, which at that point consisted of twenty-five to thirty Soviet MiG-29 fighter jets. When Washington rebuffed efforts by the previous Hungarian government to buy F-16 fighters and Patriot Missiles, it had turned to Russia and purchased twenty-eight aging MiG-29s without paying any cash. Russia simply reduced the amount it owed Hungary based on the value of the fighter jets. An impressive flight demonstration of one of the MiGs put on for Perry and me confirmed that it was an excellent plane with enormous power and maneuverability; only about one-third of the 1970s-vintage planes, however, was operational because the Russians had stopped making replacement parts. The rest of Hungary's MiG fleet had been mothballed.

After Vera and I accompanied the Perrys to Ferihegy Airport, we reflected upon the effectiveness of the Defense Secretary, who managed in such a brief visit to establish direct personal relationships with the Hungarian political and military leaders. Perry was one of the most engaging members of the Clinton Administration's senior officials. His manner was calm and pleasant, and he arrived in Hungary without presuppositions. The Defense Secretary listened intently to what I had to say and was equally attentive to members of my team and the Hungarian officials. Nothing in our future work together diminished my positive first impression, and I came to consider Perry one of the ablest senior American foreign policy officials I had met during my service abroad.

Additional senior military officers scheduled trips to Hungary as its strategic importance in helping end the bloody Balkans conflict rose to the fore. A week after Secretary Perry's visit, we greeted the Chairman of the Joint Chiefs of Staff, General John M. Shalikashvili, and his wife, Joan. I attended meetings with all the top Hungarian defense officials and Prime Minister Horn. Vera and I joined them at a luncheon and dinner. Shalikashvili had an easygoing style that helped endear him to the Hungarians, and he perceptibly strengthened their overall faith in American intentions. Moreover, the chairman returned to the Pentagon with a favorable report on Hungary's assessment of the ethnic war raging across their border as well as Hungarian military preparedness.

The meetings between U.S. officials and members of the Hungarian government and military, while highly orchestrated and pro forma, were valuable for both countries in building a strong foundation for future negotiations. Our officials were taking the measure of the Hungarians during these early sessions, and the U.S. delegation's open and cooperative manner conveyed that the United States was seeking a military relationship based on setting common objectives, sharing information, and establishing mutual trust. I felt a growing confidence that our efforts were chipping away at the Hungarians' concern that they might be dealing with another mammoth, ruthless, and nearly faceless bureaucracy reminiscent of the Soviet Union.

We all felt a strong sense of duty and history as preparations for the Dayton Peace Accords on Bosnia got underway. On October 31, 1995, the presidents of Croatia, Bosnia, and Serbia (who also represented the Bosnian Serbs and whom Holbrooke insisted not get their own seat at the table) arrived at Wright-Patterson Air Force Base in Dayton, Ohio, for the purpose of negotiating a permanent peace treaty. Everyone there understood that if the peace talks succeeded, the United States and other NATO countries would send in tens of thousands of troops to separate the warring sides. Gen. George Joulwan, the Supreme NATO Commander, was proposing a force of fifty to sixty thousand troops—one-third of whom would be American.

The potential danger to American and other NATO troops going into the war zone was very real. Already, more than one hundred U.N. peacekeepers had been killed trying to keep the peace. Two weeks before the start of the Dayton negotiations, Christopher, Perry, and Shalikashvili had appeared before the Senate Armed Services Committee. Both Democrats and Republicans voiced doubts about the wisdom of sending American troops into Bosnia, remembering the loss of life in Somalia and assuming casualties would occur on this new mission. The three administration officials tried to reassure the senators by saying that our troops would be out of Bosnia in twelve months—certainly an unrealistic estimate.

Formal negotiations to forge a peace agreement among the factions engaged in the horrific Bosnian-Croatian conflict began in Dayton on November 1, 1995. My own involvement in the process began early the next morning when Gen. William Crouch, commander in chief of the U.S. Army in Europe, entered my office at the embassy with a half-dozen top-ranking American military officers, including Lt. Gen. John Abrams, son of Gen. Creighton W. Abrams, Jr., the tank commander hero of World War II whose name graces the Abrams tank. I omitted the meeting from my printed daily schedule because the gathering was highly confidential. General Crouch had been purposely vague when requesting this meeting and would only go so far as to explain that it would deal with some aspect of NATO preparations for a peacekeeping force. We all understood that if the Dayton talks were successful, the NATO countries would have to act swiftly to send in thousands of troops to separate the warring sides. If the negotiations broke down, the less-than-adequate force of 12,500 U.N. peacekeepers already in the war zone would have to be pulled out as the fighting would almost certainly escalate.

I realized that these military leaders were under the strain of planning to send U.S. soldiers into harm's way; I tried to soften the mood and break the ice at our first meeting by showing them a brass plaque commemorating the fifteen years that Cardinal Jozsef Mindszenty had been given sanctuary in the space that was now my office. I suggested that the cardinal, a man of immense courage, would have relished the sight of so many American military leaders, their shoulders spangled with stars and their chests resplendent with medals, convening here in a free Budapest for the purpose of imposing and maintaining in neighboring countries the peace and freedom that his beloved Hungary now enjoyed.

The generals waited until we moved to the secure, fourth-floor bubble before they began to discuss substantive issues. I began by giving the military officials a briefing on the current conditions in Hungary and was joined by DCM Jim Gadsden, our military attachés Army Colonel Arpad Szurgyi and Air Force Colonel Jon Martinson, as well as our political officers Bill Siefkin and Kurt Volker. I then turned over the meeting to General Crouch, who used detailed flip charts to explain the peacekeeping assignment in the war zone likely to be handed over to U.S. forces. Crouch also identified the U.S. military units that would be committed to the peacekeeping effort, or Implementation Force (IFOR), and their likely areas of deployment in Bosnia and Croatia, which were joined in a fragile federation at the time. We all understood the high stakes; this would be the largest deployment of U.S. forces in Europe since World War II. Central to this undertaking, we were told, would be the establishment of a staging area in close proximity to—but not within the borders of—Bosnia or Croatia. The key requirements for that staging area was a site with secure facilities, a safe environment, a dependable infrastructure of roads, rails, and airstrips, and genuine acceptance from and collaboration with the host government. The country that best met their criteria, they all concurred, was Hungary.

I watched General Crouch grow increasingly concerned as the briefing progressed, and he finally pushed aside his briefing book, looked me in the eyes, and got to the core of the matter with this blunt query: "Hungary is our first choice for an IFOR staging base. If President Clinton gives IFOR the green light, will you be willing and able to persuade the Hungarian government to let us base our troops in Hungary?"

All eyes in the room were riveted on me. General Crouch assured me he did not need an immediate answer; that I should take some time to ponder the question before answering it. He went on to express his concern that obtaining the Hungarian government's approval might be a long and difficult process, with no guarantee that their cooperation would eventually be given.

I agreed with General Crouch's assessment of the situation. Since coming to Budapest eighteen months earlier, I had worked steadily to gain the trust and acceptance of the Hungarian government and its people regarding the sincerity of the United States. The subtext of our discussion in the secure bubble was whether my efforts and those of my team would prove sufficient to overcome a number of major concerns that could derail the plan: Hungary's memories of disappointments with the United States during the 1956 uprising; Hungary's reticence to antagonize its ruthless neighbor, Serbia; concerns over possible retaliation against two hundred thousand ethnic Hungarians in northern Serbia; a military culture long linked to the Soviet Union; a natural aversion to allow foreign troops back onto its soil after recently ridding itself of the Russian army. As I weighed these considerations and calculated the odds, I felt that, despite more than a year of steady progress for preparing such a historic collaboration on peacekeeping forces, an uphill diplomatic struggle remained.

Clearly, I was staring down the most difficult and delicate decision of my diplomatic career. If my answer to General Crouch was an unqualified "yes" and the White House did decide to send U.S. troops into the former Yugoslavia, I would have committed myself to one of the most challenging and critical tests of diplomatic skill that an ambassador can face: obtaining permission from a host country for the entry and stationing of a large, heavily armed foreign military force. My nation's leaders would rely on me to deliver not only the approval of a prime minister who had served at the highest levels of a former Communist enemy, but also a majority of the nearly four hundred members of Parliament, representing six contentious political parties, where extreme left-wing agitation against NATO and military involvement with the West was roiling the ranks. Furthermore, due to the urgency of the humanitarian mission, I would have to deliver in a matter of days, not months.

A favorable vote by Hungary's National Assembly was no certainty, but all my instincts signaled I could obtain it. "General," I replied, "when you're ready to call on us officially to ask for Hungarian cooperation, consider it done!"

There was visible relief on the faces of the military men after my response. They left Budapest confident that they could count on the U.S. embassy's unwavering and unconditional support, without which a Hungarian base for IFOR would have been impossible to obtain. To improve our chances of success, we did not wait for the peace treaty to be signed in Dayton. We got to work immediately.

The day after General Crouch's request at the embassy, my political counselor, William Siefkin, and Colonel Jon Martinson, the embassy's acting defense attaché, called on the Hungarian Ministries of Foreign Affairs and Defense to alert them to a possible U.S. request for the Hungarian facilities for logistical support.

The following week, USCOM Director of Operations, Rear Admiral Charles Abbot, led a delegation to Budapest to begin initial talks with Hungarian military officials and the prime minister's staff regarding the IFOR operation. Abbot explained that the United States wanted to set up a staging base in southern Hungary where twenty to thirty thousand U.S. troops could be assembled in stages and outfitted with vehicles, weapons, and other equipment before being assigned to peacekeeping duty in Bosnia and Croatia. After laying out the logistical details, Abbott asked the Hungarian officials if they could agree to allow American troops, vehicles, and equipment to enter and be stationed in Hungary.

Without missing a beat, the reply came from across the table: "We have been waiting for you since 1956."

The Hungarians made another point clear: their cooperation would not only contribute to peace in Bosnia but also further efforts to equip Hungary to operate alongside NATO and, ultimately, secure NATO membership. Reassured by Abbot, the officials agreed to meet in three days with a planning team from U.S. Army Europe to begin a fact-finding mission to determine the best location in Hungary for the staging base.

On schedule and headed by General Jim Wright, the forty USAREUR planners began organizing the massive logistical operation. They showed up for the planning sessions in civilian clothes to minimize local speculation and the possibility of stirring up public resentment. The planners first looked at possible locations in southern Hungary although Wright and his team had been advised that the ancient city of Pecs offered the best prospects. Their analysis, however, quickly showed that Pecs lacked the infrastructure to handle the troops, particularly the absence of adequate rail access and a heavy-duty airfield.

With Pecs' infrastructure deemed inadquate, the Hungarians suggested Taszar, the former Soviet air base about 120 miles southwest of Budapest that was still used by Hungary's MiG fighter jets. The Hungarians assured the planners that the base and nearby Kaposvar, a city of 70,000, had ample rail, road, and airport facilities. The Americans agreed to make an immediate inspection of the site and report back.

After their fact-finding mission, the Americans met with their Hungarian counterparts and enthusiastically reported that the Taszar airbase and the surrounding region in southern central Hungary would make an excellent staging area for Operation Joint Endeavor. The operation not only had a name, but Hungary's Minister of Defense, Gyorgy Keleti, had begun briefing his National Security Cabinet on the operation. All six Hungarian parliamentary parties were brought into the discussion to minimize the likelihood of political infighting.

Taszar soon had everyone's attention. The staging area had Hungary's nearest airfield to Bosnia and Croatia, and the long, heavy-duty airstrip had been built to handle heavy aircraft, such as American C-5s, C-130s, and military-equipped Boeing 747s. Strong road and rail facilities, including a spur track that led directly to a siding beside the air field, linked Taszar to the mid-sized city of Kaposvar a few miles away. The area's other assets included a military barracks, a large ammunition holding area, and a proven electrical and communications grids. Moreover, a pool of capable employees was ready to fill a variety of civilian jobs at the base. The decision was unanimous: Taszar was it.

Gyorgy Keleti wasted no time in briefing the full Hungarian Cabinet, which then drafted and approved a parliamentary resolution to be introduced if and when IFOR and the United States formally requested the use of Hungarian facilities. I paused during these intense, whirlwind negotiations to take a deep breath and to enjoy a brief moment of satisfaction for how well my team had done helping put these plans in place.

Even as we allowed ourselves to feel good about how far we had come, we heard a chorus of naysayers. Perhaps the most vocal was *New York Times* columnist Abe Rosenthal, who believed that Hungary would soon drop the pretense of adhering to democratic processes and return to its former ways. Rosenthal and the other critics might have thought differently if they had seen how meticulously the executive branch of the Hungarian government observed the required legal steps before formally committing itself to its new allies. Prime Minister Horn developed and mastered his political and diplomatic skills under the old communist regime, and in domestic matters he occasionally fell back on past habits. In foreign policy and security matters, however, it was my experience that he took care to respect Parliament's role under Hungary's new Constitution. That impression was confirmed the following year when a senior Hungarian military officer gave permission for a few Hungarian MiGs to take part in an air exercise over Poland without first making the necessary request to the Parliamentary Defense Committee. He resigned from office shortly afterwards, having transgressed a Constitutional imperative.

On November 21, 1995, President Clinton chose the White House Rose Garden as the setting to make the announcement we had all been anxiously awaiting. A peace treaty had been signed in Dayton. "NATO will rapidly complete its planning for IFOR," Clinton said.

"American leadership, together with our allies', is needed to make the peace real and enduring."

We swung into action alongside our Hungarian counterparts. Two days after the president spoke, a second team of fifty USAREUR planners led by Jim Wright raced to complete detailed surveys of Taszar and the surrounding area. A highly professional logistics officer, Jim exhibited extraordinary charm, and his positive energy worked wonders on the Hungarians. Their concerns, remnants of their fear of Soviet-style military decision-making, were quickly overcome by Jim's collaborative spirit.

Clearly, this peacekeeping partnership was not a marriage of equals. The United States, after all, was the world's lone superpower with a population of more than 250 million people and the most awesome military array on the planet. By comparison, Hungary was a newly democratic republic of 10 million with an outdated armed force. Despite their small size, Hungary, the Czech Republic, Romania, Poland, and Slovakia, given their strategic location near the embattled Balkans, were becoming pivotal players in America's future foreign policy and in our desire to establish peace, security, and unity in Europe by expanding NATO and finding a solution to the Bosnian dilemma. Hungarian President Göncz put it this way: "We are obliged by history to live in a very dangerous neighborhood."

Running parallel to the military logistical planning was the complex legal arrangements that needed to be hammered out between the US/IFOR Forces and the Government of Hungary. The first step was for the United States and Hungary to sign a Status of Forces Agreement (SOFA), which governed the treatment and conduct of friendly foreign forces in a host country. Key items left to be negotiated that weren't covered directly in the SOFA were IFOR contracting; transit, acquisition, and supply agreements; a protocol for the primary subcontractor, Brown & Root; a rental agreement for the use of Hungarian facilities and equipment; financial arrangements; cooperation protocol between consular, customs, and police personnel on both sides; a claims procedure for any damages; air space management and blanket air clearances; radio frequency usage; and convoy documentation.

Our to-do list was long and challenging, so I set up a series of task forces, both within our embassy and externally with the Hungarian government. The Hungarians seemed wary and uncertain as to how far they should push financial arrangements in advance of the IFOR operation, the scope of which was not yet fully determined. To keep moving forward despite some unanswered questions, first drafts of acquisition agreements were prepared by the embassy together with our U.S. military colleagues and presented to the Hungarians for consideration. During the first full year of IFOR operations, the massive staging effort cost more than $100 million; not a large number by U.S. military standards, it was extremely significant in Hungary, where the average monthly wage was $350 to $400.

With no time to lose, I felt my strongest contribution would be cutting through bureaucratic delays and red tape. Fortunately, I found a like-minded Hungarian official willing to expedite matters, acting foreign minister Istvan Szent-Ivany. Young, Westernized, and decisive, he showed flexibility and initiative by agreeing that his government would proceed with the preparations for IFOR deployment without formal documentation, subject to Parliament's approval of our request, which would be given fast-track status.

I immediately cabled Washington to report the Hungarian government's willingness to waive standard parliamentary procedures so as to speed up the introduction of the necessary Parliament resolution and to submit language for our formal request that U.S. military and civilian personnel and their equipment and supplies be permitted to enter Hungary and to set up a base for deployment of IFOR forces. Since Parliament met in Plenary Session only Mondays and Tuesdays, such a request would have to be delivered no later than the opening of business on Monday, November 27, or it would be delayed a week. With the Thanksgiving holiday coming up, I was concerned that the State Department's draft of the formal request might arrive too late.

Officials at State were concerned as well and cabled approval for us to deliver an informal text of the request, so that the Foreign and Defense Ministries would have the weekend to review the document's language and to finalize their resolution that would be delivered to Parliament for a vote.

During these intense and compressed negotiations, I received a phone call from Richard Holbrooke. Having triumphed and obtained the peace treaty in Dayton by sheer will and force of personality over innumerable obstacles, he was naturally concerned that it not fall apart at the implementation stage. He asked me where our arrangements stood and shared his concerns that the Budapest embassy and others in the region might not realize how complicated the task they faced—quickly and correctly implementing the political, military, and public diplomacy aspects of NATO's arrival—would be. I understood his concerns and admired his extraordinary accomplishment at Dayton and his passion to make sure that nothing delay or impede the peace process this close to its realization. I assured him that our embassy, our military colleagues, and our advisers were ahead of the curve and up to the work ahead. He expressed a gratifying confidence in my abilities and those of our embassy to keep the various elements moving ahead on a fast track. To his credit, I didn't hear another word from Holbrooke about the IFOR buildup in Taszar for the next several weeks, until we met at the staging area later that winter.

Happily, that Monday morning, November 27, we received the actual diplomatic note from the State Department, a remarkably quick turnaround, and we rushed it over to the Hungarian Foreign Ministry, which immediately set to work shepherding the resolution through Parliament. I felt good that my somewhat obsessive efforts to get all the officials and their respective agencies moving together at top speed were beginning to pay off.

The next evening, I sent another cable to Washington, an announcement that gave me the greatest personal satisfaction of my service as ambassador. It read:

Following consultations with the leaders of the six Parliamentary parties on the morning of November 27, the Parliamentary Defense Committee and the Foreign Affairs Committee met in an exceptional combined session at noon, November 27. The two committees approved the text of a Parliamentary resolution authorizing Hungary to provide support to IFOR. This resolution was then passed by the entire Parliament on the evening of November 28 by a vote of 312 in favor and 1 against it, with six abstentions. The resolution provides for the transit and temporary stationing of IFOR forces (not limited to U.S. forces) along with their equipment and supplies, as well as the use of Hungarian air space.

Previously, Prime Minister Horn made it clear that Hungary would not send troops to join a military operation in a neighboring country. An unexpected change of policy, however, on Horn's part—he had rediscovered his progressive, flexible, post-Soviet side of governing—made it possible for me to report more positive news. My cable continued, "The Government also sought Parliamentary authorization to send a military bridging unit to participate in the IFOR operation in Bosnia." Horn's move was a brilliant example of diplomatic compromise because, while important personnel, the bridge-building engineers were not combat troops. It was a clever compromise that allowed Hungary to say it was contributing to the IFOR operation above and beyond the leasing of bases, but in a way that would not offend its neighbors. In the end, however, Hungary's contribution turned out to be more than a mere public-relations move. The 416-member unit deployed by Hungary played a very valuable role in the operation by building and restoring nineteen destroyed bridges that reopened the approach through Croatia to Bosnia-Herzegovina for the peacekeeping troops. The unit's additional workload included rebuilding twenty kilometers of roads, restoring sixty-five kilometers of rail lines with five tunnels, and defusing numerous land mines.

Hungary's robust response to our request for IFOR assistance set the bar high for other European countries and also earned them high marks in Washington and across the other NATO capitals. By putting aside both domestic politics and residual fears from forty-five years of Soviet occupation, Hungary's swift action demonstrated in a manner no words could express that the country was intent on being taken seriously as a candidate for NATO membership. I happily wrote letters expressing the U.S. government's appreciation for their resolution of support to President Göncz, Prime Minister Horn, Foreign Minister Kovacs, and Defense Minister Keleti.

An exclamation point to the intensive and exhilarating months of negotiations and planning for IFOR was a great honor bestowed upon me by the Hungarian government. I became the first U.S. ambassador invited to speak to a committee of the Hungarian Parliament. On that occasion, just before Christmas, I offered my personal gratitude and official thanks on behalf of the U.S. government to members of Parliament, the Parliamentary Defense Committee, and, of course, the Hungarian people for their historic support and assistance to our armed peacekeeping forces. It was a powerful, uplifting, and resounding conclusion to a year of difficult diplomacy. I felt I had acquitted myself well after just twenty months as ambassador and, once and for all, had overcome any lingering concerns that a non-career State Department diplomat might not be able to handle such a sensitive and demanding post. I couldn't hope for any stronger endorsement of the job I had been doing than this letter from my commander in chief.

Dear Donald,

I enjoyed your letter describing your visit to our forces in Taszar, Hungary, and wanted to thank you and Vera for all you've done in the past year to fulfill your mission as ambassador. In just a few short weeks, our security cooperation with Hungary has taken a great stride forward. Hungary is making a

major contribution to peace in Bosnia and security in Europe, a
contribution that would have seemed inconceivable a few years
ago. I know how hard you and your embassy worked to make
this happen and I hope you take pride in this achievement.

I also appreciate your efforts to encourage the Hungarian
government to maintain its bold and challenging economic stabi-
lization program and to advance its free-market reforms. Thanks
in part to your efforts, Hungary's economy seems pointed in the
right direction and its efforts to rejoin the Western democratic
community have advanced.

Congratulations on a very good year.

Hillary joins me in sending best wishes to you and Vera
for the year to come.

> *Sincerely,*
>
> *Bill Clinton*

U.S. TROOPS ARRIVE IN HUNGARY

Obtaining approval from the Hungarians and then negotiating agreements that would govern potential problem areas was only the beginning of the embassy's involvement in our peacekeeping deployment
as we began the New Year, 1996. The arrival of three thousand permanently stationed American military personnel and the movement
through Taszar of twenty-five thousand more troops widened our
responsibilities substantially, particularly when it came to nurturing
a positive relationship with the Hungarian people who lived in the
area of the staging base.

I had a sound strategic overview already, having visited Taszar twice
at the end of 1995 to monitor progress on construction and preparations at the base. In mid-December, I flew to Taszar with Colonel
Szurgyi and Colonel Martinson, along with Kurt Volker, our political

officer, and joined an elated General Jim Wright to greet the arrival of the first C-130 cargo flights from Germany. After weeks of rain, the terrain had been churned into a sea of mud by convoys of military vehicles and heavy trucks, but the Army engineers and workers with Brown & Root, the construction arm of Halliburton, overcame the sloppy conditions by laying down wooden planks and constructing gravel roads and walkways. A tent city was sprouting, along with a mess hall, administrative facilities, and a state-of-the-art field hospital. It was an impressive sight; even more inviting for arriving troops were the hot-water showers and modern latrines (purchased from Norway, where they had been used the year before by Olympic athletes competing at Lilihammer). A PX was in operation, and an exercise gym, a chapel, and banks of phone booths were under construction. How far and how fast preparations had come in just a few short weeks!

It was an upbeat report I sent to Washington although Hungary's railway authorities were struggling to keep up with the additional rail traffic and inclement weather had delayed flights to the base, slowing the arrival of some vehicles and equipment. Still, I was pleased to note that trucks in the first fleet carrying supplies south out of Taszar had reached their destinations.

Vera and I made our second visit to Taszar on December 17, less than three weeks after the vote in Hungary's Parliament. The buildup for Operation Joint Endeavor was then approaching full velocity, as throngs of troops and vehicles in constant motion filled the base. More than 3,600 soldiers were already stationed there, and two dozen planes and dozens of railroad cars and buses arrived daily from Germany filled with troops, supplies, and equipment. This impressive build-up would not have been possible, General Crouch reminded us, without the enthusiastic support and cooperation of the embassy and the Hungarian government. We appreciated his generous remarks.

Vera and I participated in that day's media event, the dispatch of the first U.S. peacekeeping contingent into the former war zone. The 130-member U.S. Army armored unit left with more than a dozen tanks, Jeeps, and heavy weaponry on a train bound for the Hungarian-Croat border. Their mission would be to defend the technical personnel who were constructing a bridge across the Sava River at Zupanje, the only land route in northern Bosnia. That would prove to be an unexpectedly difficult assignment due to torrential rain and snowstorms that created a raging river. At the height of one storm, a deluge hit the unit's camp, sweeping away tents, vehicles, and supplies. The resulting delay in completing the 350-yard pontoon bridge over the Sava would, in turn, push back the arrival of the convoys transporting more than twenty thousand U.S. peacekeeping troops into Croatia and Bosnia.

The base was in full operation on January 2, 1996, when I accompanied Defense Secretary Perry, Commander of the Joint Chiefs of Staff General Shalikashvili, and Supreme Allied Commander of Europe General George Joulwan on their first visits to Taszar. We were joined that day by Hungarian Minister of Defense Keleti and the Hungarian Defense Force's Commander in Chief, General Deak. I was struck by how different the reception was from my World War II Air Corps experience. Here, our troops were excited to welcome their commanding officers, and more than fifteen minutes of picture-taking confirmed this impression.

The following day, rumors began circulating that POTUS would soon be coming to Bosnia and to the IFOR bases in Hungary, especially Taszar, the largest and most important. I cabled Dan Fried at the National Security Council with suggestions for the speech President Clinton would make.

A presidential visit is a peak experience for any envoy, despite grumblings about the arduous preparations. Truth be told, I never met an ambassador who did not relish the honor and access that a POTUS visit can bring. Given the demands on the presidential schedule and the large number of U.S. embassies around the world, the odds are long against it. Nevertheless, I had been in my post less than two years, and Hungary was about to get its second visit by President Clinton. Vera and I had been wise to hold out for the appointment to Budapest; it was turning out to be a very important post. We received official word with a firm date of Saturday, January 13, only a week in advance. That did not give us much time to make many complex preparations.

Many ambassadors, past and present, are wary of presidential advance teams, complaining about their indifference to local advice and their failure to show the embassy proper consideration. During my tenure, we had only positive experiences, and we always found the advance teams congenial, very professional, and always courteous. Still, the compressed time frame put all of us on edge. The plan proposed that President Clinton would first visit U.S. troops near Tuzla, on the Bosnian front line. Then, in the early afternoon, he planned to stop at Taszar to tour the base, speak to U.S. personnel, and hold a brief meeting with Hungarian leaders before heading back to Washington in the late afternoon. Tuzla's valley topography, however, was notorious for fickle weather. The airport had been closed several mornings recently due to heavy fog. Prudent planning required leaving open the possibility that the arrival order for POTUS might be reversed at almost the last moment. This complicated our embassy's arrangements because I was to escort the Hungarian president, prime minister, foreign minister, defense minister, and their top aides to Taszar in our embassy's C-12 Beechcraft and a second plane of the same type used by U.S. Air Force personnel attached to the embassy. The Hungarian officials had been asked to assemble at the VIP lounge at Budapest's Ferihegyi Airport thirty minutes prior to the noon departure time, ensuring that we would arrive in Taszar by 1 P.M.—in advance of President Clinton's arrival. I arranged with my military attachés to advise me by 7 A.M. on Sunday morning if Taszar was shifted to first stop on the presidential schedule. That would give us time to alert the Hungarians that we would be departing for Taszar far earlier than planned. If we heard nothing by 7 A.M., then the noon takeoff departure from Budapest remained the same.

Presidential protocol calls for ambassadors to dress to the level of the POTUS and neither to overdress or underdress. I asked the presidential advance team whether President Clinton preferred business suits or casual attire. The answer that came back was "informal," certainly no suits or ties, because the president would be dressed casually. He usually wore his favorite leather bomber jacket when visiting U.S. forces in the field. I passed along that information to the Hungarian government through its Foreign Ministry, and was glad I had covered this detail to avoid any embarrassment.

Late Friday night, I received a phone call from the president's advance team. They asked me to call the foreign minister and ask him to remind his president and prime minister about the next day's informal dress code. I was not thrilled with my assignment, but I telephoned Foreign Minister Laszlo Kovacs at his home and asked him, in my most diplomatic manner, to confirm that his colleagues were aware the dress code was casual. I suggested he might choose a black leather jacket I had seen him wearing around Budapest.

Vera and I laid out our "Taszar clothes," boots and warm sweaters, that night before we went to bed, ready for any eventuality, with our alarm clocks set for a quarter to six. Saturday morning dawned bright and sunny, the first good weather in several weeks, and we assumed the conditions were similar in nearby Bosnia. We were still waiting at 8:45 A.M., and had received no telephone call, our sign that everything was set for Plan A: The President was going to Tuzla first and Taszar second. We were eating a leisurely breakfast when the phone rang at a few minutes before nine. "Tuzla is fogged in," I was told. "The president's plane is headed to Taszar first."

We were cutting it awfully close and would have to move quickly to get to Ferihegyi Airport on time for the flight down to Taszar. Could the Hungarians be notified in time? We began making phone calls. Only Defense Minister Keleti, who was out of town attending a pig roast, a popular autumn weekend activity, might be unreachable.

I called our driver, quickly dressed, and raced for the airport, forty minutes away. I was relieved to see most of the Hungarians already there when we arrived, and the rest were en route. President Göncz had been about to visit his grandchildren, but had said to his wife, "No, I'll stay home in case there's a change of plans because you know the devil never sleeps." It was good to see the calls about casual attire had been heeded, except by the prime minister, who took casual to mean a suit but no tie. Deputy State Secretary Ferenc Somogyi jokingly showed off his "made in the USA label" and asked me, "Mr. Ambassador, do you think my jacket is NATO compatible?" We shared a chuckle before taking off just after 10 A.M. in two planes, with the Hungarian officials split between the aircrafts.

I was surprised and pleased to be greeted on the runway of the former Soviet air base at Taszar by Dick Holbrooke and Dan Rather, but there was no time to chat. Vera and I commandeered some vehicles and rushed to the Taszar administration building just in time to catch up with President Clinton, who had already made his remarks and toured the base. He was visiting with our troops in the massive mess tent when we met up with him. Despite the last-minute change of plan, everything had worked out, including our urgent calls to Defense Minister Keleti, who made it in the nick of time after been reached at the pig farm. Vera and I were happy to have had the opportunity to catch up with the president's senior foreign-policy speechwriter, Antony Blinken, our son.

The president seemed very pleased with what he had seen of the troops, particularly their enthusiasm during the preparations at the Taszar airbase, and he expressed gratitude during the bilateral talks with Prime Minister Horn and his colleagues. Against long odds and with unprecedented speed, Hungary had become the staging area for the largest and most complex movement of U.S. forces in Europe since the end of World War II. The president thanked the Hungarians once more for their extraordinary cooperation. They didn't miss the opportunity to remind the president that this project demonstrated that they were ready to join NATO.

After he wrapped up the talks and bid goodbye to the Hungarian and U.S. officials, President Clinton stepped into his limousine and was driven directly into the belly of the C-130 that had brought him to Taszar, a security precaution that made his arrival less obvious. As we watched the plane take off, a Hungarian passerby asked me who was flying on it. I replied with a strong tone of pride, "The President of the United States and my son."

After the president's plane climbed out of sight, we got into Humvees and gave the Hungarian officials a VIP tour of the base. As usual, Gyula Horn didn't show any emotion, but he could not fail to be impressed by the extraordinary transformation of what had been a nearly deserted, muddy field just one month ago. It was now a fully functional village employing three thousand permanent U.S. personnel with hundreds of tents, a hospital, a large mess hall, a gym, stores, places of worship, and a movie theater offering two different feature films daily. We stopped at several places on the base, and the visitors seemed most fascinated by the large, industrial kitchens. Finishing the tour, I felt a sense of accomplishment, as I am sure everyone else did, over completing such a complex and delicate set of negotiations in such a short time. My report to Washington summarized the event and its upbeat mood: "Senior Hungarian officials told us that they were pleased with President Clinton's January 13 visit to the U.S. base at Taszar, and the early arrival and departure did not hurt the success of the meeting or the positive press coverage." Although I didn't state it explicitly in my cable, I felt the Hungarians had also been very pleased by the relaxed atmosphere and casual attire. They seemed to consider the Taszar visit a symbol of passage from their not-so-distant and extremely regimented Soviet-dominated past into the democratic, egalitarian freedom that marked American values.

Hungarian cooperation had undoubtedly elevated the country and its once-suspect Socialist government in the eyes of the many American policy makers who visited or read about Taszar and the efforts that had transformed it into a peacekeeping force staging base. For NATO members, it was important to see that a country that did not border another NATO member could serve as a terminal in the heart of

Central Europe from which to dispatch troops and airplanes quickly to military hot spots. For Hungary's leaders, it was important to understand that its status as a candidate for NATO admission had been given a major boost. Although observers might wonder if those leaders were as eager for NATO's responsibilities as they were for its prestige, I was hoping that their enthusiasm might instill an equivalent eagerness in the country's voters. Polls showed that a majority the Hungarian people were still strongly against joining NATO.

Early during the buildup phase at Taszar, several officials from the U.S. military's Psychological Operations branch visited me. Psy Ops seeks to give American troops a psychological advantage in hostile environments. The officials were already active in Croatia, would be going into Bosnia, and said we needed them in Hungary too. As one of them put it, "Our job is to come in and, through a series of means, basically make sure the Hungarians know that if they mess with our troops, we'll shoot them."

I stopped him right there and said firmly: "That may be a message you need to take down to Bosnia or Croatia, but we are here under a mandate to bring peace to these areas. The Hungarians are our hosts and NATO aspirants. They want peace in those countries as much as we do."

Neverthless, we had a lot of public relations work to do in Hungary regarding our military. Military bases in Hungary for generations had been viewed with wariness; all that most Hungarians knew of the U.S. military came from Vietnam War movies. With so many Hungarian newspapers seeking stories about the U.S. peacekeeping forces, reporters who were inexperienced in fact-based, free-society reporting had begun to report misinformation, imaginative suppositions, and rumors as news. Two of the more widely circulated rumors claimed that the U.S. troops were already on the ground in Bosnia and involved in the fighting and that AIDS would most certainly arrive in Hungary with the U.S. soldiers.

I had foreseen these problems, and at the outset I had spoken to senior officers associated with Taszar and the European Command about the need to have military public-affairs officers on site to provide the media with more information and greater access to the peacekeeping forces. In the absence of such officers, the entire burden of dealing with the press and the public fell on the embassy, and our small public-affairs team was already working overtime in Budapest, Taszar, and Kaposvar, ferrying between the locations. We also had to make Brown & Root consider the impact of its work on the Hungarians and operate in a way that reflected well on the United States. It was a tall order that strained our resources.

One potentially uncomfortable public relations situation arose when entrepreneurs in Kaposvar wanted to import prostitutes from an Eastern European country; they had also acquired large quantities of beer with which they planned to open several taverns. Not knowing a great deal about Hungary, the local culture, or how the troops would be received, the U.S. Army initially confined its personnel to the base in order to avoid incidents that might leave a negative impression and thus confirm the Hungarians' suspicions about our troops. That policy caused the Hungarian entrepreneurs to become angry and vocal, and they complained in the press. Not until the beginning of 1996 did the Army wisely bring in public-affairs specialists, the 353rd Civil Affairs Command. These reservists, several of whom were fluent in Hungarian, were deployed where misunderstandings were most likely to arise, particularly at Taszar and Kaposvar. Several served as liaisons between Hungarians wishing to sell goods and services and U.S. military procurement personnel at the base, which helped avoid misunderstandings and potential conflicts. Instead of only reacting to problems, we took a proactive approach and dispatched a team of public-affairs specialists throughout southern Hungary to visit schools and town governments, discuss U.S. objectives, and be available to the local media for interviews. We also convinced the army to send a team to Budapest where most of the journalists and publications were based.

Fears among local Hungarians that U.S. soldiers would misbehave and cause problems evaporated when a series of fires and large automobile accidents occurred in the Taszar area. The U.S. military provided helicopters with medical teams to assist casualties on the scene and transported the seriously wounded to local hospitals These generous acts of U.S. kindness had a beneficial side effect. Residents of the local communities around the base asked if they could meet with the soldiers. We invited groups of local people onto the base and, consistent with our security procedures, offered them tours of the facilities. Soon, we began to receive invitations from Hungarians who wanted to host a group of soldiers in their homes for dinner. Slowly, we began to approve those visits. This spontaneous, person-to-person, grassroots effort was genuine and heartfelt and could not have been orchestrated, even with the best public-affairs specialists working behind the scenes.

Encouraged by these small-scale exchanges and to boost the Hungarians' acceptance of future NATO membership, we decided to relax some of the restrictions placed on military personnel. Permanent staffers were allowed to leave the base to make trips to Budapest and other parts of Hungary on their days off or free weekends. Hungarian bus companies agreed to provide transportation at minimal cost, even free on some occasions. Our consular section alerted restaurants and cultural centers in Budapest and other areas to expect visiting Americans in large numbers and asked that they be treated in a friendly manner. Pleased with the cordial reception the soldiers were receiving and wishing to reciprocate the hospitality, the military agreed to open the Taszar base to the general public on a more regular basis, while maintaining security. It did not take long to read positive press reports about Taszar, and the friction from the movement of more than twenty-five thousand troops and heavy equipment in and around the area was mitigated.

By the spring of 1996, it was an astounding sight to see U.S. soldiers relaxing at restaurants in Budapest with groups of Hungarians stopping by their tables to talk. Considering the two countries' recent history and previous concerns, and knowing that the last Soviet soldiers had left Hungary as recently as 1991, we could not have imagined a better outcome. This informal, unplanned contact with U.S. military personnel began to change perceptions; the average Hungarian's uncertain attitude about joining NATO began to track slightly more positive in polls. Deeper connections were beginning to form as well. Within a few months of operations at Taszar, our consulate began to process numerous residency and citizenry papers as American military men married Hungarian women, and American military women married Hungarian men.

In the end, our goal had been achieved through the human heart, and the Taszar experience proved to be an extremely successful mechanism for helping the Hungarians learn about NATO and the U.S. military, quite apart from our troops' original purpose for being there. As Defense Secretary Bill Perry told a group of National Guard officials in a speech, "I have never seen such a warm relationship between two countries as developed between Hungary and the United States—all because of our use of the Taszar base."

There had been hardly a stumble in the first full year of operations at Taszar as twenty-five thousand soldiers, two hundred thousand tons of cargo and twelve thousand pieces of equipment moved through Hungary and on to Bosnia. Given that mammoth logistical challenge, there were likely to be problems, but an unexpected disappointment came from a U.S. company. Levi Strauss, the jeans maker, had a large manufacturing plant in Hungary. I decided to ask the company to donate one thousand pairs of blue jeans in various sizes to the military men and women permanently stationed in Taszar for them to wear on their days off. I thought it would be a nice gesture that would be good publicity for the company and deeply appreciated by the service men and women. The Levi Strauss managers in Hungary said they liked the idea, but they would need approval from headquarters in San Francisco. I made four calls to the CEO of Levi Strauss to get his approval. I spoke to his personal assistant and explained the purpose of my call, yet he never returned a single call. I considered it bad business and very shabby behavior. I did not take his inaction personally, but as a slight to the United States and our troops. Ironically, the only two disappointments I had during my term as ambassador were with American business executives from Levi Strauss and managers of Credit Suisse First Boston.

Although the intense efforts to get Taszar up and running had been time-consuming, we could not neglect other central issues, such as the economy. In early January 1996, a week before President Clinton's visit to Taszar, I gave a dinner for Finance Minister Bokros to discuss how we could help move his economic reforms forward. In an article in the *Wall Street Journal* a few weeks earlier, I had publicly applauded the Hungarian government's courage in undertaking the necessary austerity measures to improve its current account balance, impose strict wage policies, and lower the budget deficit by one-third through tight fiscal policies. Privatization had begun to accelerate and would soon dramatically increase the amount of direct investment in Hungary. The best evidence I could point to of the Hungarian economy's attractiveness was the presence of such major American corporations as General Electric, General Motors, Ford, IBM, and others. Already active in Hungary, they were increasing their investment, helping to boost foreign direct investment in Hungary to the top of the heap in Central Europe.

It did not take long for resistance toward Hungary's economic reforms to increase. The critics were led by an influential Socialist deputy and former Labor minister who publicly criticized the party leadership for deviating from its worker-oriented platform by voting to earmark privatization revenue above a certain level exclusively for reducing the government debt. This allowed Hungarians, who are famously negative, to join in with the complainers, who had unreasonable expectations of capitalism due to their limited exposure to free markets under their previous system.

About this time, a U.N. study placed Hungary twenty-eighth in the world in terms of its quality of life for its citizens although the average Hungarian felt less well off than during the years of communism. One-quarter of the population was living below the poverty line, real wages had declined, and many people had been laid off as industry consolidated or failed to compete with private-sector rivals. Nostalgia for the old economic system was running high. A poll found that just one in four Hungarians thought the present system was better than socialism. Sadly, one-half of those polled thought it was worse. Concerned, I reiterated in numerous interviews with Hungarian journalists that it was essential that the Hungarian people begin to see some benefit from the government's improving macroeconomic balance sheet.

Lajos Bokros, the Finance Minister, felt he was receiving unfair blame from both the media and Parliament and threatened to resign on several occasions. Finally, he offered to resign one time too many and Prime Minister Horn felt obliged to accept. Bokros left Budapest for Washington and an important job at the World Bank where he ably helped advise newly emerging countries. After several months, Horn appointed the banker Peter Medgyessy as the new finance minister. I began periodic meetings with Medgyessy, who was personable and self-assured, and who told me he intended to continue down the path on which Bokros had started. Fortunately, Gyorgy Suranyi stayed on as head of the National Bank for another five years until he left for a position with a major Italian banking consortium.

In April 1996, U.S. Attorney General Janet Reno arrived for a two-day visit on the first anniversary of the International Law Enforcement Academy. Although she was unable to make the opening events because of the tragic bombing in Oklahoma City, Hungarian officials later rolled out the red carpet for her with high-level meetings and elaborate receptions. I joined Reno and FBI Director Louis Freeh, along with Hungarian officials, at the Academy's dedication ceremonies. The Academy soon developed a fine reputation and became a model frequently duplicated in other countries. I found Reno to be outgoing, easy to converse with, amiable, and knowledgeable about the local issues.

Another traveler to Budapest at this time was Madonna, in town to film *Evita*, in which she played the title role of Eva Peron. Set designers had transformed parts of Budapest with plastic palm trees and Spanish street signs into 1940s and 1950s Buenos Aires. A few weeks before filming began, Andrew Vajna, the film's producer, came to see me to discuss his difficulty obtaining permission to shoot a scene in St. Stephen's Basilica, and to enlist my help. I phoned the Papal Nuncio, the Vatican's representative in Hungary and a friendly and charming man, and told him about the film company's dilemma; I also suggested that the company would be generous to the Basilica if they obtained permission to film there. The producer had assured me, I added, that the scene would be dignified. "Is there anything you can do?" I asked.

The Nuncio said he would look into the matter and get back to me. A week later, he phoned back. "We cannot allow that woman to be filmed in our Basilica," he told me. He went on in language much stronger, and we were not even aware at that point that Madonna was pregnant with a lover's child. So the cathedral scene was filmed in a studio in Budapest, and several members of the embassy made appearances as extras.

In the spring and summer of 1996, we finally managed to convince the Hungarian government that it had a moral commitment to assist aging Jewish Holocaust survivors. The processs had taken more than eighteen months of proposals and counter-proposals, offers and rejections, even a meal at a kosher restaurant my stomach will never forget, but we finally forged a settlement that, while not fully satisfactory to all parties, was at least fair to all. Most important, all the parties had committed to it. In his book *Imperfect Justice*, Stuart Eizenstat was kind enough to mention favorably the part I played in the negotiations while understating his own vital contribution.

The Hungarian Parliament voted to establish a Hungarian-Jewish Heritage Public Foundation, the first of its kind in former Communist Europe. Beginning in September, 1997, the Foundation would provide modest monthly stipends to the fifteen to twenty thousand survivors of the Holocaust, most of whom were quite elderly. The payments amounted to about $50 per month. While small by American standards, the sum was very important to elderly people with scant outside income who had lost and suffered so much; now at least they could pay their gas and light bills and afford other basic living necessities.

In the end, the Hungarian government also agreed to make a restitution payment to the Jewish community of $2.7 million annually in Hungarian *forints*, a sum to be distributed in the settlement of outstanding property claims. It also returned a number of properties still being held by the government and provided funds to help restore the Dohany Street Synagogue. The Hungarians did what they had to do, even if they weren't thrilled about the cost, because they understood their moral obligation had to be met if they were to be accepted by the Western nations and, in particularly, by NATO members.

I felt a deep sense of accomplishment when I attended the ceremony celebrating the completion of major reconstruction of the magnificent Dohany Street Synagogue. The funds directed to this effort by the restitution settlement were a critical addition to the private donations that had been raised. Additionally, the government's contribution to the synagogue has proven to be an excellent investment since the Dohany Street area has become one of Budapest's major tourist attractions.

During First Lady Hillary Clinton's first visit to Hungary in July 1996, it was my pleasure to accompany her to several official events. We met with Prime Minister Horn and Foreign Minister Kovacs. Even though she had come directly from Bratislava and Prague, she always kept Hungary's situation and aspirations in clear focus.

During her visit, I also invited Hillary to join me at the new Bank Center building for the formal opening of our commercial section's new offices. She was a gracious guest who posed for photographs, answered reporters' questions, and offered generous amounts of praise for our efforts. What may have seemed like just another photo op was to me an example of how I had managed to break through a bureaucratic logjam.

Two years earlier, as soon as I learned that a new, modern office building was slated for construction one block from our embassy, I arranged to meet with the developer, a Hungarian-Canadian named Bela Fejer. At the time, we badly needed to consolidate our operations scattered across Budapest. I assumed that the Bank Center would be too expensive for our embassy budget, but decided to speak with Fejer anyway.

I told Bela Fejer that I wanted to bring our four sections together in his new building. Cost was a concern, and I asked what kind of deal, given our limited budget, he might negotiate. A week later, the developer got back to me with rental figures that were no more than what we were already paying in rent for the multiple office spaces around town. The most important concession he offered was that if the U.S. decided to close an agency for any reason, we could break the lease at any time without penalty. I was sold and felt he had given us a generous break on what the space would command from private companies.

Instead of greeting my plan for the Bank Center with enthusiasm, the heads of our branches of Commerce, USIS, USAID, and the Office of Defense Cooperation, which would be the major tenants, were skeptical that Washington would support them; they felt there was no point investing energy and emotion in something that was bound to be disapproved or ignored by bureaucrats. It was the sort of defeatist attitude among some State Department members that I encouraged them to overcome.

It was frustrating to juggle endless discussions with officials in Washington who were looking for the smallest issue with which to derail my consolidation plans. To my dismay, these conversations consumed untold hours of my time and went on far too long. Knowing that the developer was losing patience with our delays, I called Assistant Secretary for Management, Pat Kennedy, a respected colleague and sympathetic ear, at the State Department. I cut to the chase: "Pat, this is a unique opportunity for the Budapest embassy. It is not going to cost us any more than we are paying now, but I cannot get the local representatives of these agencies to sign on the dotted line. What I would like you to do is call their key people to your office for a meeting, lock the door, and do not let them out until they have agreed." Pat did just that, and I was grateful for his no-nonsense approach and skillful arm-twisting.

The Bank Center proved to be a great success. The building was only the beginning for developer Bela Fejer, who later restored the Art Nouveau Gresham Palace into the five-star Four Season's Gresham Palace Hotel.

A few weeks after Hillary's visit, former President Jimmy Carter came to Budapest to celebrate an anniversary of the Fulbright program, the outstanding intellectual exchange program that allows U.S. scholars to study abroad and foreign scholars to study in the United States. President Carter had a constructive history with Hungary and is highly regarded there because in 1978 he agreed with a plan, proposed by U.S. Ambassador Phillip Kaiser and Secretary of State Cyrus Vance, to return the Crown of St. Stephen to the Hungarian government. The bejeweled crown topped by the gold cross had been worn by the young Magyar King Stephen when he was crowned as the first king of Hungary in 1000, and each successive monarch was sworn in wearing the crown. The crown eventually came to America although it was unclear how it was removed from Hungary. According to one theory, the crown was spirited out of the country by Hungarian soldiers during World War II and buried in Austria for safekeeping. The Hungarian soldiers later told American troops where to find the crown and asked them to keep it safe during the war. The crown ended up in the United States in Fort Knox, where it was stored from the mid-1940s until 1978.

President Carter returned the Crown of St. Stephen that year, convinced it would be a prudent move to begin to repair U.S.-Hungarian relations after America failed to come to Budapest's aid during the 1956 uprising. Carter stipulated that the crown would be turned over to representatives of the Church and various representatives of the Hungarian people, but most emphatically not to the communist government. The plane carrying the crown and a small U.S. delegation arrived under the cover of darkness. It was a tearful, emotional occasion for those assembled to accept it. The crown was placed on display at the National Museum in Budapest and was later moved to the Parliament building.

President Carter's gesture of repatriation enraged émigré Hungarians in the United States, who considered it a form of capitulation to the communists. There were predictions that the Soviets would seize the crown, which did not happen. I came to empathize with the price Ambassador Phillip Kaiser paid for his decision because I too became a target of Hungarian-American conservative critics whenever I spoke favorably or acted cooperatively with the Socialist Hungarian government. These émigrés seemed unable to move beyond the injustice of the Treaty of Trianon some seventy-five years earlier, and with their obsession to annul it. I tried to encourage them to look forward, rather than focusing on a painful past.

President Carter's visit to celebrate the Fulbright anniversary was a matter close to my heart because I consider it one of America's best ongoing international exchange programs: it builds bridges among the world's future leaders. After leaving Hungary, I resumed my affiliation with the New York-based Institute on International Education, which operates the Fulbright program. I had come to know Harriet Fulbright, the widow of Senator J. William Fulbright who had originated the program. Harriet Fulbright had invited Carter to Hungary, and the former president and first lady, Rosalyn Carter, drew large crowds in Budapest.

President Carter's visit was an opportunity to highlight one of his favorite organizations, Habitat for Humanity, the American volunteer group that builds houses for people who cannot afford to buy them. Carter arrived in Budapest with a Habitat for Humanity contingent, and Vera and I joined Jimmy and Rosalyn Carter at a home site on the outskirts of Budapest where we watched the former president and first lady hammering nails, painting siding, and performing other manual labor.

I also accompanied the Carters to several meetings and events at which they were honored, and Vera and I hosted a reception for them at the residence. August 20, St. Stephen's Day, is also Hungary's national day, a day to commemorate the Magyar conquest of the Carpathian Basin eleven centuries ago. The holiday is also a religious festival and includes a service at the Basilica followed by a parade led by Church officials carrying the mummified hand of St. Stephen. President Carter, fondly remembered in Hungary for returning the crown, was asked to head the procession.

The Carters drew enormous cheers from the throngs lining both sides of the procession route. Vera and I walked directly behind them, and we found the incredible outpouring of love for them immensely moving. I could only begin to imagine how President Carter felt, receiving this tremendous ovation for a decision he had made eighteen years earlier, a decision not so warmly or universally received at the time.

At the top of our agenda at the monthly meeting of NATO ambassadors in Hungary were the Romanian-Hungarian-Slovakian negotiations aimed at settling their ethnic differences, a requirement for NATO membership. These negotiations intended to set new ground rules for the treatment of two million ethnic Hungarians in Romania and six hundred thousand Hungarians in Slovakia.

The architect of the treaties being negotiated was Ferenc Somogyi, Hungary's deputy foreign minister, whom I had come to know as fair-minded, likable, and bright. In addition to being a valued friend and skilled negotiator, he was my tennis partner. (Being diplomatic, I won't describe who won our matches.) To keep us informed, Somogyi instituted periodic briefings regarding the progress of the negotiations. We all felt it was important to seize the impetus generated by the peacekeeping troop buildup at Taszar and the desire on the part of both the Hungarians and the Romanians to be viewed favorably by the West and by NATO.

I traveled to Romania in early 1996 to support the treaty negotiations. Vera and I spent a weekend in Bucharest with our ambassador there, Alfred Moses, a lawyer whom I held in high regard after getting to know him in New York and Washington. I attended meetings with Al and Romanian officials, and he arranged for me to speak with key political figures and the foreign minister.

Moses had become quite close to Romanian Prime Minister Ion Iliescu. In fact, I worried that he might be too close to Iliescu and might lack sufficient distance and objectivity during the early negotiations between the Hungarian and Romanian governments. As an example of Al's close relationship with the prime minister, about an hour before we were due to leave Bucharest, Al suggested that I meet the prime minister. He made a call, and ten minutes later, I was shaking hands with Iliescu.

I tried to keep an open mind and ignore negative public opinion about Ion Iliescu, whom I found to be a tough, somewhat tactless character who spent the first thirty minutes of our meeting lecturing me on the inequities of Hungarian rule a century ago. Perhaps he had forgotten that he was meeting with the U.S. ambassador to Hungary, a person who could have been helpful in advancing Romanian interests with the Hungarians. Instead, he railed about how terrible the Hungarians were, a negative assessment that did not endear him to me.

Fortunately, neither Gyula Horn nor Ion Iliescu had first-hand involvement with the treaty negotiations. That task instead was given to the Romanian Foreign Minister, Teodor Melescanu, who got long well with Ferenc Somogyi. The two lead negotiators respected each other, were modern Europeans, and thought along comparable political and social lines.

Simultaneously, I collaborated with Ted Russell, the excellent career U.S. ambassador to Slovakia. He faced an especially difficult situation because Slovakia's prime minister was Vladimir Meciar, a volatile and authoritarian politician with an unfortunate reputation for nepotism, corruption, and a dictatorial outlook, but who possessed a knack for holding power. Ted and I managed to keep his end of the talks on track with the negotiations going on at the same time between Hungary and Romania.

My counterparts and I finally achieved success after many challenging months. We prevailed upon the sides to compromise and, when they could not agree, to look past some of the thorny issues so that basic treaties could be signed and progress achieved. A key breakthrough came when I was able to arrange for the delivery of a personal handwritten note from Somogyi to his Romanian counterpart Melescanu that bypassed the traditional diplomatic channels and did not appear as an official statement on Hungarian letterhead. The note offered suggestions for compromise that were accepted by the Romanians and resulted in agreement on a basic treaty that drew overwhelming support from both countries. The treaty we had hammered out cleared a major hurdle blocking the historic goal of Romania's integration with the West. Later, Hungary and Slovakia signed a similar pact as well.

All of us involved in the arduous negotiations were proud of what our labors had yielded. These treaties obligated the countries to protect their national minorities' civil liberties and cultural identity. They guaranteed that in areas of ethnic concentration the minorities' native languages could be used in schools at all levels, in administrative and judicial proceedings, on road signs, in print and broadcast media, and in almost every other aspect of communal life. Although the other fifteen NATO members represented in Budapest—particularly the British, German, and Italian ambassadors—were active and helpful in trying to advance the talks, in the final analysis, I believe it was the carrot-and-stick approach put forth by the United States (the carrot being NATO and the stick being no NATO) that eventually carried the day.

An op-ed piece Al Moses and I wrote for the *Washington Post* summed up the essence of the pact: "The heart of the treaty also is the heart of post-Cold War Europe's security challenges: how to reconcile the rights and responsibilities of minorities with majorities in a part of the world where people and borders do not match. Bosnia is a brutal reminder of the power of these ethnic and nationalistic hatreds . . . and how important it is to defuse ethnic grievances before they explode."

An example I liked to point to regarding the improvement in relations among the central European countries was the famous bridge linking Slovakia and Hungary at Esztergom on the Danube River. The bridge was destroyed during World War II, and it had never been rebuilt due to Slovakian fears of a Hungarian invasion. Five years after the treaty was signed, the rebuilt bridge opened to great fanfare. It had taken fifty-six years for the two countries to finally engage in normal cross-border transportation of people and goods.

Despite positive restitution developments, a disturbing example of Hungary's continuing unwillingness to restore property taken from its Jewish citizens during World War II was brought to my attention by a Hungarian-American lawyer, Blaise Pasztory. He came to see me with his clients Martha and Ted Nierenberg. Martha is the granddaughter of the late Hungarian industrialist and collector Baron Mor Lipot Herzog. The Herzogs were one of the most prominent families in Budapest in the early twentieth century. At Baron Herzog's death in 1934, the family's art collection contained some twenty-five hundred objects, including one of Hungary's most extensive collections of paintings by such masters as Tiepolo, Renoir, Gauguin, and Degas, as well as one of the largest privately held collections of El Greco. The Herzogs' industrial empire was initially seized by the Nazis and later nationalized by the Communists, seemingly on the grounds that the Herzogs had escaped with their lives and thus were no longer present to object. The illegal seizure of the hidden Herzog art works by Hungarian State Police during the occupation was well-documented. S.S. Commander Adolf Eichmann selected a few favorites for his headquarters in the Hotel Majestic in Budapest and had the rest shipped to Germany. A *New York Times* article described how the Herzog paintings cited in the lawsuit were eventually handed over to the Museum of Fine Arts for safekeeping. Between the end of the war and 1948, the Hungarian government reclaimed many works of art that had made their way back to Hungary from Germany. After 1948, the Hungarian state museums began to register and incorporate the Herzog works into their own permanent collections, thus nationalizing what was recognized to have been private property.

Baron Herzog's daughter, Elizabeth Wiess de Csepel, tried to recover those paintings, most of which were by now in the collection of the Museum of Fine Arts in Budapest. The Hungarian government and its museums refused to return them and instead hid behind the rationale that they had been taken during the communist-era nationalization laws. Before her death in 1992, only three works had been returned to the family, all minor works by relatively unknown artists. Since then, other Herzog family members have been unsuccessful in trying to regain the rest of the paintings from the Museum of Fine Arts and Hungary's National Gallery.

I introduced the Herzog descendants, the Nierenbergs, to the Minister of Culture, Balint Magyar, a sympathetic and caring individual. The Nierenbergs hoped the Hungarian government would acknowledge that the paintings belonged to them; then the family was prepared to present a gift of several of the artworks back to Hungary. I thought this was a generous proposal and felt confident it would resolve the controversy. Unfortunately, I was overly optimistic, and the issue of the looted Herzog paintings remains unresolved to this day.

I believe Congress lacks understanding of the value of promoting American culture abroad, and it makes a mistake by underestimating the importance of cultural exchanges as a valuable adjunct to American diplomacy. More direct exposure to American art and U.S. performers would provide a better appreciation of the high quality and wide variety of music, theater, dance, and visual art in the United States. Our political leaders seem suspicious of culture, as demonstrated every few years when Congress debates increasing its modest appropriation for the National Endowment for the Arts. We experienced this shortcoming firsthand when USIS funded a very small art exhibition at a gallery in Kecskemet. Vera and I made a point of attending the opening to signal our support of the arts, but we soon realized that trying to induce U.S. government agencies to sponsor cultural exchanges overseas was a losing battle. Our energies would be better spent on more achievable projects.

So when the Museum of Fine Arts in Budapest was planning a show of the great sixteenth-century Renaissance painter Titian and asked for my assistance, I was happy to oblige. The museum owned Titian's portrait of Cardinal Bembeau and wanted to borrow another Titian painting of Bembeau from the National Gallery in Washington. I had served on the National Gallery's Trustee Council for a decade, only resigning when I became ambassador. So I spoke to Rusty Powell, director of the National Gallery, who was sympathetic to the Hungarian museum's request and arranged to lend the Titian portrait for the Budapest exhibition. A fine addition to the show, it made for a compelling comparison with Hungary's version of the portrait and had the added benefit of creating goodwill. The impact of a single painting coming from the United States underscored for me the opportunities our government was missing by not doing more to advance America's cultural image abroad. Vera and I even gave a welcome party for the American Titian at the museum, the first such event ever held in a museum in Budapest.

Vera and I did our utmost to acquaint our diplomatic colleagues with America's great cultural and arts organizations. When conductor Christoph von Dohnányi came to Budapest in 1996 with the Cleveland Orchestra, we personally purchased fifty tickets and invited our fellow ambassadors from twenty-five countries to attend the concert and a reception afterward. This was an excellent opportunity to have these envoys hear for themselves the high standards set by such organizations as the Cleveland Orchestra and other recent performers in Budapest such as the New York Philharmonic and the San Francisco Symphony. We wanted our colleagues to remember that superb musicality when they considered how their country related to the United States.

One of our guests at the concert was Russian Ambassador Aboimov, a tough and hardline communist operative who had been in Budapest for more than a decade. Earlier that day, we played against each other in a tennis tournament for diplomats organized by the Ministry of Foreign Affairs. I won one match and lost one to him. After the concert, Aboimov came up to me and said, "With this great concert you made a big contribution to Budapest's musical life. Much more so than you did for Budapest's tennis."

I enjoyed the tennis matches and informal discussions with Aboimov. He once told me that Krushchev's decision to send tanks and troops into Hungary in 1956 had been provoked by a private message from Mao Tse-tung, the ruler of Communist China. Mao warned Khrushchev that the Soviet Union would lose all respect around the world if it failed to suppress the rebellion.

A few months later, I called Aboimov two days before our scheduled tennis match to remind him. "Oh no," he said. "I completely forgot when we made the tennis date that Sunday is our election day back in Russia. I have to stay by my phone to monitor the results." During the communist regime, Russia's election results were predetermined. By 1996, they had become a source of uncertainty. Welcome to democracy, Mr. Aboimov.

Our love of classical music led Vera and me to make several good friends among Hungarian performers, including Andrea Rost, the celebrated international coloratura soprano, at whose invitation we heard sing the role of Violetta in *La Traviata* at Milan's grand La Scala Opera House. Andrea has appeared at the Metropolitan Opera, the Chicago Civic Opera, and the Kennedy Center, where her artistry gives listeners much pleasure and also boosts Hungary's cultural reputation. Our friendship continues, and Vera recently served as Andrea's matron of honor when she was married in a lavish ceremony at the Opera House in Budapest.

Administrators of Hungarian orchestras often asked for my advice. Using my experiences on the board of the New York Philharmonic and other arts groups in the United States, I gave examples of how to boost their fundraising and offered some suggestions to the new board members of Ivan Fischer's Budapest Festival Orchestra. I assured them the time would come when Hungarian companies, banks, and a growing number of individuals would become prosperous enough to help fund the nation's orchestras and cultural groups.

During my time as ambassador, a growing number of Americans were visiting Budapest and enjoying the city's cultural attractions. Unfortunately, many were also getting ripped off by a handful of unscrupulous restaurant owners and nightclub managers. Tourists were lured into these establishments, often by attractive young women who asked them to buy them a drink. The scam came because the Americans could not read the fine print on Hungarian menus. At the end of the meal, the bottle of wine they thought cost $20 ended up as a charge for $500 on the bill. A dinner for four that should have cost $50 instead cost $750. In many cases, these complaints were passed along to our embassy and routed to our Consular Office. It was discouraging to find that the Hungarian police ignored these extortionists and showed no concern for the victims. I suspected, but could not prove, that the police were being paid hush money to give the swindlers a pass.

I finally became so frustrated over this ongoing problem that I declared that we were going to publish a list of offending restaurants and nightclubs. I turned to Teddy Taylor, our Consul General and an immensely capable man, and he and I developed an action plan. His office had gathered complaints over several months and our investigation determined that most of the scams took place in about a dozen establishments. We began to publish a monthly list of these offending restaurants and nightclubs in the English-language paper *Budapest Sun*. We also printed the names in the embassy's pamphlets given out to American visitors, warning that these places should be considered off-limits and that customers went there at their own peril. To my knowledge, this was the first time such a tough approach had been taken in the region.

The published lists raised an outcry from the establishments we had named. None of them managed to disprove our charges, though, and some were forced to close their doors due to a lack of business. Even though complaints decreased, we went one step further and persuaded the Hungarian government to create a Hungarian Tourist Police. A subdivision of the Hungarian Police Force, it deals only with problems regarding tourists. Our program also started a public debate about business ethics in the tourist industry. Stories appeared in the

International Herald Tribune, Financial Times, and *New York Times*. Finally, our efforts revitalized the Hungarian Tourist Office.

Westel, a Hungarian-based telephone company, hosted a U.S. election night celebration at the Marriott Hotel ballroom on November 5, 1996, for the American community and a group of Hungarian political leaders. Together, we watched the returns in the race between President Clinton and Vice-President Gore, the incumbents, and the Republican challengers, Senators Bob Dole and Jack Kemp. Westel hired a Dixieland band and installed a replica of the Statue of Liberty to create an all-American ambiance.

Hungary is six hours ahead of Eastern Standard Time, making the party too early to see votes being tallied. Who would win was a foregone conclusion by then, however, and everyone in the room knew where my loyalties lay. I felt comfortable when at the start of the party I quoted that great American philosopher Yogi Berra, "It ain't over 'til it's over," but added, "I think that, although the polls are still open, the American presidential election has been decided."

Politically-appointed U.S. ambassadors submit their resignations after an American presidential election, even if the incumbent wins a second term; career ambassadors are posted for a three-year tenure. Four months remained until the end of my third full year, and I anticipated that my service would end at about that time. I wasn't even close.

FINAL EFFORTS

I had witnessed Hungary's painful transition from state-run socialism and a command economy to a free, parliamentary-governed, market economy. Now as 1997 began, I felt confident that I would be leaving the country in better shape than I found it, particularly in its relations with the United States. After Prime Minister Horn finally grew concerned enough about the huge deficit looming over the national budget to take our advice, the Hungarian government launched a full-court press to speed up privatization. During the previous year, 1996, about $6 billion of Hungarian-owned state enterprises had been sold directly to foreign investors, reducing Hungary's foreign debt to manageable proportions. This sell-off also cut in half its total percentage of debt in relation to gross domestic product. By doing so, Hungary's international credit rating had improved to the point that the International Monetary Fund shifted the country from a watch list of problem countries to a roster of countries who were meeting their obligations.

By 1997, total foreign investment in Hungary had reached $16 billion. That figure amounted to one-third of the total amount for Central and Eastern Europe, including the former Soviet Union. Nearly three-quarters of Hungary's once-nationalized and largely inefficient industries were now in private hands with modern management know-how. Hungary was firmly established as a location for Western companies to do business. Most encouraging of all, exports had begun to climb. That would boost the growth of the country's total output, its GDP, to 4.4 percent by the end of the year. The government finally had sufficient breathing space to implement a fully funded pension system, to improve higher education, and to create a national treasury. Of all the countries in the former Soviet bloc, Hungary was by far the most effective at turning from a socialist, centrally-owned and controlled economy into a growing, competitive, capitalist society.

My embassy and I felt a great deal of satisfaction for all we had accomplished together over the course of three years. Much work remained to be done, however, and the most important bit of unfinished business was helping Hungary achieve its goal of joining NATO. The Hungarian government was eager for NATO membership as proof that Hungary was now firmly locked into the West. What remained to be seen, however, was whether the Hungarian people shared the goal of NATO membership. None of the other former Soviet-bloc countries hoping to be invited into NATO that year faced the same uncertainty over the outcome. The other former Soviet bloc countries needed only approval by their legislatures, which the governments controlled, to approve NATO membership. Only Hungary would be putting the NATO decision up to a vote in a national referendum. It was a high-stakes process with no guarantee of victory and a strong chance of defeat.

In 1993, an extremist left-wing party not represented in the Hungarian Parliament succeeded in obtaining the necessary number of signatures to initiate a referendum on NATO membership. At the time, such a vote would almost certainly haved failed because the public was not sufficiently informed to focus on the issue. The extremist provocateurs caused enough of a stir to get the government to agree to a plebiscite if and when Hungary was actually invited to join NATO, even if Parliament voted against the proposed referendum. Since then, while Hungarian animosity towards American military personnel moving through Taszar for the most part had disappeared, it was still far from certain whether ordinary Hungarians would vote to ally themselves with NATO. Many Hungarians were tired of being taken advantage of by stronger nations and simply wanted to be left alone to become a sort of Central European Switzerland, concentrating on international trade but remaining neutral in geopolitics. So the NATO conundrum drifted along while my days as ambassador dwindled.

Meanwhile, my responsibilities assisting American commercial efforts in Hungary continued to keep me busy. From the start of my ambassadorship, I had made it clear that the United States was not going to sell offensive weapons to Hungary until it was integrated into NATO, partly because it would be a waste of Hungary's precious financial resources. In February 1996, however, five senior officials from McDonnell Douglas came to see me about their efforts to sell

F-18 fighter planes to the Hungarian military. The Hungarians, who had been attempting to modernize their armed forces, were mulling over the purchase of twenty-five jet fighters to replace their aging Soviet-made MiGs. They seemed to be leaning toward the American plane versus a Scandinavian competitor, the Gripen. As Hungary was seeking membership in NATO, in which America is a key member, the plane order became a bargaining chip.

There was not much technical or operational difference between the competing fighter planes. Furthermore, it was debatable whether Hungary even needed an air force with twenty-five jet fighters jets. One had to wonder as well why nearby Poland needed fifty fighter jets when a single U.S. aircraft carrier housed twice as many. I suppose these former Warsaw Pact countries considered a modern air force a symbol of national sovereignty and, to a lesser degree, a defense against the new fighter jets being purchased by neighboring, theoretically hostile countries.

The Hungarians showed more restraint than other potential fighter plane customers, realizing that the purchase was more useful as a NATO bargaining chip than necessary for defense. Hungarian officials were polite to our overtures on behalf of McDonnell Douglas, but they continued to stall about a purchase. They knew how to play the political game. (In later years, while seeking European Union membership, they flirted with buying European planes.) Throughout the 1990's, they stuck with their old MiGs. Finally, a decade after I completed my ambassadorship they began to replace the MiGs with Gripen fighter planes built in Sweden and powered by American jet engines. Then they took the prudent step of leasing the planes rather than purchasing them outright.

In our financial reform assistance efforts, I had often stressed the importance of honesty, impartiality, and transparency in the Hungarian government's attitude toward business and the bidding process. In 1997, the time had come to privatize two Hungarian television stations. Once again, unfortunately, the American companies who joined the bidding weren't playing on a level field.

After his years as U.S. Ambassador to Austria, Ronald Lauder saw an opportunity to build a commercial TV network in former Soviet satellite countries in Central and Eastern Europe. Until then, the media there had been government-owned and tightly controlled. By the time Hungary invited bids on its two commercial TV stations, the Lauder Media Group already owned stations in Poland, the Czech Republic, and Romania. Ronald asked for the embassy's support in pursuing its bid. Even if he had not been a former ambassador and a good friend, I would, of course, have tried to assist the bid of an American company, and Ronald's company was the only American-owned bidder. John Fogarasi from Commerce and Susan Elbow from USIS joined me in a meeting with Tamas Revesz, president of the Television Board of Hungary. We made the case on behalf of the Lauder Media Group, which was offering considerably more money and better programming than the competing German and Scandinavian consortiums. Ronald and I made the same case to Prime Minister Horn as well.

Tamas Revesz and the Television Board rejected the Lauder bid in favor of the German offer. He denied being pressured by Hungarian political leaders, but I had it on good authority that German Chancellor Helmut Kohl directly lobbied Prime Minister Horn. I am certain that the Germans beat out the Americans because of politics rather than economic considerations. The bidding process was rigged; the Lauder Group never had a chance. They had wasted time, money, and effort submitting a bid that was never seriously considered. The *Budapest Sun* confirmed as much, reporting that officials of the Free Democrat Party, who were in league with the Socialists in the ruling coalition, along with government officials had approved the sale to the Germans in a secret meeting on March 3. Such examples of the old communistic cronyism are what disappointed me most about Prime Minister Horn. By awarding the bid to the Germans for less money and inferior programming, he had shortchanged the Hungarian people in exchange for a political payoff.

In 1996, Hungary faced a serious problem: human traffickers, using trucks with secret containers and hiding areas, were smuggling desperate illegal immigrants through Hungary into Western Europe. I addressed this troubling issue in a speech to new students at the International Law Enforcement Academy in the spring of 1996; in it I stated that if former Soviet-bloc countries wanted acceptance by their Western neighbors, they would have to prevent the transit of illegal aliens. Immigration had to be controlled and acceptable to the recipient countries. I hardly needed to remind my audience that alien smuggling was a criminal operation. Thugs conveying the refugees sometimes let them suffocate in packed trucks or containers without proper ventilation. The smugglers demanded exorbitant fees, as well, and forced many of the women into sexual slavery. I spoke about the shifts in crime across Europe, much of it emanating from cities such as Kiev. Hungary was taking serious steps, including adopting stiffer drug penalties, appointing a U.S.-style drug czar, and signing the Council of Europe Convention on Money Laundering.

I was happy to host a visit from then-Senator Joe Biden, a truly fine public servant and also a good and longtime friend of ours. My son, Antony, subsequently worked as a senior advisor to Senator Biden and as chief of staff of the Democratic majority of the Senate Foreign Relations Committee. Kurt Volker and I met Senator Biden at the airport and gave him a very full day. We started with a briefing by the country team at the embassy, followed by meetings with the prime minister, foreign minister, and defense minister. Then we had lunch with several members of Parliament. It was a good opportunity for

the senator to evaluate firsthand the performance of the man he had
confirmed to be Ambassador to Hungary at the Senate hearing three
years earlier. With his visit, I felt as if I had come full circle.

In early April 1996, I invited Dick Nathan, Director of the
Rockefeller Institute of the State University of New York in Albany,
to come to Budapest to analyze the dichotomy between the national
and local governments in Hungary, and to talk about how we deal
with those competing governmental interests in the United States.
Many years earlier I had helped lure Dick away from Princeton University to run the Rockefeller Institute, which Cliff Wharton and I
had established when I was chairman of the SUNY Board of Trustees.
The Institute brings together leading scholars and political scientists
to examine the interplay between national and local policy issues and
governments.

Radio Free Europe was an indispensable resource during the Cold
War. Its broadcasts were often the only truthful information available
to people behind the Iron Curtain, countering their governments' lies
and propaganda. With the fall of Communism and the advent of
open, democratic political systems throughout Central and Eastern
Europe, the need for Radio Free Europe ceased. Its broadcast office in
Munich was being shut down, and its radio archives could no longer
be stored there. Officials planned to discard this trove of audio tapes
and transcripts.

For several months, I had been meeting with A. Ross Johnson,
a counselor to Radio Free Europe in Washington, to try to save the
tapes. We both felt that it was essential for the United States to
practice the democratic values it preached by putting the Hungarian-
language material into Hungarian hands, so that it would be freely
available to scholars for generations to come. I was gratified that our
efforts succeeded. It was my honor on May 27, 1997, to turn over to

Hungary's National Szechenyi Radio Library more than five thousand audio tapes and six hundred and fifty thousand pages of program scripts generated by Radio Free Europe from 1951 to 1994. I spoke at the ceremony and noted that the materials from the 1956 uprising were especially important historically, even if they reflected poorly on U.S. foreign policy. "They provide an opportunity both to reconsider the past and think about the future, as well as an opportunity for the Hungarian people and Hungarian historians to regain a missing segment of their history." A once secret 1956 U.S. report that had reviewed Radio Free Europe's role in the Hungarian Revolution concluded that the agency had not incited the Hungarian people to revolution; instead, the report noted "the uprising resulted from ten years of Soviet repression and was finally sparked by the shooting on October 23 of peaceful demonstrators."

What remained open to debate was whether the Hungarian Freedom Fighters were misled by broadcasts *after* the revolution began. Charles Gati, head of the State Department's Planning Office and an American of Hungarian birth, had been highly critical of RFE's actions during the insurrection. Charles had been a valued mentor to me during my preparation for my ambassadorship, and he and his wife, Toby, also a senior official in the State Department, had been our dinner guests at the residence. Gati strongly criticized Radio Free Europe's encouragement of its listeners to persist in their uprising despite the apparent futility of armed conflict with the Soviet Union. I sidestepped that contentious issue and concluded that by turning over the tapes to Hungary, America was providing the evidence to the Hungarian people so that they could make up their own minds about Radio Free Europe's role in the 1956 uprising.

George Soros created the Open Society Archives to provide secure storage for additional materials he acquired from the remaining Radio Free Europe tapes and scripts. Valuable primary sources on the history of the Cold War and Communism are thus accessible to the public. Ably directed by historian István Rév, the Open Society Archives is today part of Central European University. This internationally recognized institution of postgraduate education, emphasizing social sciences, humanities, history, business and law, was founded and generously supported by George Soros.

Soon after the presidential elections of November 1996, Vera and I were having dinner with friends at the Kempinski Hotel when I got a phone call from Washington. The caller was Strobe Talbott, deputy secretary of state under Madeleine Albright. Strobe said he was surveying politically appointed ambassadors and asking what they wanted to do now that the election was over. I replied that "while I do not want another posting, I want to be able to stay through July when the conference of NATO members in Madrid will extend Hungary an invitation to join NATO."

I wanted to see my years of hard work through to the end. Vera and I had discussed it, and we were both prepared to go home to New York after that. We believed we had made a positive difference in Hungary and served our country well. A July departure date was also beneficial to the State Department because the residence could be prepared for the next ambassador during the summer.

I learned my successor would be Sandy Vershbow, a highly respected careeer Foreign Service officer. Vershbow, who worked at the National Security Council at the time, indicated a preference for either NATO or Hungary. Because our present ambassador to NATO was due to stay in place until November, Vershbow was slotted for the Hungary post. Vera and I set our departure date for July, when Sandy Vershbow would succeed me.

In late spring, however, I received a call from Washington to inform me of a change of plan. The departure of our current ambassador to NATO had been moved up, and Sandy Vershbow was now going to Brussels to replace him as ambassador to NATO. A political appointee would be coming to Hungary as my replacement as ambassador. Because he was just beginning the confirmation process, months would pass before he could take over. Was I willing to stay on? "Until when?" I asked. "Give me a date."

Washington had no idea but guessed it might be near the end of 1997. I decided to set my own timetable. "There is going to be a national referendum on whether Hungary should join NATO on November 16, 1997," I explained. "The vote is so important that the ambassador needs to be in place here when it happens, and I can be useful in the effort to pass it. I will stay for that, and then Vera and I will be on the first direct flight to New York." It was agreed.

THE NATO VOTE

Despite the agreement that the White House and I had made that I would depart right after the referendum on November 16, when my successor's Senate confirmation came through sooner than anticipated, he began pressuring the White House to replace me earlier. This made no sense; given the experience I had after three and one-half years in Budapest, my help was needed to convince voters that NATO membership was in their best interest and that America and the other NATO countries were reliable allies. As it turned out, my successor, a former Marine, wanted to get to Budapest in time for the annual Marine Ball, which takes place in early November. The White House phoned me again when I was deeply involved in the NATO vote campaign. I made my position absolutely clear to them, reiterating that I would be leaving right after the November 16 referendum as we had agreed. "And tell my successor to cool it," I added. "There is a Marine Ball *every* year."

We had a difficult task ahead of us because less than 40 percent of voters generally turn out for a referendum in Hungary. Mainly ardent opponents become motivated in these low-turnout votes. Could the pro-NATO faction put together a campaign that would overcome that traditional advantage for opponents? We chose to intensify our efforts to motivate the electorate to turn out and to vote for NATO membership. We organized meetings, printed literature, and planned ways of reaching the public, and I took every opportunity to give media interviews in favor of NATO membership.

This was the rationale for voting for NATO membership that I made repeatedly to the Hungarian people: "For hundreds of years, you Hungarians have been unable to control your own destiny. You were controlled by the Turks, the Austrians, and the Soviets, but only briefly by yourselves. You made the wrong decisions before World War I and, consequently, lost a good deal of your territory. Unfortunately, when World War II came along, you were caught in the middle. You could not join the alliance against Germany because you were surrounded by the Germans, who finally invaded your country in 1944. And then you were occupied by the Russians. The NATO referendum next month will be the first time in four hundred years that you, the Hungarian people, are not being controlled by an outside force and can make a decision that affects your own destiny and future. It is a chance for you not to complain about the past, but to take some action about the future. You have the future in your own hands."

I also had strong arguments for criticisms raised against joining NATO. Some critics complained that the cost would be too high. I explained that if Hungary did not join, it would have to face the unhappy prospect of modernizing its defense forces on its own and at its own expense. Hungarian leaders were concerned about a poor turnout; the lack of voters might indicate to Washington that the Hungarian people did not care enough about NATO security to go to the polls. If Hungarians did not care, why should the United States bear the expense of including Hungary in NATO, estimated at up to $33 billion over twelve years for Hungary, Poland and the Czech Republic? I made sure that Hungarians understood that, as with their own government, the White House and the State Department had to make the case for NATO expansion to the U.S. Senate, which must, according to our Constitution, ratify treaties with foreign nations by a two-thirds vote.

Our extraordinary push for the NATO vote was derailed slightly by an article in the *International Herald Tribune* allegedly written by two British journalists who warned Hungarians not to vote for NATO because they had no guarantee the alliance would come to the country's defense in case of attack. The article gained notoriety around Hungary and was discussed widely. When questioned by reporters, I said that it sounded like Russian propaganda and that every member of NATO received the same full support and defense.

The referendum took place on November 16, 1997. The next morning, Hungarians opened their newspapers to learn that more than 51 percent of the electorate had gone to the polls and nearly 75 percent of them had voted to join NATO. These were stunning numbers! It was a landslide victory, a bigger margin than any of us had predicted. We felt extra pride in the fact that the largest plurality came from the Taszar-Kaposvar area, where our NATO peacekeeping forces and community relations efforts had paid off. We celebrated our resounding victory, both for Hungary and for the efforts of our Embassy.

Our farewell took place in the embassy's conference room on November 19. My colleagues presented me with a beautiful drawing of the embassy with their names signed on the back. I felt that I had earned their respect, one of the most gratifying aspects of my tenure. They recognized that by working together as a team, we had provided outstanding representation for the United States at a critical historical moment. Vera and I were grateful for their cooperation and support and we hoped, in turn, that we might have helped them perform their jobs better and to advance their careers.

Jim Gadsden, the person with whom I worked most closely, told me that I had been a positive influence on his career in several ways. When he later became ambassador to Iceland, he introduced several of my initiatives, including monthly brown bag lunches that gave junior members access to the ambassador and quarterly reviews that focused on how well each section and agency was achieving its goals. I felt proud that Jim was carrying on my work and legacy. I am also gratified that the outstanding work of our team in Hungary has been recognized by the Department of State. A number of my former colleagues have been promoted to high positions, including several ambassadorships.

As a postscript to these events, at a ceremony in Washington on July 22, 1998, I was awarded the U.S. Defense Department's Medal for Distinguished Public Service. Presented by Deputy Secretary John J. Hamre, the dedication reads: "His tenure in Budapest immeasurably strengthened security in Europe at a crucial time and brought Hungary and America closer together." Congressman Tom Lantos would later tell an interviewer how important and effective my work had been in strengthening Hungary's shaky progress from a poverty-stricken former Communist state to a free people making free choices on their way to greater prosperity.

Back home in New York, I received the following letter from President Bill Clinton.

Dear Donald:

I have received your letter of September 29, 1997, and it is with regret that I accept your resignation as Ambassador to Hungary. America has been well represented during your tenure, and I thank you for all you've accomplished.

By advocating the democratic values and free market principles that have always made our nation strong, you have played a key role in promoting our economic and foreign policy objectives in Hungary. Your unwavering commitment both to advancing our interests and to assisting the government and people of Hungary has helped make that country the leading Central European destination for American investment. You have also played a pivotal role in securing and developing Hungary's support for our peacekeeping efforts in Bosnia, and in so doing helped create the framework for a more peaceful, more stable Europe. I salute you for the important role you have played in strengthening U.S. ties in the region and advancing Hungary's integration into the transatlantic community.

Along with my gratitude, I send my best wishes to you and Vera for every future success and happiness.

Sincerely,

Bill Clinton

EPILOGUE

In the time since we left Hungary, some things have changed for the better, while others remain the same. The country still faces many challenges, but on the whole, it has made enormous progress.

In early 1998, a right-of-center government headed by Victor Orban took office. The good news was that the geopolitical policies we strove to establish remained largely in place, and Hungary met its NATO obligations.

On March 24, 1999, twelve days after Hungary officially became a member of NATO, NATO forces launched an air war to halt Serbian aggression in Kosovo. The presence of three hundred and fifty thousand ethnic Hungarians in the Serbian province of Vojvodina, as well as Hungary's common border with Serbia, posed a serious problem for Hungary, which did not want to get pulled into this conflict. Hungary met its responsibilities to NATO by preventing a Russian convoy from bringing military supplies to Belgrade and by refusing to allow Russian transport planes to fly over Hungarian territory. Most important, it made available the IFOR base at Taszar to

U.S. and NATO air forces, thus passing its first test by placing NATO membership obligations over its own security concerns.

Unfortunately, the Orban government set back Hungary's progress toward more transparency and accountability in government operations. The national deficit and unemployment stayed stubbornly high, foreign investors remained burdened with complex tax regulations, and, during the first two years of the Orban administration, no major state-owned companies were privatized. Also troubling, relations with Romania and Slovakia were set back after the previous years of progress toward a reconciliation of ethnic issues.

In 2002, Victor Orban and his Fidesz party, lost the elections. They were replaced by the Socialists, or MSZP, and former Finance Minister Peter Medgyessy became Prime Minister. Soon after being sworn in, Medgyessy's administration was rocked by an allegation that he had been an informer for the Secret Service. He responded that from 1977 to 1982 he had been a counterintelligence operative protecting Hungary's economic secrets from the Warsaw Pact countries that were determined to undermine Hungary's ultimately successful bid to join the International Monetary Fund. That explanation bought him time and kept him in office for two more years.

In 2004, Peter Medgyessy stepped down and Ferenc Gyurcsany became Prime Minister. Gyurcsany had belonged to the Young Communists in his youth, and when privatization began, he acquired a number of formerly state-owned companies and built them into successful private businesses. By his mid-forties he was one of the richest men in Hungary. The electorate responded positively to Gyurcsany's strong executive abilities by re-electing the Socialist in 2006, marking the first time since the end of communism that a government had been able to retain office for two election cycles. This was an encouraging sign of the political maturation of Hungary.

Unfortunately, the political situation soon took a turn for the worse when Gyurcsany—in a private speech to members of his party—admitted that he had been less than truthful during the campaign about the state of the economy. Spending on the welfare state, health care, pensions, and education had gotten out of hand. Instead of approaching the European Union target of a 4 percent fiscal deficit, Hungary's deficit exceeded 9 percent. The government introduced emergency corrective measures, reminiscent of 1994–95, affecting taxes and government spending. Hungary's credit rating and aspirations for adoption of the euro have been set back.

Also troubling is Hungary's dependence on energy supplies from Russia and the emergence of a small extreme right-wing movement that dismays the majority of Hungarians as well as the international community. The present government and its predecessors have also disappointed many by backing away from the settlement we had achieved for the return of the Nierenberg art. As recently as January 2008, the Hungarian government overturned several prior court orders to return the paintings.

Despite these developments, Hungary has continued to move forward. The private sector has blossomed. Exports rose 18 percent in 2006 and new investments in manufacturing, financial services, and tourism have surged. Budapest now enjoys new hotels, restaurants, and retail shops and endures Western-style traffic jams. But in late 2008 the country again faced a credit and liquidity crisis reminiscent of the early 1990s: Hungary will be required to return to strict and painful economic policies.

Nothing better symbolized Hungary's journey from the twentieth century to the twenty-first than its membership on December 20, 2007, in the Schengen travel zone. Border controls were lifted between the old European Union members and the new states which joined in 2004. Hungarians could now travel by car to all points west without stopping for passport control while crossing national borders. And in late 2008, Hungary successfully met the U.S. "refusal" standards that will now enable visa-free visits to the United States by Hungarian citizens. How much the world has changed in the fifty-eight years since Vera and her mother ran through the woods, trying to avoid the barbed wire and border patrols that imprisoned Hungary and the Hungarians.

We return to Budapest regularly where we both enjoy and value Donald's membership on the board of Central European University and Vera continues her association with PRIMAVERA.

Both of us cherish the memories of the fascinating years we spent in Hungary representing the United States. During a time of transition we seized the moment and made a difference by helping guide Hungary from its four and one-half decades of repression toward what it is today—a respected and contributing member of the Euro-Atlantic community.

As we write in 2008, renewed attention is focused on Hungary's economic and security responsibilities in Europe. Emboldened by surging oil revenues, Russia's use of excessive force in Georgia has illuminated Hungary's NATO and European Union obligations and its participation in the ongoing Nabucco and South Stream pipeline discussions.

On November 4, 2008, Barack Obama's election as President of the United States restored the world's admiration for American democracy. We remain optimistic that democratic Hungary will continue to play a constructive role, not looking to the past, but focused on the future. It has been a great privilege for us to have participated in these historic times.

KEY EVENTS IN
HUNGARIAN HISTORY

Spring 895 AD   Led by Arpád, the Magyars take over territories previously occupied by Slavs in the Carpathian Basin.

1000 AD   St. Stephen, the first King of Hungary, is crowned, opting for Christianity and Roman Catholicism.

1458–1490   Reign of Matthias Corvinus, King of Hungary: His fascination with the achievements of the Italian Renaissance leads to Mediterranean cultural influences in Hungary.

1526–1699   Turkish occupation of Hungary.

18th Century   Hungary increasingly tied to Austria as a colonial province under Habsburg rule.

March 15, 1848– Oct. 6, 1849	Revolution against Austrian rule.
April 14, 1849	Lajos Kossuth declares independence from Habsburg rule.
1867	The Compromise—the Habsburg Empire transformed into the Dual Monarchy—Austro-Hungarian Empire.
1918	Collapse of the Austro-Hungarian Empire at the end of World War I.
March 1, 1920	Admiral Horthy elected Regent and proclaims Kingdom of Hungary with a vacant throne.
June 4, 1920	Treaty of Trianon—Hungary loses two-thirds of its territory.
Dec. 12, 1941	Hungary declares war on the United States.
March 19, 1944	German forces occupy Hungary.
April 13, 1945	End of World War II on the territory of Hungary.
Dec. 14, 1955	Hungary is admitted to the United Nations.
Oct. 23, 1956	The first day of the 1956 Revolution and the fight for freedom.
Oct. 30, 1956	Armored military units free the Hungarian primate, Cardinal József Mindszenty.

Nov. 1, 1956	The government announces Hungary's withdrawal from the Warsaw pact, declares the country's neutrality, and appeals to the United Nations for help.
Nov. 4, 1956	Soviet troops attack Budapest. Members of the Nagy government take refuge in the Yugoslav Embassy. Mindszenty is given asylum in the U.S. embassy, where he will live in what is now the Ambassador's office, staying in the embassy building until September 28, 1971. The Kádár government, backed by Soviet forces, restores the Communist regime.
Jan. 6, 1978	The ceremony marking the return of the Crown of St. Stephen is held in the Hungarian Parliament.
Sept. 10, 1989	Hungary opens its border with Austria. It is one of the most important events that led to the fall of the Berlin Wall.
Oct. 23, 1989	Declaration of the Hungarian Republic.
June 19, 1991	The last Soviet soldier leaves Hungary.
Nov. 28, 1995	The Hungarian Parliament allows NATO troops to be stationed in Hungary.
December 1995	Taszar air base, a Soviet airfield during the Cold War, becomes the first U.S. and NATO military base in a former Warsaw Pact country, serving as the primary staging facility for peacekeeping forces entering Bosnia.

Nov. 16, 1997   Hungarian referendum supports Hungary's bid
                     to join NATO.

March 12, 1999   Hungary joins NATO.

May 1, 2004   Hungary joins the European Union.

ACKNOWLEDGMENTS

After our return to the United States, many friends and colleagues urged us to write a book recounting our experiences in Hungary. In doing so we have benefited from the advice and expertise of Joseph Amiel, Barbara Taylor Bradford, Fredrica S. Friedman, Paul Grondahl, Florence Fabricant, Patricia Fabricant, James Peltz, István Rév, Duncan Searl, and Laurie Searl. Their generous advice and expertise were invaluable.

INDEX

ABOUT THE AUTHORS

VERA BLINKEN was born in Budapest, and graduated from Vassar College with a degree in the History of Art. She practiced interior design, first at the architectural firm of Edward Durell Stone, and later founded Vera Evans Interiors. Mrs. Blinken has been a member of the Board of Directors of the International Rescue Committee since 1978, serving most recently as Secretary. She was Special Assistant for the Arts and Cultural Affairs to Senator Daniel Patrick Moynihan and is currently Vice Chairman of FAPE—Foundation for Art and Preservation in Embassies. While living in Hungary as the wife of the Ambassador, in 1996 she founded PRIMAVERA, the first mobile breast cancer screening program in Central and Eastern Europe. In 2002, for services to the Hungarian people, she was awarded the Middle Cross of the Republic of Hungary.

DONALD BLINKEN, U.S. Ambassador to Hungary from 1994–1998, is a native New Yorker. He graduated magna cum laude in economics at Harvard University and cofounded the investment banking/venture capital firm of E. M. Warburg, Pincus & Co. He was Chairman of the Board of Trustees of the State University of New York, President of the Mark Rothko Foundation, and President of the Brooklyn Academy of Music, and has also served on the Board of the New York Public Library. He is currently co-Chair of Columbia University's European Institute and is a member of the Advisory Board of its School of Public and International Affairs. He also serves on the Boards of the New York Philharmonic, the Citizens Development Corp., the National Committee on American Foreign Policy, the Project on Ethnic Relations, and Central European University in Budapest, and is a member of the Council on Foreign Relations.